AD Biography
Orbach Jer 2011

prince of
s to Law &

DISCARDED BY
MEAD PUBLIC LIBRARY

JERRY ORBACH,
PRINCE OF THE CITY

· ·

Once on a New York City sidewalk, a mother with a six-year-old boy saw Jerry walking by and told her little son, "That's Lumière." Jerry overheard them, and when the little boy said, "No way!" Jerry stopped, knelt down, and asked the boy to close his eyes. He then sang "Be Our Guest" to him in his Maurice Chevalier accent with the voice of Lumière. The little boy's eyes grew wide and stunned, and he said, "How did you do that?" It is a question we all continue to ask about Jerry. —JON OLEXY, Jerry Orbach's cousin and friend

JERRY ORBACH, PRINCE OF THE CITY

HIS WAY FROM *THE FANTASTICKS* TO *LAW & ORDER*

John Anthony Gilvey

APPLAUSE
THEATRE & CINEMA BOOKS

An Imprint of Hal Leonard Corporation

Copyright © 2011 by John Anthony Gilvey

All rights reserved. No part of this book may be reproduced in any form, without written permission, except by a newspaper or magazine reviewer who wishes to quote brief passages in connection with a review.

Published in 2011 by Applause Theatre & Cinema Books
An Imprint of Hal Leonard Corporation
7777 West Bluemound Road
Milwaukee, WI 53213

Trade Book Division Editorial Offices
33 Plymouth St., Montclair, NJ 07042

Frontispiece photo of Jerry Orbach: Time & Life Pictures/Getty Images

"Try to Remember" by Tom Jones and Harvey Schmidt © 1960 (renewed); Chappell & Co., Inc. (ASCAP). Lyrics used by permission of Warner/Chappell Music.

Unpublished poems written by Jerry Orbach used by permission of Rita Cancilla Hubbard.

Poem by Jerry Orbach on pg. 107 is reprinted with the permission of Touchstone, a Division of Simon & Schuster, Inc., from *Remember How I Love You: Love Letters from an Extraordinary Marriage* by Jerry Orbach and Elaine Orbach. Foreword by Sam Waterston. Copyright © 2009 by Elaine Orbach and Ken Bloom. All rights reserved.

Printed in the United States of America
Book design by Kristina Rolander

Library of Congress Cataloging-in-Publication Data is available upon request.

ISBN 978-1-42348-845-3

www.applausepub.com

9001045190

To Emily Olexy Orbach,
with appreciation and gratitude

CONTENTS

FOREWORD

THERE WAS ONE SHOW THAT ANYONE VISITING NEW York between the years 1955 and 1961 could not miss, and that show was *The Threepenny Opera* in Greenwich Village. I happened to see it when a charismatic young actor named Jerry Orbach was playing the lead character of Mack the Knife. He seemed to slide across the stage, insinuating stealth and menace coupled with an easy charm. And when he opened his mouth to sing it was pure gold. The same held true for Jerry's seminal portrayal of El Gallo in *The Fantasticks* a few years later. The great song "Try to Remember" became his then and remained his for the rest of his life. No one could top him. From that point on I never missed a show Jerry was in, not until my own career took off and my life on stage and screen became too busy for me to see his.

I got lucky. In 1972 a sweet romantic comedy called *6 Rms Riv Vu* brought Jerry and me together on Broadway for seven months. He was everything I had imagined him to be and more: buoyant, funny, and a consummate professional. He never missed a performance even when an all-night poker game inched towards a two o'clock matinee. I looked forward to those magical hours on stage with him eight times a week, and when the run of the show ended our friendship had been sealed.

There was no one quite like Jerry. He had a big heart and loved people, all kinds of people. He was a New Yorker's New Yorker, but his embrace included the world. He seemed at home wherever he was, and people everywhere returned his affection, from the chorus kid backstage to the cop on the beat.

My husband Ed Sherin often played golf with Jerry, either at his swanky club in Westchester County or at our scruffy club in rural Nova Scotia when he and Elaine visited during the summer. He was a very good golfer but an outstanding pool player; to see him run the balls on a table was a thing of beauty. He was as graceful with a pool cue as he was with a soft-shoe. Games were his thing—all kinds of games, from crossword puzzles and scrabble to poker and pinochle. But the game I most loved to play with Jerry was a guessing game. I would hum a few notes of music, and then he would sing the song. I never caught him out; he knew every song that had been written. The pleasure of this game for me was hearing him sing; it was sheer joy. I adored his voice.

His revels now are ended, but he lives on in the indelible memories of those of us who received his thoughtful phone calls, laughed at his inveterate jokes, read his romantic doggerel, or witnessed his song and dance, and the remarkable panoply of characters he created for stage and screen. He was our sweet prince.

Jane Alexander

PREFACE AND
ACKNOWLEDGMENTS

. . . .

ONE AUTUMN MORNING IN 2005, THE SUBWAY DOORS opened, and I took a seat lost in the thought of how to follow up my first publication, a biography of Broadway director-choreographer Gower Champion. Idea after idea crossed my mind, but none caught my enthusiasm. Then, I looked up, and beaming down at me from an advertisement for Manhattan's Eye Bank for Sight Restoration was Jerry Orbach. "Well, what about me, John?" he seemed to say. *Jerry Orbach!* Yes, of course! When I was a doctoral student in the educational theatre program at New York University, Jerry had contributed an important interview to the research for my dissertation on four of Gower's musicals. "Here's my number, John. I'll be back in New York in a few days. Give me a call," he told me one evening following a performance of *42nd Street* at the Valley Forge Music Fair. He meant it. Days later, there I was speaking with Jerry about *Carnival* (1961) and *42nd Street* (1980). "They're the bookends of my Broadway career," he said.

What an extraordinary career it was, too — one that encompassed not only the theatre, but also film and television. Few performers adapt so adeptly to that kind of challenge as Jerry Orbach. Whether Billy Flynn, Lumière, or Lennie Briscoe, his sharply drawn characters captivated from start to finish. My first experience of his magic came in 1973, when I watched his Alvaro Mangiacavallo come charging down a serpentine flight of stairs to woo the great Maureen Stapleton, reprising her Tony-winning role as Serafina Delle Rose in a revival of Tennessee Williams's *The Rose Tattoo* at Philadelphia's Walnut Street Theatre. Moments like that — and countless others throughout Jerry's career — have made writing his biography a happy task and an especially productive one, thanks to the mentorship and patience of my agent Eric Myers of the Speiler Agency, publisher John Cerullo, editorial director Carol Flannery, and project editor Bernadette Malavarca of Hal Leonard Performing Arts Publishing Group. My thanks also to the staff of the Billy Rose Theatre Collection of the New York Public Library for the Performing Arts, Janet C. Olson of the Northwestern University Library Archives, Ron Mandelbaum of Photofest, Rita Cancilla Hubbard for Jerry and Elaine's photographs, and Rick McKay, whose interview with Jerry has aided this work.

Achieving this goal has been possible thanks to Jerry's colleagues and friends who have given generously of their time, memories, and insights, among them Jane Alexander, Zora and Richard Brown, Ellen and Lewis Gould, Tom Jones, John Kander, S. Epatha Merkerson, Patricia and Bert Michaels, Jon Olexy, Chita Rivera, Harvey Schmidt, Edwin Sherin, Ted Sod, Sam Waterston, and Dick Wolf. The support received from the members of Jerry's family has also been extraordinary. At the outset, the late Elaine Cancilla Orbach, Jerry's wife, gave this project the kind of insight only a soul mate can give. She was gone all too suddenly and soon. As work progressed, it was my good fortune to have the contributions of Jerry's sons, Tony Orbach and Chris Orbach, whose stories and reflections about their father add a distinctly personal touch. They also have done a fine job of channeling the perspective of their mother, Marta Curro, Jerry's first wife, who was too ill to participate. But the greatest contribution by far has been from Jerry's mother, Emily Olexy Orbach, who generously answered questions, schooled me in the family history, contacted family members on my behalf, gave me access to the Orbach archives, and, most particularly, shared precious memories of her son. For these reasons, this book is dedicated to her.

Along the way, there also has been great support from friends and family—including Cathleen Albertus, Michael Brady, Harry Chung, Rev. John Dennis, Carol Maher, Nick Miraflores, Nick Soleotis, Lee Stuart, Alan Thomas, Rev. Thomas Tucker, my teachers and colleagues, the Oblates of St. Francis de Sales, and, most especially, Fran and Dad. Finally, a bow to Jerry for the joy on my parents' faces the night they saw *Chicago*.

LYRICS OF "TRY TO REMEMBER" FROM *THE FANTASTICKS*

. . . .

LYRICS: Tom Jones, MUSIC: Harvey Schmidt

Try to remember the kind of September
When life was slow and oh, so mellow.
Try to remember the kind of September
When grass was green and grain was yellow.
Try to remember the kind of September
When you were a tender and callow fellow.
Try to remember, and if you remember,
Then follow.

Follow, follow, follow, follow, follow,
Follow, follow, follow, follow.

Try to remember when life was so tender
That no one wept except the willow.
Try to remember when life was so tender
That dreams were kept beside your pillow.
Try to remember when life was so tender
That love was an ember about to billow.
Try to remember, and if you remember,
Then follow.

Follow, follow, follow, follow, follow,
Follow, follow, follow, follow.

Follow, follow, follow, follow, follow,
Follow, follow, follow, follow.

Follow, follow, follow, follow, follow,
Follow, follow, follow, follow.

Deep in December, it's nice to remember,
Although you know the snow will follow.

Deep in December, it's nice to remember,
Without a hurt the heart is hollow.
Deep in December, it's nice to remember,
The fire of September that made us mellow.
Deep in December, our hearts should remember
And follow.

Since his death on December 28, 2004, a growing number of Jerry's neighbors, friends and colleagues felt it fitting that he should be honored in a special way by having a corner of Fifty-Third and Eighth named in his honor. So, in March 2007, with their support and the blessing of his mother, Emily, Elaine took up the task.

PROLOGUE:
HEARTS SHOULD REMEMBER

FOR NEARLY TWENTY-FIVE YEARS, HE AND HIS WIFE, Elaine, had lived in a high-rise on Eighth Avenue at West Fifty-Third Street in the area of the city best known as Hell's Kitchen. The stronghold of working-class Irish Americans who for decades had tolerated scores of mobsters, bootleggers, and street toughs, the neighborhood, with its rough-and-tumble life, was well known, immortalized in the stories of Damon Runyon and the musical *West Side Story*. But by the time he arrived in summer 1980, the grit of Hell's Kitchen was slowly giving way to the high-toned gentrification that less-threatening names like Clinton and Midtown West conveyed. The neighborhood was turning safer and, with its proximity to the theatre district, was becoming an ideal place for actors to live. Amid its burgeoning restaurants, condos, and shops, Jerry Orbach quickly became a welcomed and respected presence.

Everyone knew him—some from earlier days when he trod the boards as one of Broadway's great leading men in *Carnival*, *Promises, Promises*, *Chicago*, and *42nd Street*, others from films like *Prince of the City*, *Dirty Dancing*, and *Crimes and Misdemeanors*. Children recognized him as the voice of the beloved candlestick Lumière in Disney's animated feature *Beauty and the Beast*. But it was his twelve-year stint as wisecracking New York Detective Lennie Briscoe on NBC's *Law & Order* that brought him national acclaim and gave him an honored place in the hearts of New Yorkers. As *Law & Order*'s creator and producer Dick Wolf put it, "Jerry is the quintessential New Yorker. He brings the city with him in every scene."[1] Being a New Yorker by birth clearly aided that naturalism, but greater by far was the bond Jerry cultivated with fellow New Yorkers. Whether dining at Da Tommaso, his favorite restaurant, visiting friends and fans in the Midtown North Detective Squad, or simply playing poker with the boys at the Lone Star Boat Club on West Fifty-Fourth, he was a New Yorker's New Yorker—a common man with an uncommon gift for creating characters that resonated with audiences because they were drawn from his love affair with the city and its people. No wonder his glossy publicity photo hung in places like Ms. Buffy's French Cleaners, his Eighth Avenue tailor.

PART I:
TENDER AND CALLOW FELLOW

Chapter 1

ENTRANCE, 1935–1955

· ·

IN 1932, PLYMOUTH, A SMALL TOWN SITUATED ON THE Susquehanna River four miles west of Wilkes-Barre in northeast Pennsylvania's Luzerne County, was not an easy place to earn a living, especially for a young woman. At the height of the Great Depression, the economy in this hard coal region, like most of the country, was at a standstill as the mines, as well as the hosiery, silk, and lumber mills, drastically downsized their workforces or folded completely. To survive, many young people were abandoning the area and flocking to the big cities in search of better prospects. Emily Olexy, an attractive twenty-two-year-old with sparking blue eyes and blond hair, soon found herself among them, navigating the waters of change that swept her from the stability of Plymouth life with her Eastern European Catholic family to the flux of New York City with its mass of cultures and faiths.

Straight away, Emily mainstreamed herself into the city's bustle, taking a job as a waitress and cashier. But the afternoon she entered Walter's Pharmacy at Second Avenue and Thirteenth Street and headed to the soda fountain for a five-cent Coke, her life changed forever, courtesy of the genial, outgoing man with the mustache behind the counter. The fact that Leon Orbach, called Leo, was a German-Jewish immigrant of Sephardic (Spanish) ancestry and eleven years her senior did not deter her in the least from accepting his invitation to dinner—a decision many might consider rash even today. Not Emily. "My dear, it was the Depression," she later explained to a young reporter. "When anyone asked you out for dinner, you went!"[1]

That evening, as the two chatted over lamb chops, they shared family histories. Leo was nine years old when he, his three brothers, and their parents, Isadore and Bertha, emigrated to the United States from Berlin in 1906. They were fleeing the rising anti-Semitism that had first ignited in their hometown of Neustettin, Germany (today Szczecinek, Poland), when the large synagogue there was burned to the ground by arsonists in 1881. When Isadore, a textile braider by trade, landed in New York City with his family, his brother helped him get established in his thriving laundry business on St. Mark's Place in the East Village. Leo grew up and attended school there while also working in his uncle's laundry until the family moved to the burgeoning neighborhood of Morrisania in the city's South Bronx section after World War I. Following stints as a prizefighter and a vaudeville comic playing Catskill vacation spots like Grossinger's, he finally transitioned into the drugstore concession business.

Emily's parents, Alexander and Susanna, raised her and her two brothers in Plymouth until the family moved to Lynnwood on the other side of the Susquehanna in 1924. Alexander, born in the village of Bartlovka, near the city of Bialystok in northeastern Poland, immigrated to the United States as a young man, arriving in New York City in 1905, then moving on to Ohio, and finally settling down in Plymouth. There, he found work as a carpenter constructing the supports and walkways for local coal mines. H also met and married Susanna Klauba, whose parents were Lithuanian.

In the days following that first dinner, as Emily's visits to the soda fountain became a daily ritual, Leo decided to mark their week's anniversary with a special treat—tickets to Irving Berlin's *Face the Music*. It was Emily's first Broadway show and unlike anything she had ever seen. Like Leo, she was fascinated by the stage and had already put her talents to the test as a singer on a weekly Wilkes-Barre radio program. But the two discovered they had more in common than a fondness for show business. A two-year courtship was soon under way and remained strong even during the year Emily returned to Lynnwood to take a better job.

Unlike most Catholic parents of the day, Alexander and Susanna were surprisingly accepting of their daughter's Jewish boyfriend. There were two reasons for this: first, their own marriage ran counter to the bitter enmity between Polish and Lithuanian Catholics that dated back to the Middle Ages and as recently as 1889 had erupted violently on the streets of Plymouth;

and second, Susanna's mother was a Jewish orphan who had been raised by a Lithuanian Catholic family. Even so, Leo was not fully embraced by the Olexys until he acquired U.S. citizenship, which he did shortly before his marriage to their daughter. The Orbachs were equally taken with Emily and the remarkable ease with which she picked up the Yiddishisms that peppered her speech.

Emily Olexy and Leo Orbach were married in Manhattan at City Hall on July 11, 1934, and began their life together in an apartment on Findlay Avenue near 167th Street in the Morrisania section of the South Bronx. On October 20, 1935, at 12:45 P.M. in Bronx Maternity Hospital, Emily gave birth to an eight-pound, four-ounce baby boy. Both she and Leo wanted a name that no one else had in their families and liked the sound of the one proposed by their sister-in-law Elsie, the wife of Leo's brother, Al. Weeks later, Jerome Bernard Orbach was baptized at St. Mary's Polish Catholic Church in Plymouth. Though the boy would be raised Catholic, his father would make certain that he also acquired an appreciation of his Jewish roots. As a result, Jerry would become so at ease in both faiths that he could later claim with a grin, "I can be all things to all people. I was raised a Catholic, and I can support their causes. When I go for a fund-raising dinner for Israel, I'm Jewish."[2]

Nine months after his birth, Jerry was taking in the world from the carriage proudly pushed through Claremont Park by his father, who never lost an opportunity to show neighbors how his son could devour with delight the slices of green peaches he fed him. But Leo and Emily quickly learned that their child could be as inquisitive and daring as he was lively and entertaining—signature characteristics that would remain with him throughout life. One day when the family was living on the top floor of a Topping Avenue apartment house near 173rd Street, Emily left her one-and-a-half-year-old playing on the floor of the bedroom while she went to get something from the adjoining bathroom. When she returned, there was Jerry staring in at her from the fire escape outside. He had climbed through the twelve-inch opening in the window and was now staring down into the street six floors below. "I didn't faint," she remembers. "I just went over to the window . . . and said, 'Jerry, come here just a little further to me.' I kept asking him to come. . . . I think he finally realized he had to come in, and I grabbed him. I've never forgotten that picture in my life: a small child who could climb and do anything. He was a daredevil."[3] The escapade was just the first of many risks Jerry would take in life.

Like many people during the Depression, Leo had to go where there was gainful employment, which meant his family would be uprooted frequently. By 1937, when Jerry was two, they were living in Mount Vernon, New York, on the border of the Bronx in Westchester County, where Leo managed a soda fountain at a local drugstore. During their four years there, he and Emily satisfied their son's wanderlust with frequent trips to Tibbetts Brook Park in Yonkers and summer excursions to Rye Beach, where by age five Jerry was conquering rides like the Whip and Derby Racer (alongside his father) and witnessing thrilling acts by the country's top circus performers at "America's Premier Playground," the Playland Amusement Park.

At five, Jerry also began kindergarten. One day, when Emily received a call from his teacher, "I thought, oh, this is trouble. [But instead] she said, 'Everybody wants to imitate Jerry. Whatever he does, the whole class wants to do.' So he was more or less of a leader and just got so popular. He always had a lot of friends. He wanted to entertain everybody because he was an only child. That's the way he'd get their attention, and he needed the friendship. So wherever we moved, and we moved a lot, that's what happened."[4] While his peers were busy imitating him, he was busy imitating every voice he heard on the radio, from Bing Crosby to the Lone Ranger. A perfect blend of his father's vaudevillian humor and mother's singing skill, he was soon enlivening family gatherings with songs or bits of entertainment delivered with the confidence of a pro. He instinctively knew how to amuse those around him by making them laugh and, thanks to Leo's tutelage, by age six could play a winning game of poker, which would become a lifelong pastime.[5]

Jerry's sixth year was significant for another reason—the family quit Mount Vernon and moved to Lynnwood, Pennsylvania, where Emily's family now lived. There, the second grader (who had skipped first grade because he had already mastered reading) was introduced to music by way of the coffee shop his father managed above the family's basement apartment. "Guys older than me are always amazed that I know all the songs from 1941," he later joked. "Well, I had a jukebox over my head every night."[6] Above, jitterbuggers danced to Jimmy Dorsey's "Amapola," Duke Ellington's "Take the 'A' Train," and Vaughn Monroe's "Racing with the Moon" while Emily and Leo took turns filling orders, flipping burgers, and helping Jerry with his homework below. That Halloween, Jerry decided on a trick calculated to win treats galore: he and his buddy, the boy next door, would be musical hoboes, Jerry playing the harmonica while his partner sang and danced. Just one problem: he needed a costume. From her father's old clothes, Emily created one for him and then painted his face. Amazingly, the two little tramps knew just where to find the best audiences and treats. By the evening's end, they were the hit of every taproom in Lynnwood, with a hatful of coins to prove it.

But everything came to a standstill on Sunday morning, December 7, 1941 when the Japanese attacked Pearl Harbor. As the nation steeled itself for World War II, life changed significantly for Americans, and the Orbachs were no exception. By 1942, the jitterbuggers had gone off to war, the coffee shop closed, and Leo, too old to enlist, went to Baltimore to do his part for a time as a worker in a munitions plant. Months later, when he returned, he took a position as banquet manager for the Sterling Hotel in Wilkes-Barre before landing what would be a permanent position managing lunch counters for Neisner Brothers, a national retail store chain. The nature of the job demanded that he relocate as the needs of the company demanded, and so for the next seven years the family crisscrossed the country via stores in Scranton, Pennsylvania; Springfield, Massachusetts; and Waukegan, Illinois.

In Scranton, where the Orbachs' home sat atop one of the highest points of the city and across from a firehouse, seven-year-old Jerry immediately made friends with the firemen, and also with a neighborhood boy who coaxed him into joining the choir for the 1942 Christmas pageant sponsored by the local Episcopalian Church. It was his first performance on stage, and it made a deep impression. Another significant experience came in May 1943, when he made his First Communion and Confirmation during Mass at St. Peter's Cathedral. By summer, the family was preparing to move to Springfield. It was then that a spontaneous swim on a hot afternoon almost turned deadly for Jerry. Earlier that day, he and his buddy Francis, had gone to the public pool and found it closed. Their solution was to try the creek that ran just ten blocks from Jerry's home. As they waded through the water, Francis slipped and fell down a steep incline, taking Jerry with him. A sixteen-year-old boy sitting on the bank saw Jerry's legs flailing about and immediately plunged in and brought him to safety. "Where's Francis?" Jerry cried. The young man, who had only seen Jerry, immediately went back and retrieved Francis, but it was too late. The boy was dead. The police arrived, brought Jerry home, and reported the matter to Emily. She immediately contacted the doctor because the muscles in Jerry's throat were so constricted he could scarcely speak. A week's bed rest was prescribed. By the end of it, Jerry had completely recovered his speech and was practically his old self. But Leo wanted his son to learn from this life lesson. Ten days after the accident, he enrolled him for swimming lessons at the YMCA, and by summer's end Jerry was one of the best swimmers in the class. By then, Leo had arrived in Springfield, Massachusetts, to start his new job and scout out a furnished apartment for the family. Back in Scranton, Emily put their furniture in storage and made preparations for the long train trek that would take her and Jerry to their new home where Leo waited. But before they could board the train, Jerry had to part with his first and only pet—a black cocker spaniel that had been his constant companion during their time in Scranton. Brokenhearted, he returned the dog to the lady who had given it to him.

Daily after school in Springfield, Jerry continued developing his swimming skills at the local "Y." One afternoon, in his enthusiasm to master a new dive, he sprang into an area of the pool too shallow to absorb the impact, hit bottom, and cracked two lower teeth. Emily had to rush him to a dentist, who removed the remains of one tooth and stitched up the gum. Jerry's risks were more calculated at school, where his performer's instinct surfaced in a manner that surprised him as much as it did his teachers: "When I was nine years old, they picked me for the leading role in the school play. We were doing a puppet show, and the teacher was auditioning the kids for the part of Aladdin. My first reaction was 'Those kids aren't reading it right.' And when I read the part, the teacher said, 'Okay, you're Aladdin.'"[7] He had landed his first leading role. In 1948, the Orbachs were about to complete their fifth year in Springfield when Neisner's transferred Leo to Waukegan, Illinois, three miles north of Chicago. Once more, he went ahead to pave the way for Emily and Jerry, who returned to Lynnwood in the interim to retrieve what the family had in storage. In May after an eight-hundred-route-mile, fourteen-hour train trip from springtime Scranton, they arrived in still-snowy Chicago minus winter gear, settling in a temporary apartment until they secured a permanent home at 1518 Lloyd Avenue.

When he arrived at the Andrew Cooke School, the twelve-year-old eighth grader with an IQ of 163 had already skipped another grade and immediately won the role of Huckleberry Finn in the class play, *And Then What Happened?*

He made friends easily thanks to a vital defense mechanism he had perfected that helped him blend, chameleon-like, into every new situation — a consequence of the constant moving that always made him the new kid on the block. Now, at last, he could sink roots and flourish in Waukegan, a town of about sixty thousand with over thirty industries, the Great Lakes Naval Base, and a mix of middle- and upper-middle-class whites, blacks, sailors, and Southerners. This "wild town,"[8] as Jerry termed it, was all the more so on nights when he joined other teens for the car racing, beer drinking, and random fist-fighting typical of their age. To avoid being picked on, "I hung out with the baddest guys in school. I was with a very rough crowd — leather jacket, Levi's, engineer boots, a ducktail haircut, and cigarettes rolled in the sleeves."[9] Acting seemed the farthest thing from his mind. A self-described "semi-hoodlum,"[10] he whiled away hours at Waukegan's numerous pool halls testing his nascent skills. With the presence of the naval base, the town was much like Newport News, Virginia, with "two pool halls and bowling alleys per block."[11] Jerry's classmates were "mostly Greek kids whose fathers and uncles owned poolrooms. They'd go in and rack balls after school, so I started to learn how to play.... We were playing pool all through high school. I did my tenth grade geometry paper on three-cushion billiards. It was all on the angles. I was using those angles to show different types of triangles — isosceles triangles, scalene triangles — so I did pretty well."[12]

At Waukegan Township High, he soon added other interests. He joined the football and swim teams, and "I always sang, sang with my mother, sang in the choir. They sent me down to the University of Illinois for a singing contest and I won a gold medal in the baritone division without really any training. [I] didn't know what I was doing."[13] Then drama teacher Melba Wixom spotted his talent, and he became a regular in the school shows: "She was a bundle of energy, and everyone loved her. The major event in my life was my starring role in a high-school play called *Mr. Barry's Etchings*. That drama set the course of my life. It was about a retired old gentleman who starts forging $50 bills. That part made me famous in Waukegan."[14] From Wixom, who believed in the good, old-fashioned methods, he learned basic stage mechanics like how to enter with the upstage foot and gesture with the upstage hand. In no time he was chalking up leading roles in the school's productions. His high school buddies were as impressed with his stage interests as they were with his billiard skills. "Jerry had an old phonograph," friend Mike Balsamo recalls. "He'd play *The King and I*. Guys like us weren't too familiar with that kind of music. But he was. He said he wanted to do musicals like that someday."[15]

By 1952, the popular, charming high school senior—with his thick black hair, deeply set blue eyes under heavy brows, and a nose, he once quipped, that 'covers three counties" —stood a full six-foot-two, weighed in at 165 pounds, and was rarely without a date come Saturday night. He also knew exactly how to wear the "look" of the day—jeans, sneakers, tight-fitting T-shirt, and a slouched, "don't mess with me" attitude. Now an up-and-coming pool player, he might well have made a living at the game if not for one thing: "It was just sort of understood that it would be an actor's life for me. It was never a decision that I made at a certain point...I think I always knew I was going to be a performer."[16] A young breed of film actors who were breaking the conventional rules of the craft further fueled his interest. James Dean, Montgomery Clift, and Marlon Brando impressed him greatly, especially Brando in *The Wild One* (1953). "Marlon Brando changed the face of American acting," he later observed. "The great American actor prior to Brando was John Barrymore, and that grand, theatrical style. People weren't noticing what Spencer Tracy was doing in the movies. He was really leading the way into naturalism. But when Brando hit with *A Streetcar Named Desire*, even before that on the stage with *Truckline Café*, he changed acting."[17] As graduation neared, the influence of Jerry's film idols and school stage experiences made him wonder if he could get more from what had been only an extracurricular activity. "Although I had the lead in the junior and senior class plays and had always had the leads throughout my school years, I never thought of acting as a career until Melba Wixom gave me a push. She had a job at the Chevy Chase Playhouse in Wheeling, Illinois, [and] the day I graduated she got me and [classmate] Judy Jones in as apprentices. I was sixteen. That was 1952—a long time ago."[18]

Apprentice Orbach did everything from hauling gravel, to building scenery, to being driver for the star of *Come On Up, Ring Twice*—the legendary Mae West. "The owner of the theater threw me the keys to his Cadillac and said, 'Go pick up Miss West.' And when I parked in front of the hotel, I parked the car so beautifully—right on the red carpet with a running board sticking over the curb. She said, 'What do you do around the theatre?' And I said, 'I do everything.' And she said, 'Well, you tell them you're my driver.' So I drove her around all week."[19] It was quite a week. Following each performance, she would treat him and the rest of the crew to sandwiches, beer, and tales of Hollywood's bygone days. "She was wonderful, like my Aunt Elsie from the Bronx. Very sweet and down-to-earth. She was also one of the first women's libbers and was among the few women of her day who both wrote and produced plays. But all of that sexual put-on was purely comic, which made her even more charming."[20] On the day of her train's departure from Chicago, Jerry had the honor of driving the star to the station with two police motorcyclists leading the way and several squad cars covering the rear. It was the ride of a lifetime: "We ended up with a police escort taking us into Chicago to LaSalle Street Station so she could make her train with her company. And we went right through Chicago at about eighty-five miles an hour into the station, and she threw me a $100 bill, which was like four weeks' pay. Imagine a sixteen-year-old kid with a police escort driving a big Cadillac with Mae West in the back seat. Everything's been downhill since."[21]

Actors John Ireland and Vincent Price were also among Jerry's troupemates that summer. Price's friendship and mentoring in the principles of acting contributed greatly to Jerry's professional debut as the Typewriter Man in a production of *Room Service* by the season's end. Other actors taught him comic timing, how to project his voice without damaging it in a three-thousand-seat tent theatre, and how to restrain his overactive eyebrows. One of these was a soon-to-be television comic by the name of Tom Poston on whom Jerry made a lasting impression: "He was such a nice person, so quick and bright, very outgoing, very friendly, loved to laugh, great sense of humor. You might have thought it obvious that he was going to do something very successful when he grew up, so to speak."[22] Poston also taught him how to dress. The teenager had been wearing peg pants, blue suede shoes, and robin's-egg-blue suits until Poston took him to Brooks Brothers in Chicago and made him buy a three-button charcoal-gray suit with natural shoulders. "I didn't know what a three-button suit was," Jerry later confessed. "I thought it was disgusting. I dressed like a high-school kid."[23]

To the relief of Jerry's parents, especially Leo, who understood well the risks in trying to launch a career in show business, Poston succeeded in persuading his friend to attend college. Certain he was only postponing the inevitable, Jerry reluctantly enrolled as a drama major, first for a year at the

University of Illinois in Urbana, where to his surprise he won a medal for being the best-drilled R.O.T.C. cadet on campus, and then for two more years at Northwestern University in Evanston, one of the top theatre schools in the country: "I began to learn Stanislavsky-based teachings on improvisation and imagination—all the internals. For a time, I went through a period where nothing sounded real to me unless I was talking at a conversational level on stage. I was working so internally, I went through what they call the mumbles. I was an incomplete Method actor. Gradually I found out that real acting takes a good deal of energy and slightly bigger-than-life attitudes."[24] The theatre department productions at Northwestern provided him with significant roles like Mercutio in Shakespeare's *Romeo and Juliet* and Azdak in Brecht's *The Caucasian Chalk Circle*. The classroom training also gave him a solid foundation in the craft by effectively combining the contemporary, what had come out of the Group Theatre and the Actors Studio in New York, with traditional instruction in fencing, movement and speech.[25] Ever resourceful, Jerry developed a unique way of combining the theory he was getting in school with the practice that would test it: Northwestern theatre student by day, resident actor by night at the Evanston Showcase Theatre, a year-round stock company where he earned the weekly $25 salary that paid his tuition. There, at age seventeen, he also earned his Equity Card while playing a bit part in *A Trip to Bountiful* with Lillian Gish and Kim Stanley.[26] Stanley's acting made a big impression: "I watched Kim every night. Every night. It was so startling what she did that nobody had ever done before. I had never seen acting like that. Just totally mind-blowing."[27]

By the end of his junior year in 1955, the nineteen-year-old was growing increasingly restless with academia and ever more determined to strike out on his own as an actor. "I always hoped he'd go on to be a scientist," reflects Emily, "but I knew that would never happen. He was constantly going to movies, and he was in the Elks Club show each year. The theatre was his goal, and his father and I knew it."[28] Even so, his parents continued to press him to finish college, go on for his master's degree, and teach as insurance against the possible failure of his acting career. He wanted none of that: "It was kind of unique for the time because I never wanted anything to fall back on. I just assumed that I was going to be okay. That I was going to make it as an actor. I had, I guess, a really indestructible ego."[29] With his parents' blessing, he was bound at last for the city of his birth.

Chapter 2

STREET SINGER/ STORYTELLER, 1955–1961

. . . .

"I REMEMBER SEEING THE *NEW YORK TIMES* THEATRE section in 1950," Jerry once reflected, "and if you look at that theatre page you'd say all of these shows couldn't be running at the same time. Not *South Pacific* and *Mister Roberts* and *A Streetcar Named Desire* and *Death of a Salesman*? They couldn't be all on Broadway at the same time in the same year? Yeah, they were."[1] At the time of his arrival in New York City in fall 1955, this renaissance was still in full bloom with no end in sight — *Damn Yankees*, *Bus Stop*, *Cat on a Hot Tin Roof*, and *Inherit the Wind* likewise running simultaneously in an era later to be known as the Golden Age of Broadway. Fresh from the summer season at the Gristmill Playhouse in Andover, New Jersey, where he had appeared in *Picnic* and *The Caine Mutiny Court-Martial*, Jerry immediately launched plans for becoming the next Brando or Dean. After finding a cheap, tiny flat on West Sixtieth Street shared with a classmate from Northwestern, he began studies with Herbert Berghof, the actor, director, and writer who with his wife, actress Uta Hagen, created the renowned HB Studio where performers like Anne Bancroft, Jack Lemmon, Jason Robards, and Maureen Stapleton studied. He also studied voice with Mazel Schweppe, who taught him, "Emotion — *emotto* — on the word is an outgoing process, feeling is an ingoing process. If you're feeling something, really feeling it, it's very hard to express what you're feeling, especially in singing. If you're really breaking down and crying you can't sing. But you can remember what you just felt and tell about it. So you express emotion and you're telling about how it felt a moment ago or a year ago."[2]

In the heart of the theatre district, drugstores, like Ray's or Walgreen's, were Communication Central for people in the business. Jerry spent hours in these places networking, making contacts, and taking in the latest news and gossip, because they were the chief means of getting the inside track on the entertainment scene. All the comedians hung out at Hansen's Drugstore at Fiftieth Street and Seventh Avenue, where Jerry's pal Tom Poston often took him. There he became a test audience for comics Jackie Leonard and Lenny Bruce, whose deadpan looks and latest jokes had him practically under the table with laughter.[3]

But there was nothing funny about the intense competition he had underestimated, or the five months of fruitless auditions that almost forced him to take a job as a short-order cook. This stretch of bad luck finally broke in December 1955, thanks to friend Jo Wilder (Mrs. Joel Grey), who helped him land an audition for an understudy job at $45 a week with *The Threepenny Opera*. The acclaimed revival of the 1928 Kurt Weill / Bertolt Brecht musical based on John Gay's *The Beggar's Opera* was playing the Theatre de Lys (today the Lucille Lortel) in Greenwich Village. A radical commentary on modern society, it graphically depicted eighteenth-century London street life, complete with cutthroats, thieves, and prostitutes. Its distinguished cast included several performers who would soon become familiar to theatre and television audiences: Ed Asner (*Mary Tyler Moore*, *Lou Grant*), Beatrice Arthur (*Mame*, *Maude*, *The Golden Girls*), Jerry Stiller (*The Stiller and Meara Show*, *Seinfeld*, *The King of Queens*), Charlotte Rae (*Diff'rent Strokes*, *The Facts of Life*), John Astin (*The Addams Family*, *Night Court*), Jane Connell (*Mame*, *Crazy for You*), Jo Sullivan (*The Most Happy Fella*, *Perfectly Frank*), and the renowned Lotte Lenya (wife of composer Weill and the definitive interpreter of his songs), recreating her acclaimed role as Jenny Diver. Following an initial run of 96 performances, from March 10 to May 30, 1954, it returned on September 20, 1955, for a phenomenal six-year run totaling 2,611 performances.

Although Jerry's knowledge of Brecht from his *Caucasian Chalk Circle* experience at Northwestern was useful, in the end it was his singing ability that impressed director Carmen Capalbo and helped him clinch the job.

The evening he went on in the role of the Street Singer for vacationing Tige Andrews, he electrified the audience with his rendition of "Mack the Knife." His talent and personality quickly won him friends like Ed Asner: "He was so damned magnetic I cottoned to him immediately. We began hanging around in the show, out of the show, going out having a beer or coffee together afterwards. Jerry's a spellbinder. I always wanted to be his friend. I loved being his friend. He's a vastly entertaining creature—funny, interesting, very, very bright."[4] Just how bright was soon evident as Jerry advanced his way through seven different parts over the next three and a half years, including a six-month stint in the leading role of Macheath. "I played Mack opposite Lotte Lenya [then 50] when I was 20 years old.... Playing Mack the Knife opposite Lotte Lenya! Unbelievable.... I was so young for it, it was a joke, but I had the [character's] saber scar, the hair and everything. It worked."[5]

But while keeping pace with the formidable Lenya, he was also discovering new aspects of the craft, like the power of the pause—targeting the audience's attention the way a director does with a camera: "There was a pause...where Macheath says, as he's about to be hanged, 'Which is worse—to rob a bank or to own a bank? And which is worse—a man dead lying on his back or a man alive on his knees?' I could hold that beat for as long as I wanted to. Then I'd let them go, and I'd go up the stairs to be hanged."[6] The sensation of grabbing the audience by the throat, holding them for an instant, and then releasing them was thrilling.

Backstage, Jerry, Asner, Astin, and Stiller whiled away time between entrances playing poker in a room above the stage, pausing only to come crashing down the stairs just in time to make their cues. Jerry was also an equal opportunity poker player—one of the best he ever bet against was none other than Lotte Lenya herself. He loved to play because "It's an acting game. If you've never played poker with six actors you've missed something. Talk about a poker face! A guy might burst into tears, or go into the bathroom and run the water and sound like he's throwing up—all part of bluffing. It's a great way for an actor to improvise."[7] Over the course of his thirty-year New York stage career, the backstage poker game would be customary with Jerry.

Now that Jerry was doing musicals, it made sense to improve his movement and ability to quickly learn a dance routine, so he joined Asner and Astin for lessons with famed Broadway choreographer Peter Gennaro. In class, the agility of the three made such an impression on the dance master that he gave them a special name — "the oxen."[8]

Dressing rooms backstage at the Theatre de Lys were the size of telephone booths. Jerry's was situated next to that of a young, doe-eyed, raven-haired actress from San Francisco, who, like him, had been hired as an understudy. A striking Sicilian/Irish beauty, Marta Curro was a statuesque, five-foot-nine standby for the four women playing the roles of the Prostitutes. Bright and loquacious, she reminded Jerry of his ideal — film actress Ava Gardner. Her mother, Evelyn (Eve) Rose Malone, was an artist and illustrator of children's books; her father, Anthony Curro, like Jerry's dad, had been a prizefighter under the name of Eddie Frisco before turning to insurance and real estate sales. Marta was a young child when her parents divorced and since then had been raised by her mother. She was instantly taken with Jerry's manly grace, amazingly powerful voice, and unassuming charm: "You know the first time I realized I was crazy about him? We were standing in the subway station on our way to a 42nd Street movie, and he reached up and buttoned the top button of my coat. Nobody ever dared to do that before with me, or cared whether I was cold or not. I said to myself: 'I think I love this guy.'"[9]

After Saturday evening performances, the pair headed to Forty-Second Street for a night on the town — a fifteen-cent subway ride, a beer and hamburger, hot dog, or fried clam sandwich on the corner at Brandt's or Hector's, then a double feature. At 4:00 A.M., they left the theatre and headed for the bakery to wait for the fresh doughnuts to come out warm from the oven at 5:30. Total cost of the evening? Two bucks![10] Within New York's young-actors' circle, Jerry and Marta were soon considered a fashionable couple, quick-witted, socially aware, and freethinking. A whole decade before the sexual revolution, they were living together in a $70-a-month apartment at 26 Perry Street in Greenwich Village. "You know, it was a different era," Jerry later observed. "Living together was kind of a Bohemian, modern, racy thing to be doing. Not everybody did that."[11] As their relationship grew, they pooled their talents and resources. Marta's gourmet cooking and her extraordinary zest for Italian dishes made dinner a grand occasion. Sunday morning Jerry would whip up the kind of short-order egg-and-omelet fare he had learned when helping Leo at the luncheonette back in Waukegan. He also could be handy in the dinner department, as his broiled chicken soused in sloe gin, lime, and honey-flavored marinade attested.[12]

It seemed strange to Marta that Jerry, while outgoing and talkative at home, was uncomfortable with small talk at parties, where he "stared at the ceiling a lot … [figuring] you just didn't go around doing your nightclub act for people you just met."[13] Then, one evening, he suddenly started conversing with strangers who, to his delight, immediately warmed to his repartee. Marta also found him easygoing by nature, rarely losing his temper save for an occasion when a young Englishman living in their building urged them to go along with a move to fire the superintendent, "a 63-year-old lady who cleaned the halls in a housecoat and tiara."[14] Jerry's response was to lift the Englishman by the collar and pin him against the wall. The superintendent went right on cleaning—tiara and all.

Marta had been studying with Lee Strasberg, distinguished director of the Actors Studio. Founded in 1947 by Elia Kazan, Cheryl Crawford, and Robert Lewis, the school was rapidly gaining international renown for Strasberg's refinements and adaptations of Constantin Stanislavski's "Method" originally devised for the Moscow Art Theatre. Jerry's film idols—Dean, Clift, and Brando—had studied there too, and Marta encouraged him to do the same. Soon he was taking classes with Strasberg, and also with Mira Rostova of the Moscow Art Theatre. As for Marta, an actress of considerable talent herself, she eventually decided to abandon the theatre for a writing career. Her article about Method acting, later published in the *Village Voice*, was, Strasberg said, the finest description of the process he had ever read. Director Elia Kazan even posted it on the set when filming *Splendor in the Grass* in 1961.[15]

After a two-year trial, Jerry and Marta officially tied the knot during a service held at St. Joseph's Church in Greenwich Village, Sixth Avenue and Washington Place, on June 21, 1958. Afterwards as they dodged the rice while exiting the church on their way to the reception at the Mandarin House on Thirteenth Street, Marta had no misgivings about their prospects, convinced as she was of her husband's potential: "I had enormous faith in Jerry's future, simply because he loved what he was doing so much and he was so good at it. And I couldn't imagine that he wouldn't be a success. Also, when you're young like that, you have no idea of what the world is really like, and you think you can do everything you want to do."[16]

Everything, for Jerry, included a film career, which he desperately wanted. However, it would not come easily, since he was not the kind of young actor producers wanted: "Hollywood at that time was, God forgive us, Tab Hunter and Tony Curtis. I wasn't the type. If you wanted to go to Hollywood they'd say you'd better get a nose job first. You blink too much. You're too swarthy. I was twenty the first time I heard I was too tall and dark to play the juvenile lead. My nose was also a factor. I considered getting a nose job for, oh, a minute. Of course, it made me mad…but I don't let things bother me for very long."[17]

Though "too tall and dark" for juvenile leads, Jerry could play other roles, like that of Joe "Mumzer" Sanchez, the Latino street gang leader of *Cop Hater* (1958), the big-city police drama in which he made his screen debut. A vividly brutal film for its day, it dealt with an investigation led by Robert Loggia, as Detective Steve Carelli, to track down the murderer of several policemen during an oppressive heat wave. Based on the detective novel of the same name written by Ed McBain (a.k.a. Evan Hunter, who later wrote the screenplays for *Blackboard Jungle* and *The Birds*), the film also featured Vincent Gardenia. But the Grade B movie was soon gone, taking with it Jerry's hopes of suddenly being discovered by Hollywood.

As he neared the end of three and a half years with *Threepenny*, he concentrated on landing a role in a Broadway play, but there were no offers. In late spring 1959, his career was stuck in neutral even as Emily and Leo, about to retire from Neisner's, were preparing to leave Waukegan and move permanently to New York City that fall. So, soon after James Mitchell (his fellow actor later in *Carnival*) took over as Macheath, he quit *Threepenny* and headed with Marta to Ohio to do summer stock yet again. There he sharpened his skills playing Mannion in *Mister Roberts*, the Kralohome in *The King and I*, Dr. Sanderson in *Harvey*, and Benny in *Guys and Dolls*. Though the job kept things afloat financially and professionally, it also meant missing Leo's big retirement dinner back in Waukegan — which he wanted to attend more than anything. At the end of the summer, Jerry returned with Marta to New York. Audition after audition, nothing came his way, his goal of making it as a New York actor as elusive as ever. He was desperate for a break. Four jobless months later, it came.

Two hundred fifty bucks a week! A fortune for the day, it was the sum producers were offering Jerry to appear in *Lock Up Your Daughters*, the

London musical hit by composer Lionel Bart (later of *Oliver!*) based on *Rape Upon Rape*, Henry Fielding's eighteenth-century comedy about British licentiousness. Jerry considered the musical, due on Broadway that spring, a good omen, bringing 1959 to a happy end for him and Marta. They celebrated with a night out at Julius Monk's intimate Upstairs at the Downstairs, a popular club on Fifty-Sixth Street between Fifth and Sixth Avenues noted for witty revues. There they ran into Word Baker, the club's associate producer, whom Jerry knew from his days at the Gristmill Playhouse in Andover.

"I've got an interesting show, a great part for you," spouted Baker enthusiastically. "Yeah, that's nice," nonchalantly countered the actor, not about to give up his $250 weekly Broadway wage for the paltry $45 Baker was offering for his off-Broadway venture. But as Baker elaborated, Jerry quickly became intrigued: "I didn't know what he was talking about, but when Word explained it was a musical by a couple of fellows named Tom Jones and Harvey Schmidt based on [*Les Romanesques*, an obscure work by Edmund] Rostand, I became interested because I knew *Cyrano* [*de Bergerac*] very well."[18] Interested though he was, he hesitated about following up because the role in *Lock Up Your Daughters* meant not only more money, but also the prestige of being on Broadway. Yet Marta thought Baker's project held more promise and coaxed him into auditioning.

Baker had directed the University of Texas revue that first united songwriters Jones and Schmidt in 1950, as well as the ones they had written since for Upstairs at the Downstairs. Baker had seen Jerry as the Street Singer in *Threepenny* and pressed him to audition for *The Fantasticks*, particularly for the principal role of suave bandit El Gallo, who tells the story of the romance between a girl and boy and the opposition their fathers fake to test their children's sincerity. Also a participant in the action, El Gallo influences the destiny of the lovers and, ultimately, the outcome of the story.

For Baker, Jones, and Schmidt, the scope of the role made it the most urgent and problematic one to cast. They had already seen several actors, and none of them fit the bill — a younger version of Broadway's Alfred Drake, with the requisite masculinity, singing ability, facility with poetry and wit. Then, one rainy afternoon as Schmidt and Baker sat through audition after audition in the West Village's tiny Sullivan Street Playhouse, there stood Jerry center stage in a yellow plastic raincoat. "He just instantly looked like El Gallo to me," says Schmidt. "He came out of the rain looking like a Navajo prince."[19]

Schmidt and Baker soon discovered that the Navajo prince, with his sinewy frame, elegant gestures, quick wit and astonishingly powerful baritone, was rather mature and sophisticated for his twenty-four years. Above all, there was a mesmerizing "counterculture danger"[20] about him that conveyed the dark, mysterious quality they were seeking. Much as he pretended to dismiss it, Jerry was actually a beatnik with an insatiable proclivity for chain-smoking his way through late-night film marathons at Forty-Second Street cinemas then, early next morning, analyzing what he had seen while sipping espresso with friends at a coffeehouse.

Days after his first audition, he arrived for a second one at the brownstone on West Seventy-Fourth by Riverside Drive where Jones and Schmidt shared an apartment with two other roommates. He zigzagged his way through a phalanx of aspiring El Gallos seated on the stairway and, at length, arrived at the door of the songwriters' third-floor apartment, where he knocked and was told to enter. This time Jones and producer Lore Noto were on the scene, and at once he impressed them as much as he had Schmidt and Baker. Jerry had it all — the looks, voice, poetic art, and playful sense. When the audition ended, he politely bowed and was gone. The four creators were unanimously decided — Jerry was their El Gallo. "Jerry! Wait!" yelled Jones, Schmidt, and Noto from the window as Baker charged down three flights of stairs, dodging actors all the way until he reached the street. He caught up with Jerry at the corner and told him everyone agreed that the role was his. "I think Jerry was impressed with the enthusiasm and the immediate commitment that we made," says Jones. "And it was a good thing that we made it, too, because we didn't know he had been offered a part in *Lock Up Your Daughters*."[21]

The team's decision simply confirmed what Jerry knew the moment he first read the script — he had to do it. So what if it was $45 a week? It was beautiful, funny, and gave him a leading role almost tailor-made for him: "El Gallo is a magician; he's a narrator; he's a romantic. He's all the things you'd ever want to be, so what better part to play? I had decided I wanted to do it, and that was it."[22] As for *Lock Up Your Daughters*, he turned it down, trusting his intuition — and Marta's — that *The Fantasticks* was the better bet: "That was indicative of my life and taking a chance. Always taking a chance. Being out there with no net under the wire, I guess."[23]

Jerry soon forgot the risk once rehearsals got under way in spring 1960. The working atmosphere was extraordinarily creative because of Baker's open directorial method, which encouraged the actors to experiment to find distinctive approaches to the material and then distilled their contributions by determining exactly what they should use and how they should use it. Jerry and the cast soon learned that Baker was not a dictator, but an editor who exercised his authority by helping them bring to life his overall vision for the production—a troupe of commedia dell'arte players living, traveling, and performing together from the back of a wagon they pull from town to town. "So that's how we began to work," Jerry explained. "We had the freedom to say, 'Hey, I've got an idea: How about this?' and Word was wide open to anything. That was very unusual at that time...[because]...you were supposed to just sit there and do what the director told you."[24]

"Try to Remember," which in time became the show's hit, was the first song Jerry learned. Composer Schmidt recalls how Jerry bonded with the song: "He first heard it after he was cast in the show, when he'd come by my apartment and I'd work with him on the songs with musical director Julian Stein. I asked if he wanted the key changed, and he said, 'No, it's just perfect. I don't want to change it.' ... He was innately musical. There was never anything fussy about the way he sang. His voice was like his persona, unadorned. Just Jerry. The song was instantly his the minute he started doing it."[25] From that point forward, "Try to Remember" was Jerry's signature song.

In rehearsal, there was a simplicity of style emerging that would be key to the production's success, and Jerry perfectly matched his El Gallo to it with a realistic approach that rejected pretentiousness. "My goal was naturalistic, realistic acting," he explained. Because he could sing, he was getting jobs in musicals at a time when friends who were not singers were jobless. Even so, he wanted to bring aspects of "the Method" he had learned as an actor to the musical theatre. Anything mawkish or corny was to be avoided—the one exception being a comic moment in the "Rape Ballet." As for the rest—the direct addresses to the audience and the poetry—truth was what he wanted. "That was very, very important to me.... I think that was my particular contribution to the structure of that play: you have to have that reality when you're doing the little poetic speeches, ... otherwise the high-flying poetry and comedy have nothing to bounce off of."[26]

The exception to the reality rule, the "Rape Ballet," gave Jerry a perfect opportunity to show El Gallo's comic side by evoking actor John Barrymore's exaggerated style—the complete antithesis to "the Method" he had studied under Berghoff and Strasberg. Once again, his instinct was right on target. As soon as the Boy [Matt, played by Kenneth Nelson] stabbed him, he clutched at the fake chest wound and stared at his assailant in utter disbelief, in the manner of Barrymore "doing a sort of broken-wristed point. So when Kenny stabbed me, I went like that, and suddenly it was a big laugh."[27] Though a bit exaggerated, the comic touch suited the moment perfectly.

Although Jerry was the youngest in the cast, he was also, as Donald Farber and Robert Viagas note in *The Amazing Story of "The Fantasticks": America's Longest Running Play*, "the dominating presence [whose] obvious talent, strong and well reasoned opinions and dark good looks would have stood out in any crowd."[28] Beyond these things, the members of the company noted how pool and poker filled Jerry's spare time. His skill at billiards endeared him to producer Lore Noto, an accomplished player himself and also an inveterate poker player who, along with Tom Jones and a few others, would often end up supplementing Jerry's paycheck via their weekly poker games.

Jerry's dark looks and height might have been intimidating if not for his good-natured personality and self-effacing way "of making jokes at his own expense,"[29] as Kenneth Nelson observed. Rita Gardner, who played the Girl, Luisa, was impressed with him from the first day of rehearsal:

> When we all sang, I certainly knew who was the real star. I looked over and there was this wonderful actor—so strong and alive. And he was always coming up with things. I would just say, "Oh, and he can juggle, too," because he'd come out and he'd be throwing up oranges and balls. He was the glue of that show, someone who made you feel that everything would be all right. Every time we played the scene where I had to stand up on a chair and fall back in his arms, I knew Jerry would catch me. You could trust him implicitly.[30]

Among the remaining cast members were Jerry's friend from Northwestern, Richard Stauffer, who played the Mute and, for a time, would be his dresser; William Larson and Hugh Thomas as the fathers, Hucklebee and Bellamy; Thomas Bruce (a.k.a. Tom Jones) and George Curley as the actors; and Jay Hampton as the Handyman.

When *The Fantasticks* opened on May 3, 1960, at the Sullivan Street Playhouse, it was barely noticed, but in the following weeks the show found its audience and soon was a phenomenal hit, eventually becoming the longest-running play in the history of the American theatre before closing January 13, 2002, after forty-one years and 17,162 performances. Jerry's bet had paid off handsomely, especially with the Broadway-bound *Lock Up Your Daughters* dying on the road only weeks after he cast his lot with Baker, Noto, Jones, and Schmidt: "I said at the time, *The Fantasticks* could close in a week or if it became a legend like *Threepenny Opera*, … that maybe it would become the thing to see when you're in the Village. And maybe it would run four or five years. I said that would be the wonder, the ideal thing. And of course I was wrong by about thirty-seven years. So I guess I picked the right one."[31]

New York Times critic Walter Kerr thought so too, noting, "Mr. Orbach, whose task it is to set a suitably fey tone without letting archness run away with him, most notably suppresses the incipient cutes, speaks as straightforwardly as though he were trying to convince an investigating committee he had never heard of payola, and tacks cardboard moons onto handy pillars with the utmost sobriety. Having an interesting face, a controlled voice and a clear intelligence, Mr. Orbach is no doubt on his way."[32]

His parents, now living in the Village on Delancey Street, could not have been prouder. Leo was especially delighted to see his son achieve the success that had evaded him as a young vaudeville comedian. "My husband went to see the show every night," remembers Emily. "As a matter of fact, one night soon after the recording of the show was made, he invited everybody over to our apartment to hear it. It was a summer night around eleven o'clock or so, and they started playing the record over and over. The sound right went out the open windows and up into the courtyard. And the neighbors all kept yelling, 'Turn that down!'"[33]

While in *The Fantasticks*, Jerry obtained a small part in *Twenty-Four Hours in a Woman's Life*, a television play starring Ingrid Bergman. "Of course I fell in love with her," he explained. "You couldn't help that. I just wanted to lay down in the gutter and let her walk on me."[34] His follow-up was another Grade B film, a mostly fictitious account of infamous Prohibition-era Irish mobster Vincent "Mad Dog" Coll (1908–1932), also the vicious henchman of New York bootlegging kingpin Dutch Schultz. The film, *Mad Dog Coll* (1961), in which Jerry appeared as Coll's best friend, Joe, who betrays the gangster and then steals his girlfriend, also included newcomers Telly Savalas as Lieutenant Dawson, Vincent Gardenia as Dutch Schultz, and Gene Hackman as a cop. But the end product was so undistinguished that Jerry wished the studio had canceled its release. Even worse was the grief he was getting about portraying a rat who turns on his buddy, especially from pool-hustling friends Brooklyn Joey, Hundred Ball Blackie, and Johnny Eyebrows, to whom he was known as Jerry the Actor.[35]

While his film career still failed to ignite, Jerry's stage work was now so fully ablaze that some powerful people in the business were taking note. He'd been with *The Fantasticks* only a few weeks when Broadway director-choreographer Gower Champion saw his performance and then returned for a second look with producer David Merrick and songwriter Bob Merrill. After the performance that evening they offered him the lead in their new musical based on the popular film *Lili* (1953). Astonished and ecstatic, Jerry was suddenly Broadway bound as the leading man of *Carnival.*[36]

Chapter 3

LEADING MAN/ SURVIVOR, 1961–1966

· ·

JERRY RACED UP SECOND AVENUE AGAINST THE ICY blast of mid-January 1961, destined for the Phyllis Anderson Theatre, his mind buzzing. Here it was the first day of rehearsal for *Carnival*—over three months after being told he had the role of Paul Berthalet, the mordant, lame puppeteer transformed by the lovely waif Lili—and he was still without a contract. "Don't worry about it," Gower Champion had assured him, "You're in as far as I'm concerned." But that was little consolation to the actor, who had not even been asked to audition! Warily, he had accepted the director's word and prepared for months, even bonding with a practice puppet he constantly wore on his hand around the house. To avoid embarrassment in case the job fell through, he and Marta had agreed not to discuss it with anyone, not even their closest friends, until he officially signed on. Turning onto Fourth Street, he entered the stage door, wondering if Champion, Merrick, and Merrill realized what they were doing: "I did a lot of singing, and they knew I could handle that, but they had no idea if I could do the puppet work or have the kind of bitter, world-weary, disenchanted qualities that Paul is supposed to have."[1]

Champion had already been working with the dancers for a week when Jerry entered the backstage area and greeted stage manager Charlie Blackwell. "Hi, I'm Jerry," he beamed. "Shhh! Mr. Champion is thinking," admonished Blackwell. Jerry surveyed the scene: the director was standing at the center of the stage, literally pondering the next step while the entire chorus froze in place, too terrified to move. "*Oh*, he's *thinking*," Jerry mused. Clearly, Champion's method of working was worlds apart from Word Baker's experimental give-and-take. Jerry's first impression of him was that of an imposing figure in whose presence people were afraid to even whisper. His control over performers was absolute and centered on where they fitted in terms of the impressive stage pictures he created. He was forever thinking in terms of visual images. Fortunately, Champion, along with Merrick and Merrill, still visualized Jerry as Paul and, true to their promise, signed him on that day. "I guess they knew I wouldn't turn it down," Jerry kidded.[2]

Gower Champion (1919–1980), who with wife and partner Marge had graced numerous television shows, nightclubs, and film musicals as a popular dance team, had recently turned to directing and choreographing Broadway musicals with the smash hit *Bye Bye Birdie* (1960). He was a master at streamlining musicals and making them flow seamlessly. His continuous choreographed staging, which he would perfect with *Carnival*, made every element of a musical—even scene changes—dance from start to finish. His vision or concept for this production was also groundbreaking. For the prologue, the action unfolded on an empty, curtainless stage with a troupe of players gradually filling the area before raising a vast circus tent under which the entire story unfolded. At the finale, the troupe dismantled the tent and little by little deserted the stage, leaving it bare once more. But, impressive as his staging was, at this point in his new career, Champion's vernacular was still in dance, not acting, and this complicated his communication with actors greatly.[3]

A case in point was a day when Jerry and star Anna Maria Alberghetti were working with the director on a scene where Paul heartlessly rehearses Lili beyond endurance. "Gower asked me if I would do the scene walking around Anna Maria in a circle," Jerry explained, "making the circle smaller and smaller until I would end up face to face with her. I said, 'Do you mean you want the scene to get more and more intense and that I should get more and more angry?' He said, 'Yes, *that's* what I mean.' At that point, all of his communication was in the visual sense. He was still much, much more of a choreographer than he was a director. His communication skills about anything resembling acting were very, very limited."[4]

Unless there was something plainly wrong with the acting, Champion generally left the specifics to the performer. Ironically, in creating the character of Paul—a great dancer turned puppet master as a result of a war injury to his right leg—Jerry drew upon the physicality of Champion himself, studying the dancer's hands and upper-body movements but adding a limp. As for internals, the director had only one instruction: Paul was to be completely black and unrelieved. Though Jerry wanted to give the character more nuance, he delivered precisely what he was told. Shortly after the opening, Lee Strasberg attended a performance. Afterward he remarked to Jerry, who was then studying with him, "Gee, it's so one-note, dark and unrelieved." "That's the way Mr. Champion wants it," responded Jerry. "He doesn't want any warmth spilling out at all." "Well," protested Strasberg, "couldn't we once in a while see him fighting *against* the warmth spilling out?" "Oh, good idea!" the actor exclaimed, grateful to have his instincts confirmed.[5]

Despite limitations with the language of acting, Champion was a master at casting, able to perfectly suit actor to role. At the time of *Carnival*, he was keenly aware that critics and audiences were tiring of what had been the acting level of musicals—booming-voiced singers, relics from operetta, who spoke in stentorian tones and lacked any credible characterization. This practice began to alter with the introduction of performers who were primarily actors, like Yul Brynner in *The King and I* (1951), and later Rex Harrison in *My Fair Lady* (1956). For Jerry, a serious actor whose idols were Marlon Brando and James Dean rather than Gordon MacRae and Mario Lanza, the timing was perfect for his arrival on Broadway because the part of Paul was a very serious, bitter, dramatic piece. These qualities were reflected in the songs "I've Got to Find a Reason," "Everybody Likes You," "Her Face," and "She's My Love," which Jerry initially heard performed by composer Bob Merrill on tape.

> When I first heard the songs, I almost wept because I thought, "Oh, my God! This kind of obtuse, off-the-wall stuff is not even in the same league with 'Try to Remember,'" because a lot of it was recitative, self-pitying and in character. I found them very difficult, very challenging and *actable*. They were songs you could act out and, being an actor first and a singer second, I liked the idea of that challenge. Also, I was doing four different screaming puppet voices and then going back into a song, which was probably one of the more difficult things I've ever attempted.[6]

Although Jerry did not realize it at first, his performance in *The Fantasticks* had been his audition for Champion, who had known at once that he was ideal for Paul. So had Anna Maria Alberghetti: "Jerry was a wonderful actor. The reason he was so wonderful in the show and made the play so believable is that he is an actor first and a singer second. To me he *was* Paul. There wasn't one moment on stage that I didn't believe him being the total character he was. That's why our scenes really worked."[7]

On Sunday, March 5, prior to its out-of-town tryouts in Washington and Philadelphia, *Carnival* had a run-through at the Phyllis Anderson for an invited audience whose exuberance raised the rafters. Clearly, Jerry's talent had matured beyond his twenty-six years, and Emily and Leo proudly awaited his Broadway debut. Adding to their pride was news that Marta was pregnant and due in late fall. At the same time as the expectant grandparents were preparing to move into a roomier apartment in the same building as Marta's mother, Eve, on Eighteenth Street, their son and daughter-in-law were packing for their five-week road trip and making arrangements for the care of their four Siamese cats. Days later, as their Washington-bound train pulled out of Penn Station, Jerry and Marta ecstatically anticipated his stage success and their first child.

On Easter Sunday morning, April 2, Leo died suddenly from a heart attack at age sixty-four, the day before he and Emily were to move into their new apartment. "When my husband retired, he had glaucoma," explained Emily, "so we came to New York for him to have eye surgery. But I had made up my mind we were going to stay here, because Jerry was here, and I knew he would want to help taking care of Leo, who also had a heart condition. I knew it wouldn't be long, but never expected it to come so soon."[8]

In the face of his father's unexpected death, Jerry immediately left for home, Marta by his side, to join his mother and help with his father's funeral arrangements. When he returned to Washington, he kept focused and professional, never permitting his personal grief to affect his performance or the morale of the company. "He just got very quiet," recalled Tom Poston. "He didn't impose his mourning on anyone else, but he suffered the loss. They were very, very close."[9]

Before *Carnival* left Washington's National Theatre to move on to Philadelphia, the company had the honor of performing for the President and First Lady, who came backstage to greet the cast after the performance.

"President Kennedy was surrounded by at least half a dozen Secret Service agents," recalled Jerry. "Suddenly there was an explosive noise, everyone hit the floor, Secret Service agents were crouching and guns were drawn. It turned out to be nothing more than a bottle of shaving cream that exploded when an actor on the level above accidentally dropped it. I turned to President Kennedy and said, 'You know what happened to the last president who saw a play in Washington.' Kennedy laughed and said, 'Yes, but I wasn't sitting in Lincoln's box.'"[10] The memory of that evening would haunt Jerry for life.

On April 13, 1961, *Carnival* opened at the Imperial Theatre to raves and later won the New York Critics' Circle Award for best musical. The critics also recognized Jerry as a new kind of leading man with the voice, authority, and conviction of an actor destined for stardom. The audience response was no less affecting. As Jerry later recalled, "*Carnival* was a wonderful experience and a show that touched people in a very special way—especially young girls. Every now and then, somebody comes up to me and says it changed their whole life and made them fall in love with the theatre."[11]

Soon Jerry learned that the impact of being a Broadway actor reached beyond the Imperial's stage into the heart of the theatre district itself, where he was now considered a member of the community—something that impressed him greatly as he made the acquaintance of restaurateurs along the Great White Way. Apart from their cuisine, theatrical restaurants, like Sardi's and Joe Allen's, became famous because they cultivated a relationship with performers. Often customers would dine in such places (as they still do today) in hopes of spotting a celebrity. One evening, shortly after the opening of *Carnival*, Jerry and three friends left the Imperial and headed across the street for dinner at Sardi's.

> There was a mob scene outside. The whole sidewalk was filled with people. There was some opening or something, and I looked to see how we could possibly get in there. Vincent Sardi saw me out on the sidewalk, I didn't even know he knew who I was, and he said, "Oh, Mr. Orbach, your table is ready." And I said, "Whoa, does this guy know how to handle the actors!" So I was loyal after that. Joe Allen knew that, too. Joe always said, "A friend with a reservation first, a friend without a reservation second, a stranger with a reservation third."[12]

By now, Jerry was also keeping company with stars like Pearl Bailey, Milton Berle, and Richard Burton. Years later, in 1992, Jerry related a story to his cousin and friend Jon Olexy about his introduction to the charismatic Welsh actor, then appearing in *Camelot* just blocks away from *Carnival*. Although Jerry generally spoke of performers in the friendliest and most complimentary terms, he bent that rule a little on this occasion. Explained Jerry to Jon,

> Lee Strasberg and members of the Actors Studio were celebrating Burton's birthday. At the time, Burton was having an affair with Susan Strasberg, Lee's young daughter. Strasberg himself was picking up on the rumors and was concerned. I bought a small crystal-like kaleidoscope and had it wrapped. Nothing, really. But when Burton opened the gift, he began to thank me profusely and genuinely. Holding up the crystal, his Welsh cut-glass accent rumbled clear and warm — "Crystal is a symbol of the soul of life. The many hues of man's personality pass through in all their splendor and color and emotion" — and on and on. Of course, everyone nearby is listening intently to this minute-long thank-you soliloquy, from some play or other, I thought. And I said to Burton when he finished: "Richard, thank you, those were beautiful words. Where are they from?" And Burton said: "Why, Jerry, they're from *me* ...." And in the background, Susan Strasberg said, "And that's not the only thing he's good at!"[13]

But with all the hobnobbing, kudos, and perks, there was a downside to *Carnival*: Jerry's puppetry skills were never really acknowledged. Because he performed behind a curtain, neither critics nor audiences were aware that he handled all the puppets and did the voices for each — the lively boy-clown Carrot Top, the shy walrus Horrible Henry, the haughty grand dame Marguerite, and the cunning fox Renardo. Consequently, people were not interested in *his* autograph; they wanted Horrible Henry's.

> When we opened in New York, the reviews basically said that Jerry Orbach was fine, good, whatever, *but the puppets were out of this world!* The puppets got reviewed like a separate entity, like somebody else was doing them. A couple of years later, when I did the show again, now having the value of hindsight, I had the entire front of the puppet

booth put on with Velcro and after that big scene when Lili walks off with Marco [the Magician], I came out and ripped off the whole front of the booth. When the audience realized there was no one else in there, I got a three-minute standing ovation.[14]

Gradually, word did spread about Jerry's expertise with the puppets, and soon he was appearing on puppeteer Shari Lewis's children's show with his menagerie from *Carnival*. Producers were offering him "a three-year contract on TV for a children's Saturday morning show. I didn't want it, but it was security … three years on salary. Marta said she didn't marry a puppeteer. That was that."[15] But at home his puppetry skills soon found new purpose entertaining his son Anthony (Tony) Nicholas, born December 6, 1961. Fatherhood also gave Jerry fresh insight into his relationship with Leo, making him appreciate more than ever the debt he owed him: "When you're growing up and in your twenties, you think your father's pretty dumb and pretty old-fashioned, but then as you become a father you start to realize how smart he was."[16]

Jerry settled in for what he thought would be a long-term commitment to *Carnival*, but he had only been with the cast a little over a year before producer David Merrick (1911–2000) tapped him to join the national tour in Chicago. Though far from thrilled about leaving Marta and Tony for four months, Jerry found it hard to deny Merrick, who could make or break an actor's career. A later-day Florenz Ziegfeld with a host of successful productions to his credit (*Look Back in Anger, A Taste of Honey, Becket, The Matchmaker, The World of Suzie Wong, Jamaica, Gypsy, Irma La Douce*), his impeccable instinct for worthwhile properties was as famous as the chicanery and ruthlessness to which he often resorted to insure their profitability.

Chief among Merrick's controversies were his legendary battles with actors over salary, and in coming years Jerry would have his share. On this first occasion, however, Jerry was concerned that the national tour's out-of-town expenses—lodging, lessons, and meals—could quickly eat away at his take-home pay. "David wanted me to go out to Chicago … and I really didn't want to leave, … but I saw a chance to make some money and I said, 'Well, David, I've got to have more money, to go there.' And he said, 'Well, just talk to Jack and tell Jack that I said to give you whatever you ask for because I know you'll be fair.'"[17]

"Jack" was Jack Schlissel, Merrick's business manager, whom Marta dubbed "Black Jack." As Jerry told film director Rick McKay, "Black Jack Schlissel, he liked that nickname. So I go out and say to Jack, 'Jack, I gotta have $1250 a week because I have to send money home.' He said, 'Oh, we can't give you that much.' And I said, 'David just said to give me whatever I asked for.' He said, 'No, but he meant maybe like $1000, but not $1250.' I said, 'Well, that's how much I need.' He said, 'I'll tell you what I'll do, I'll split it with you, we'll give you $1125.' I said, 'Okay,' and left. I'm sure Jack went in [to Merrick] and said, 'I just saved you a hundred and a quarter.' That's the way it was with Merrick."[18]

The impresario did have some advice for the young leading man: "You know, you're never going to get rich in the theatre. You can only get rich in the movies and television. If you're trying to get rich, don't work with me."[19] *Carnival* was the first of three musicals Jerry did with Merrick, with *Promises, Promises* (1968) and *42nd Street* (1980) to follow.

As Jerry departed for Chicago and the happy reunion with friends from nearby Waukegan that would be part of it, he reflected on the changes in his life since opening night:

> The nicest was the birth of my son Anthony, known around the house as "The Friendly Giant." He was born at Lenox Hospital about 8:30 in the evening, just before I went on stage. A nurse called me from the delivery room and held the telephone into the nursery so I could hear him holler. I felt great, but I think I gave a distracted performance because I was thinking about everything except the show. Anthony now has eight teeth, blond hair and blue eyes, and he doesn't wake me before 9 or 10 in the morning which is most considerate of him.[20]

Fatherhood became her son well, thought Emily, who wished that Leo could have lived to see their grandson, as well as their son's success.

Although he returned to the Broadway cast of *Carnival* four months later and remained until closing on January 5, 1963, little by little he was growing uneasy about the kind of roles he was getting. The Street Singer and Macheath in *Threepenny*, El Gallo in *The Fantasticks*, and Paul in *Carnival* had all been shadowy figures firmly rooted in musical theatre. Every actor dreads being typecast, and it was also Jerry's worst fear: "They'd say, 'He plays those dark, brooding characters; he doesn't do comedy,' or 'He does musicals, so he's not an actor.'"[21] His solution was to take Marta and Tony and head for Hollywood. That only compounded the problem—five miserable months with nothing to show but a bit part driving a jeep in the opening of the film *John Goldfarb, Please Come Home* (1965). "It was the low point of my life," he said. "I don't even know how to describe it. It's that thing of for years the New York actor has really been shoved down their throats. They've been told that New York actors are better, so everybody's on their guard. They ask what you've done. You say, 'I was in *The Threepenny Opera*, and they say, 'The what?' I told one casting guy I was in *Carnival*, and he said, 'You were in a carnival?' Now, he couldn't have been that dumb ... I think he was putting me on. Then again, he may have been just that dumb."[22]

After the Orbachs' return to New York in summer 1963, Jerry's post-*Carnival* slump continued. Having been the romantic lead in a hit Broadway musical, he resolved to accept only roles of equal distinction, even after a number of ostensibly firm offers fell through, the role of the magnetic rainmaker, Bill Starbuck, in *110 in the Shade* (1963) and the dashing Nick Arnstein in *Funny Girl* (1964) among them.[23] The price he paid for his inflexibility was a colossal depression that only worsened when Marta became the family's breadwinner after taking a job as a TV talk-show host. "I was depressed, I think, in terms of work," he admitted, "like when a television name whom everybody knew was really terrible would get the lead in a big Broadway show that I wanted desperately. I'd walk around for six months mumbling, 'That miserable, no good ...' A lot of things like that went on in the business [and] used to make me brood."[24]

In summer 1964, Jerry's spirits revived a bit as he and Marta moved from their crowded Perry Street apartment into a spacious four-story brownstone at 232 West Twenty-Second Street in Chelsea, for thirty-four years the meeting hall of the Italian Bakery Workers' Union. But just as they made the $1000 down payment sealing their $50,000 purchase, the studio canceled Marta's talk show. With both spouses now out of work, the reality of a huge mortgage to pay jolted Jerry out of his depression. "Before we got the house," Marta explained,

> people would call up and ask him to do commercials and he'd say, "I don't do commercials." Or they would call up and say, "We have a part

for you," and he'd say, "Where is it?" and they'd say Poughkeepsie or some place, and he'd say, "I'm sorry but I don't go there." And he'd hang up and we'd laugh — we'd get hysterical at all the things he wasn't going to do if they weren't convenient. Okay, now we get this house, and ten minutes after we get the house we have no money. And they call him up and say, "Would you like … ?" and he'd say, "I'll do it." He said yes to everything — like a hooker.[25]

He emerged from his yearlong exile sufficiently chastened to raise his baritone in an off-Broadway revival of *The Cradle Will Rock*. This 1937 "play in music" by Marc Blitzstein championed industrial unionism and counseled against surrendering one's honor to the political and commercial establishment. As Larry Foreman, the musical's principled hero, Jerry at last had a role with a positive thrust and, equally important, a chance to work with some renowned names in the theatre and music worlds. Howard DaSilva, the director, had also created the character of Larry Foreman when Orson Welles directed the original production. Music director Gershon Kingsley, who later would be the first to use the Moog synthesizer in live performance (and would also compose the international electronic hit "Popcorn"), had performed similar duties on *The Entertainer*, *La Plume de Ma Tante*, and *Jamaica*. Out of respect for Blitzstein, who had recently died, composer Leonard Bernstein served as musical consultant for a cast that included Lauri Peters, Nancy Andrews, Clifford David, Rita Gardner (Jerry's castmate from *The Fantasticks*), Micki Grant, and Joseph Bova (who later appeared with him in *42nd Street*). Despite the distinguished contributions and glowing reports from the press, the revered virtual-opera ran only eighty-two performances after opening at Theatre Four on November 8, 1964.[26]

A second revival followed — the New York City Center's production of Frank Loesser's *Guys and Dolls*, in which Jerry played Sky Masterson. It also starred comedian Alan King as Nathan Detroit, Sheila MacRae as Adelaide, Anita Gillette as Sarah Brown, and World Middleweight Boxing Champion Jake LaMotta (later the subject of the 1980 Martin Scorsese film *Raging Bull*) as Big Julie. Jerry's role required him to deck LaMotta's Big Julie at every performance. "Jake used to say I was the only guy who ever knocked him down — eight times a week. Even Sugar Ray Robinson [LaMotta's contender in three fights] never knocked him down. That was okay. I didn't want anybody to think I really could knock down Jake LaMotta."[27] Even though he was playing a dark character once more, at least it was a gangster with a heart of gold. In the end, Jerry made such an impression as Sky that, shortly after the production opened on April 26, 1965, he received a Tony nomination as Best Supporting or Featured Actor in a Musical, the first time an actor from a musical revival was so honored. Although Victor Spinetti of *Oh, What a Lovely War* received the award, Jerry was pleased to have his work recognized by the theatre community.

By the time he landed the role of the sinister Jigger Craigin in the Lincoln Center production of Rodgers and Hammerstein's *Carousel*, his career was well into what he later termed his "revival period." (His mother-in-law, Eve, thought "survival period" more apt.) *Carousel* opened in New York on August 22, 1965, after touring Toronto, Detroit, and Minneapolis, where, as part of his role, "I took a dive at a guy on stage and stabbed myself in the leg right down to the bone. I limped for a while after that. It was the same leg that was supposed to have been crippled in *Carnival.* Two ladies who saw the show in Miami and had seen *Carnival* said: 'Jerry Orbach really does have a limp.'"[28]

Working with composer and producer Richard Rodgers was another plus. Jerry also understudied John Raitt, who was re-creating the role of Billy Bigelow, which he had originated twenty years before. "John saw me in an understudy rehearsal one day, and said, 'You are *never* going on. I don't care how sick I am,'" Jerry recalled with a laugh. "Billy is almost a tenor's role—kind of high for me and tough, but it was all a lot of fun."[29]

While rehearsing for *Carousel,* he played five Sunday night performances in the Music Theatre's workshop presentation of *Berlin Is Mine* and had a solo album to his credit, *Jerry Orbach Off Broadway* (MGM, 1962). That summer he appeared at the Vancouver Arts Festival playing Joey to Robert Weede's Tony in *The Most Happy Fella.*[30] Things were going so well that during *Carousel's* stop in Detroit, Jerry purchased a six-legged antique Brunswick Arcade pool table that he had shipped to the family's new townhouse. "Peter Falk's starting a billiard club with Paul Newman, Sidney Poitier, and Robert Ryan," he told a reporter. "He asked me to join. I said: 'Peter, I'm going to have my own table.' He said: 'Yeah, but you've got to have action—other people to play with.' No one can beat me except Johnny Johnston and Jackie Gleason."[31] He had come a long way from the day he played his first game when school let out for the summer in the eighth grade. The same could be said of his first trip to Brooks Brothers with Tom Poston for a business suit, for by now he was considered one of the best-dressed men in New York and usually a year ahead of fashion trends.

After touring with *Carousel*, Jerry returned to New York and auditioned for the Lincoln Center revival of Irving Berlin's *Annie Get Your Gun* with the renowned Ethel Merman recreating her stage success as Annie Oakley. Both Merman and her friend Benay Venuta, who was playing Dolly Tate and was also Jerry's costar and fellow poker player in *Carousel*, were pushing for him to be Charlie Davenport, the manager of Buffalo Bill's Wild West Show. As the production edged closer to rehearsal, "Benay said, 'Are you going to do *Annie*?' and I said, 'I don't think so, the director [Jack Sydow] thinks I'm too young for it.' Well, she called Merman, whom I'd never met, and Merman called the producer [Richard Rodgers] and said, 'Is Jerry Orbach going to play Charlie Davenport?' The producer said, 'I don't think so.' So she said, 'Well, then, get yourself another girl singer!' So I got the job."[32]

Merman amazed him.

> She was a great, great lady — a lot of fun personally [and] great to hang out with. When my son Tony was young, she was like an aunt — this wonderful, down-home person in a home situation. In the theatre, she was something else, because in the middle of a dress rehearsal or technical rehearsal she'd say, "Charlie, the third light on the number two rail, isn't that supposed to be a baby pink? It looks like a bastard amber to me." And they'd look at the chart and say, "Oh, you're right, Miss Merman." She knew everything. Everything. A great, great pro.[33]

Opening night, May 31, 1966, was quite an occasion at the New York State Theater, with Irving Berlin beaming down his approval from a box above the stage. When Merman sang the first eight bars of the chorus to "There's No Business Like Show Business," the entire audience burst into applause and gave her a standing ovation that stopped the show. After its run in New York, the production toured the country before it was taped for NBC television and broadcast on March 19, 1967. "I looked like Milton Berle," Jerry joked.[34]

A tour as Tom in Tennessee Williams's *The Glass Menagerie* at last gave Jerry a totally non-musical role that led to the lead in the ill-fated Broadway comedy *The Natural Look*—a part Jerry took on as a favor to director Martin Fried, then married to leading lady Brenda Vaccaro. Other cast members included Gene Hackman, Ethel Griffies, Doris Roberts, and Zohra Lampert. After eighteen preview performances, the play opened and closed on March 11, 1967, the only flop of Jerry's career. The trouble was that first-time playwright Leonora Thuna "wouldn't change a word, wouldn't take any suggestions."[35] But there was a plus: *The Natural Look* gave Jerry a whole new look. "I got to keep the wardrobe. I figured I ought to get something out of it. The day they asked us to clear out the dressing rooms, the stage manager said, 'Oh, by the way, the producers asked if you want to buy any of the wardrobe.' There were a couple of Cardin blazers, a great suit, Gucci loafers—it was beautiful. I said, 'No, I don't think so,' grabbed it all off the rack, and walked out."[36]

PART II:
THE FIRE OF SEPTEMBER

Chapter 4

MANIACAL WONDER/ SCHNOOK HERO, 1966–1970

· ·

"I'LL DIE IF I DON'T GET THAT PART," JERRY CONFESSED to Marta. "And you know, I don't think I will. Hell, they've got big guys [Alan Arkin, Dick Shawn] flying in from the coast, from all over, paying their own expenses, who want that part."[1] The part was that of a super-liberal Jewish intellectual whose tolerance is pushed beyond limit when his wife, seemingly bent on dumping him for a black scuba diver, takes up with a black intellectual instead. The unbridled and ultra-harried Harold Wonder, who constantly wavers between forgiveness and revenge in Bruce Jay Friedman's wild, acerbic comedy *Scuba Duba*, was just what the thirty-two-year-old actor needed to expand his range and break the cycle of revivals and typecasting. And Friedman's unconventional, blush-inducing romp did the trick for Jerry when it opened off-Broadway on October 10, 1967, at the New Theatre on East Fifty-Fourth Street.

The play's larger-than-life antihero was the pivotal career role every actor seeks, a tour de force for Jerry, whose manic performance, according to *New York Times* reporter Joan Barthel, included "hurling enraged, bone-marrow obscenities into the moonlight; brandishing a wicked scythe as he plunges headlong into tangled Faulknerian greenery; frantically, desperately juggling grapes and doing push-ups; having his knee bitten by a girl in a purple bikini and gobbling a green apple while ferociously humming and dripping sweat"[2]—all the while rampaging about in striped pajamas. In addition, Jerry was onstage throughout entire play—two hours and thirty-five minutes, minus the intermission. Sustaining the credibility of a hyper-neurotic for that length of time required tremendous physical and emotional stamina that Jerry seemed to have in endless supply. He hardly sat still or kept quiet for a moment, frequently roaring and writhing with anger when not tussling with the fetching, bikini-clad girl next door (Brenda Smiley), hindering a thief (Judd Hirsch), reviling and then pardoning his wife (Jennifer Warren) and her black lover (Rudy Challenger), or coming face-to-face with the dreaded Scuba Duba himself (Cleavon Little). Manic indeed, but what was the point?

All the characters, explained Friedman, were essentially "the animated hallucinations of Harold Wonder. Sexual terror is at the root of many of Harold's fears. And Scuba himself is the metaphor for the final, terminal demands that the Negro seems—to the white—to be making in this country."[3] At a critical time in the Civil Rights era, *Scuba Duba* was cutting edge, dealing not so much with race relations as with the white person's lurid and erroneous beliefs concerning what constitutes a black person and, likewise, the black person's idea of whites. Hence, the effect of *Scuba Duba*'s rowdy humor, as *Life* magazine described it, was to "jar the audience, white and Negro alike, into exploding laughter—and a great release of tension. Negroes are tickled to see the white hero expose his hang-ups, the whites seem exhilarated by having their obsessions exorcised. The total experience comes close to the emotional catharsis of tragedy. But here it is something even rarer: the catharsis of outrageous comedy."[4] That was precisely what drew Jerry to the work.

> I loved the play when I read it; the construction of language, and the humor is my favorite kind of humor. I don't think it's a put-down of the Jewish intellectual-liberal; it's just an explanation of this one in this situation…. When you show people who can't understand, it's a plea for understanding. It should help people watching understand why people *don't* understand. That's why it's a very serious play. Some plays show the bigot, some show the saint, but this play shows the big main group of white Americans who think of the Negro, or any other minority group, as a group. Whether they think of them as strange or no-good or wonderful, they think of them as a group, not as individuals.[5]

But getting *Scuba Duba* to opening night was almost as intense as the play itself. According to Friedman, whose later works included the play *Steambath* (1970) and screenplays for *The Owl and the Pussycat* (1971), *Stir Crazy* (1980), and *Splash* (1984), "It was my first play. There were disasters along the way—director [Jacques Levy, later of *Oh, Calcutta!*] leaving at the last minute. The final preview might as well have taken place at a funeral parlor. Predictions of doom. And then 'Voila,' it all came together on opening night. I was completely inexperienced about the way of actors and the theatre, and didn't realize they were all 'saving it' for the only performance that counted."[6]

On opening night, when restraint finally yielded to abandon, the result was nothing less than phenomenal. "It's wild; it's like a field day," explained Jerry. "Actually, I do get something of a rest during the last twenty minutes. By then, Harold Wonder is a defeated guy. He's going downhill. It's not the same frantic pace anymore."[7] The loss of a few pounds from sustaining the intensity each night was a small price to pay for the once-in-a-lifetime opportunity to display "every facet of my personality"[8] in one broad, riotously vigorous, and exceptionally vulgar-tongued characterization. But the vulgarity was not purely for its own sake. "The language, which has been criticized," Jerry observed, "comes out of a great reality. Everyone I know talks like that when they become emotional. The language is not just for shock value. It is never just dirty words directed to the audience."[9]

Deep within himself, he was discovering resources that would take him to a whole new level of performance. "I know it sounds like an old cliché," he mused, "but it's true. I'm finding all kinds of things in the part."[10] In so doing he was showing himself to be an actor of substance. After this breakthrough, his work would no longer be damned with faint praise like "attractive," "winning," or "engaging." Yet, oddly enough, it was these very qualities that rescued his portrait of the cuckolded maniac from tastelessness. There was a personal breakthrough, too. With the success of *Scuba Duba* and its 692 performances, Jerry stopped grasping for a film career and embraced life as a New York actor, planting himself firmly on the stage. "I like it here. I don't have anything against television or the movies. But it's more exciting here. And I don't like getting up early either which you have to do in Hollywood when you're working."[11]

His home life was evolving considerably, too. By March 1968, Marta, now pregnant with their second child, and six-year-old Tony were his chief concerns. His second priority was the care and upkeep of their Chelsea brownstone, now valued at $105,000—more than double the $50,000 purchase price of four years before—a gamble that had paid off considerably. The old rituals of his bohemian past had yielded to new ones: all-nighters at Forty-Second Street movie houses were replaced by a single feature on Saturday evening followed by pizza; vintage champagne substituted for cigarettes. His characteristic earnestness and subdued sense of humor were still plain, along with the genial, soft-spoken temperament that made him slow to take offense—except when behind the wheel. "He drives like he's in the country," Marta declared to a reporter.

It's funny, that's really the only area where he's aggressive and testy at all. He's a pussycat in every area of his life except in the car. We'd been married six months and we drove home to see his folks in Waukegan, and we got in the car and he started tearing down the highway yelling rank obscenities out the window—and I looked at him and thought: My God, I've married a crazy person! Then I realized that I'd never seen him in a car before, having been wooed and won in New York on subway platforms and things. He never gets in any accidents, but the car is totally dented up, and it's only three months old. It's a Dodge Coronet and the 'C' is missing now so it's just a Dodge oronet.[12]

Word of Jerry's extraordinary performance in *Scuba Duba* quickly circulated, and one by one the creative team of the Broadway musical *Promises, Promises*—producer David Merrick, director Robert Moore, librettist Neil Simon, and songwriters Burt Bacharach and Hal David—dropped in for a look. After a tense ten-day period of scrutiny, Jerry auditioned and finally won the role of C. C. (Chuck) Baxter in this musical adaptation of the film *The Apartment* (1960), written by Billy Wilder and I. A. L. Diamond. The dramatic comedy had starred Jack Lemmon as a corporate ladder-climber who gains favor with his adulterous coworkers by lending them his apartment key for their trysts until he falls for Shirley MacLaine, boss Fred MacMurray's latest girlfriend, after rescuing her from a suicide attempt.

In September 1968, as rehearsals began, Jerry's career was heading for a crucial shift, one greatly aided by his recent ten-month stint in *Scuba*. In four months he would be a major star, not by copying Lemmon's film performance, but by making the most of the role the musical's authors had created and adding his own distinctive touch. "During rehearsals of *Promises*," he told Craig Zadan, "I decided to make the character an extension of my personality rather than to fit myself into the role of the character. I think that Chuck, as I play him, is as close to myself as I can get."[13]

What Jerry chose to emphasize was his vulnerable side, that easily imposed-upon, self-effacing, trusting aspect of his nature that at times could be his undoing. Essentially, his Chuck Baxter was what musical theatre historian Ethan Mordden terms "a schnook hero, an oxymoron that works better in '60s film than in the '60s musical."[14] To make it work for the musical, Simon, Bacharach, and David gave their schnook hero greater power than Wilder and Diamond did theirs. Simon assigned him the best comedy lines, Bacharach and David some very extroverted songs, like "Half as Big as Life," "She Likes Basketball," and "Promises, Promises." Furthermore, Jerry's type of schnook, though beleaguered and morally self-effacing like Lemmon's, was more outgoing—a loose-jointed hero who, despite his idiosyncrasies and blunders, was a tempest of compressed energy. With the exception of the bowler hat that occasionally topped his tall frame, *Jerry's* schnook, notes Mordden, "was every bit the hero—just, maybe, a New York kind of hero."[15]

But two weeks into rehearsal Simon called Merrick in a panic over Jerry's failure to show convincing characterization. In fact, he seemed out of place in the role—dour, gloomy, and unlikable—more Paul the puppeteer of *Carnival* than Chuck Baxter the schnook of *Promises*. Though there had been no run-through as yet, Merrick accepted Simon's word and his advice to replace Jerry with a particular actor he wanted to read for the part. The actor was vacationing in Hong Kong, and it took six phone calls before Merrick finally reached him. When he did, the actor told him he could shave a few days off his vacation if they were serious about him. The following day at the run-through, Merrick arrived with his retinue to find that overnight Jerry's performance had undergone a phenomenal transformation. "Maybe it was Merrick's presence," Simon conjectured, "but I think it was just due to the way some actors need some time before they break through a part. He went from sullen to charming, from grim to delightful, from unlikable to winning—in short, he was terrific. I suddenly couldn't imagine anyone ever playing the part but Jerry." Afterwards the producer stared curiously at Simon and asked, "What's wrong with him? I think he's sensational." "So do I," admitted the writer. "I don't know what gave you the impression I didn't like him."[16]

Simon's second thoughts may have had something to do with the fact that the character's stature contrasted considerably with Jerry's. "Physically, I was all wrong for the part," Jerry readily admitted. "He should have been shorter, a Bobby Morse type—his opening number is called 'Half as Big as Life'—but it worked out great. 'Doc' [Neil Simon]...had me talk to the audience a lot because I'd done that in *Scuba Duba*. He liked me sharing thoughts with the audience."[17] Ultimately, Jerry's ingratiating personality and agile comic flair were what would warm audiences to his Chuck Baxter as the show was hewn to perfection during its Boston-Washington tryout tour.

When *Promises* debuted in Boston, it ran too long and was in need of pruning and reshaping. As is typical during a tryout, some scenes and numbers were jettisoned in favor of better-quality ones. Even so, critic Elliot Norton perceived the promise of *Promises* at once and, most particularly, Jerry's potential star turn as Chuck Baxter.

> Jerry Orbach saunters through the evening, easy and affable, cheerful and appealing, a new star for Show Business: a big new star with his own style, which is unforced, his own charm, which is boyish and natural. He is a comedian, a romantic leading man and—in certain songs—a good singer.... He takes his troubles directly to the audience. His smile is warm, his manner agreeable as he talks about the girl, even when the girl won't talk about him. He is defensive when he lets the key [to his apartment] go out [to office higher-ups], apologetic, rueful.... He tells it like it seems in words, in rueful jokes and in songs.... He works in a low key, never pressing for effect; able to rouse the whole stage or the whole theatre with a scene or a song, and just able to make a sentimental moment seem honest.[18]

At the end of the Boston run, Jerry stopped home to pick up Tony and take him to Washington, where the show would conclude its pre-Broadway tour. With Marta pregnant and due to give birth any day, Jerry would be

Tony's daily caregiver. He would also be his guide around the Capitol and teacher in matters theatrical. It was an experience the seven-year-old would treasure for life—and not simply because he got to skip a couple of weeks of school. "That was a great time for me," recalls Tony.

> I really got to bond with Jerry and also get a glimpse of backstage life. We went around DC a little, but I was drinking in every bit of the show. I saw things as they changed from performance to performance, and then I got to see the show when it came to New York, too. But it was always nice that I could hang around backstage, although it was an unusual thing for a little kid … But Jerry never had any qualms about setting me up somewhere and saying, "Here, Tony. Hang out here." And, of course, there was always someone—a stagehand or chorus person—charmed by a little kid. Everyone was looking out for the little kid.[19]

When he returned home, Tony found a great surprise—a baby brother. On November 11, 1968, Marta gave birth to a second son, Christopher (Chris) Ben, named after actors Christopher Jones and Ben Gazzara. For Jerry, having a new baby was the one thing that topped being hailed in Washington as the great new star Norton had predicted. But now, with another mouth to feed, it was all the more crucial for him to succeed. As *Promises* began its seven previews prior to opening night, Jerry remained calm and steady, even in the midst of the unexpected. Remembers Adrienne Angel, who played the role of Sylvia Gilhooley, the heroine's ally,

> One night, in previews, the scenery fell down. And he just talked to the audience, and said, "We're having a little problem here," and he would just go on. He could forget lines and it wouldn't bother him at all. Whenever I forgot lines on stage, I would go to pieces. Nothing seemed to affect him. One night there was a fire in Shubert Alley, and smoke started filling the theatre. The audience was murmuring and getting nervous, and Jerry was told by the stage manager to make an announcement. So Jerry just stepped out of character and said, "I've been asked by the management to tell you that there's no fire in the theatre. It's in some garbage out in the alley so let's just go on with the

show. But let's take it from after where he hits me. I don't want to do that again." He even made that work for him.[20]

Jerry's onstage cool sprang from one of his most valuable qualities—an unwavering trust in his ability to deliver the goods. "I know my own worth,"[21] he stated plainly on one occasion, meaning that when standing before an audience he never doubted for an instant that he could satisfy their expectations. This professional self-confidence gradually began to color his private life as well. Generally, an actor experiences a sense of emotional release when performing, a feeling of transcending the boundaries of the self for a few hours each night while the character holds sway. But for Jerry, it worked in reverse. "To me, acting has taken the place of psychoanalysis because I started to carry that sense of release more and more into my daily life. When I was younger, I used to be rather withdrawn and inhibited in social situations, but not on the stage. Over the years, acting brought me out more, made me release more in private life. It's no longer a sublimated release onstage—it all sort of flows together."[22]

That flow was evident as Jerry cavorted across the stage of the Shubert Theatre gloriously loose and alive the night that *Promises, Promises* opened on December 1, 1968. "As the put-upon and morally diffident hero," wrote *New York Times* critic Clive Barnes, "Mr. Orbach has the kind of wrists that look as though they are about to lose their hands, and the kind of neck that seems to be on nodding acquaintanceship with his head. He makes gangle into a verb because that is just what he does. He gangles. He also sings most effectively, dances most occasionally, and acts with an engaging and perfectly controlled sense of desperation."[23]

That same evening, as the company proceeded to the stylish El Morocco on East Fifty-Fourth Street to celebrate, Merrick sent Simon a small gift to mark the occasion. Opening it, the writer discovered a framed telephone bill listing a huge charge for six calls to Hong Kong.[24] The status of the show, despite its unprecedented price of $15 per ticket, was no less huge.[25] It ran three years on Broadway and two more on the road, and in spring 1969, Jerry won not only a Drama Desk Award for Outstanding Performance, but also a Tony for Best Actor in a Musical Play. He also introduced the show's two hit songs: "Promises, Promises," and "What Do You Get When You Fall in Love?," a duet with costar Jill O'Hara.

The professional recognition kept coming. One evening after the show, a bouquet of violets arrived with a note reading, "You are only terrific. I wish every actor could see you. Terrific!!! Garson and Alfred and Lynn second the motion." Actress Ruth Gordon, wife of director-author Garson Kanin and friend of the world-famous husband-wife acting team of Alfred Lunt and Lynn Fontanne, had signed it. All four had seen the show the preceding evening.[26] Jerry had earned the respect of his peers — the most significant achievement an actor can merit. "[Mira Rostova], an acting teacher of mine, once asked me why I wanted to act, and I said I suppose it's because I want to be loved. She said: 'No you don't. You want to be respected.' And she was right. You don't even care if people seeing you are jealous of you or hate you for doing something good, but if they respect you, you're happy about it. The main thing is to be respected in the profession by other actors. That's why the stage is so important to me. It's the hardest test of an actor."[27]

Important as it was to Jerry, the stage was changing radically. "I had an appointment with Richard Rodgers the day after *Hair* opened [April 29, 1968, on Broadway]. He said, 'I think my kind of music is over. Look at the reviews this got. It's rock 'n' roll now.' And I said, 'No, what are you talking about? Your kind of music will never be over.' But it was."[28] Billed as "The American Tribal Love-Rock Musical," *Hair*, with its improvisational staging; racially integrated cast; and riveting depictions of the hippie counterculture, sexual revolution, and Vietnam War protests, attracted thousands, especially young people for whom musicals had been relics of the past. With music by Galt MacDermot and book and lyrics by James Rado and Gerome Ragni, *Hair* at once created the genre of the rock musical and defined it for generations to come. It also ignited tremendous controversy with its profanity-laced dialogue, derision of American patriotism, and portraits of freewheeling sexuality and illegal drug use — topped by a nude scene that ended the first act. With all its sensationalism, the musical, which debuted downtown at Joseph Papp's Public Theater in October 1967, brought to Broadway a phenomenon that had been building on its outskirts for some time.

Hair's impact on mainstream New York theatre also spawned a rush of these new trends, particularly nudity — the sum of which Jerry took in stride.

I think that it's like anything else, the first wave of getting used to something new. I think it's fine that we found all these new freedoms on the stage. We had a topless girl in *Scuba Duba* that was used for shock effect by the director. Now, I find that certain shows will open and for no reason at all contain a nude scene, just to jump on the bandwagon. These things are invalid and not good.... The moral climate has really changed in this country. The ladies who see matinees of *Promises, Promises* think that the four old men cheating on their wives are adorable. Ten years ago *The Apartment* was a very shocking picture; they were thought of as miserable, dirty old men. Now we just laugh at them.[29]

Jerry's newfound celebrity changed him little. His offstage hours were still filled with Marta, Tony, and Chris; their two cats, Sgt. Pepper and Choo Choo, and dog, Spot; along with occasional rounds of poker and pool with buddies in the makeshift game room on the second floor of the family's brownstone. "He has a poker night once a month," Marta explained. "We haven't finished remodeling the house yet and the second floor is a wreck, but Jerry couldn't wait any longer. So he put up a Tiffany shade and put his poker table under it with bricks and stuff lying around on the floor, and it's like playing cards in Munich in 1944."[30] Among the poker night regulars were a stockbroker, a stagehand, a lawyer, some actors, and Neil Simon, who remarked that the room was such a mess he felt as if the night watchman would enter at any minute to evict them. Jerry was also teaching the game to little Tony, just as Leo had done with him. Already Tony was showing promise: he was betting against his father's pals with the money the tooth fairy left him — and winning!

In another area was the pool table Jerry had purchased in Detroit — likewise surrounded by a pile of rubble. Décor was of no consequence. It was more important to have a space where he could play his buddies — all except actor and master player Peter Falk, who steadfastly refused to go up against him, maybe because of what he'd observed on television one night. In 1968, while performing in *Promises*, Jerry substituted for an ailing Falk, who was scheduled to play the famed Minnesota Fats on the *Dick Cavett Show*. The competition began with a game of eight-ball. Fats missed and Jerry ran the table. "Fats said, 'You been spending more time in the poolroom than the acting class,'" Jerry later told Kenneth Shouler of *Billiards Digest*. Fats countered with a few trick shots, and then Cavett asked Jerry if he would do a few: "I wasn't sure, but I tried [Willie] Mosconi's finale—you know, his 1 in the corner, 2 in the side, cue ball three rails for the 3 in the corner. I popped it the first time. I get back to the theatre and this stage hand says, 'How did it go on the Cavett show?'" Jerry explained what had happened. Later that night, the stagehand sat at a bar, knowing the outcome of the match—and that the Cavett show was tape-delayed. "So he bet $600 on me and says, 'I bet Jerry beats Fats.' The other guy says, 'C'mon, no way.' I break, run out, and the stagehand wins $600!"[31] Jerry was in top form, making the most of his home-based billiard parlor.

Downstairs, the recently refinished, roomy, stainless steel kitchen, with its low ceiling, exposed brick walls, and dark wood tones, was the place to be. An adjacent alcove held head-high racks filled with vintage wines witnessing to Jerry's newly acquired membership in the Sommelier Society, the nation's oldest wine-teaching organization. Huge windows that looked onto a charming little backyard garden framed the room. At the grand dark oak dining table with bentwood chairs that glowed under a yellow-and-brown Tiffany lamp, Jerry sat one spring afternoon in 1969 over coffee with reporter Gordon Gould of the *Chicago Tribune*. As baby Chris started fussing in his bassinet, Jerry rose to calm him. He fed him a little milk and then hoisted him to his shoulder, without regard for the elegant dark blue sport shirt with the Nehru collar that could become a sacrifice to paternity at any moment. Surveying the room fondly, he remarked to Gould, "I'm happiest when I'm right here in this kitchen. It's like being in the country in the middle of the city."[32] In the yard just outside the kitchen, he pointed with pride to the small plot of grass, flowering cherry and magnolia trees. "It's funny, but just sitting here, New York completely disappears," he added. "In summer, it's so dead quiet, you can be awakened by the sound of the lawn mower next door."[33]

Still, it was a city life the Orbachs were leading—a life with its own unique risks and concerns, none of which were lost on Marta. One afternoon when Gould arrived to interview her while Jerry was doing a matinee of *Promises,* she appeared visibly shaken. "You know what's the matter now?" she asked the reporter. "I've thought that Jerry was dead for the last ten minutes, and I've been crying!" That day at 1:00, Jerry had driven off for the 2:00 matinee, assuming it was at 2:30. Thinking he had time to kill, he stopped at the neighborhood pool hall. "He's a terrible driver," Marta continued, "and he left for a 10-minute ride … and at 1:40, the stage manager called me and said he wasn't there, and I thought he was dead. Jerry came walking up the street at 2:00 and everybody except David Merrick was out in the street screaming."[34] Fortunately, the episode was a false alarm, and Marta, now a frequent guest on *The Les Crane, Orson Bean*, and *Jack Parr Shows*, could calmly return to her family duties and to hosting the dinner parties she loved to give for friends on Jerry's day off.

As for Jerry, producers were now offering him scores of plays and films, all with six-figure salaries attached. Even film versions of *Scuba Duba* and *Promises, Promises* were in the works. Warner-Seven Arts had bought *Scuba Duba* and was asking him to repeat his stage role, and David Merrick was already negotiating the film rights to *Promises, Promises*. "I'm selling Jerry with the package," he stated, "because where can you find a Walter Matthau and Jack Lemmon in one man?"[35] Somehow it all seemed surreal to Jerry. "They're really saying they'll do any property I'd like...which is really wild. I came home from Hollywood with my tail between my legs. Now it's like, 'Wow! By gosh, you're a star! It goes on and on 24 hours a day, and it's a lot of fun ego-wise, but I think it will settle down after a while. People get used to it," he smiled. "*I'm* getting used to it."[36] At last he was a hot property with a film career at hand.

Chapter 5

JOEY'S PAL, 1970–1972

· ·

WHAT BETTER WAY FOR BROADWAY'S BEST ACTOR IN a Musical to conquer Hollywood than to star opposite Julie Andrews in the 1970 film version of the Broadway musical *She Loves Me*? Penned in 1963 by *Cabaret* librettist Joe Masteroff and *Fiddler on the Roof* songwriters Sheldon Harnick and Jerry Bock, this adaptation of Hungarian playwright Miklos Laszlo's play *Parfumerie* told of two clashing Budapest shop workers, Georg Nowack and Amalia Balash, who unknowingly reply to each other's newspaper personals and become secret pen pals.[1] The pairing of Andrews and Orbach as Amalia and Georg was pure inspiration. making Jerry's first major film offer almost impossible to refuse. But refuse he did. "My *then* manager said my first major movie shouldn't be a musical because they would pigeonhole me, so I turned it down. I turned down a big money offer. Hedda Hopper or Louella Parsons wrote about it, 'How dare he turn down this movie!' The movie was later shelved, and they had to pay Julie her whole salary. I would have been paid off."[2]

There was also a new offer from David Merrick and Gower Champion to consider: the lead in *Sugar*, a musical version of the film *Some Like It Hot*. But it was too soon after *Promises, Promises* to take on another Jack Lemmon role from another Billy Wilder film, so he declined.[3] Just when the films of *Scuba Duba* and *Promises, Promises* failed to happen, along came another with the kind of dramatic heft Jerry wanted. Based on Frederick Earl Exley's prize-winning fictional memoir, *A Fan's Notes* (1972) recounted a failed writer's struggle with mental illness, alcoholism, and divorce. But the crux of the story concerned his obsession with the triumphant New York Giants and their star running back Frank Gifford, his former college classmate and idol. Ultimately his fixation yields only vicarious success, unearned and empty, and he is left on the sidelines of not only the gridiron but also life itself. The sardonic plot was timely and the vulnerable character of Fred ideal for Jerry.

Canadian film director Eric Till assembled a cast that also included Burgess Meredith, Rosemary Murphy, Patricia Collins, Conrad Bain, and Julia Robinson and employed a striking mix of stream-of-consciousness, flashback, and fantasy techniques to illuminate the conflicts of the central character. But studio brass found the effects confusing. "Warner Bros. didn't know if it was about football or a mental hospital or what, so they shelved it," said Jerry. "It was shown in Canada and called a masterpiece, and I got some votes for it at the Cannes Film Festival but it never showed here."[4] The reason angered him greatly. Although *A Fan's Notes* was not a big-budget film, there were deferred payments owed on it. "This is film-industry talk," Jerry declared. "They owed me money; they owed the director money. If they show it once commercially anywhere in the United States, it costs them about $150,000 in deferred payments, and if it dies they lose the money, and if it were to do well then they would have been proven wrong, so there's no point in them ever showing it."[5]

His hope was that *A Fan's Notes* would not only establish him as a serious actor, but also impress audiences and critics with his versatility in light of what followed. Inspired by journalist Jimmy Breslin's satiric novel about New York City's criminal underworld, *The Gang That Couldn't Shoot Straight* (1971) was loosely based on the activities of mobster Joseph "Joey" Gallo and his Brooklyn gang. In it, Jerry played a caricature of Gallo, Salvatore "Kid Sally" Palumbo, alongside Leigh Taylor-Young, Lionel Stander, Jo Van Fleet, Hervé Villechaize (later Tattoo of TV's *Fantasy Island*), and a young Robert De Niro in an odd comic turn as a bicycle racer posing as a priest. The result was a "very broad, silly, musical-comedy-style thing [that also] was the first thing people saw me in, so [their response was] 'Broad! Hokey! Comes from the musicals.' That really set back what film career I might have had for quite a while."[6]

Despite his best efforts, Jerry was frustrated from the start. The director, James Goldstone, was from California and consequently knew little about

New York City, its humor and milieu. "I had 40 or 50 arguments with him," said Jerry, "and won one or two of them. I think the picture would have done much better if it had come out after *The Godfather*. It would have been a nice counterpoint."[7] Jerry's bitterness over the misfire of *The Gang That Couldn't Shoot Straight* was somewhat eased when the opportunity to meet the real Joey Gallo rose in mid-January 1972, shortly after the film debuted. It was only natural to want to know how close Kid Sally came to his real-life counterpart. So when NYPD detective Eddie Lambert told the actor that he knew Gallo personally and might be able to arrange a meeting with the gangster fresh from a nine-year stretch in prison for extortion, Jerry was extremely curious. So was Marta. But neither was prepared for the vortex that would spin their lives out of control within three months' time.

Jerry's towering Kid Sally could not have differed more from the genuine Joey. Slimly built, at five-foot-six, 145 pounds, with thinning hair framing a bony face that bore a large mole on the left cheek, Gallo was hardly an intimidating figure. But his eyes conveyed a reality his physical appearance concealed. "Ancient," journalist Pete Hamill called them. "Devoid of time or any conventional sense of pity or remorse, they seemed to range from the color of slush to the color of fogged blue steel. They watched everything…. For a few years, in the early sixties, I would see him in police stations; … he would joke with the cops, and smile for the reporters, but the eyes never changed. Tormented …."[8] Their chilling intensity reflected the confluence of extremes deep within that could turn Gallo from hospitable to hostile in an instant. When that happened he was virtually unstoppable, having learned early in life to compensate for any physical shortcoming by attacking first and with a devastating brutality. Once, when a burly off-duty cop elbowed one of his buddies off a barstool, Joey was on him in a flash, clawing, punching, kneeing, and biting him so severely an ambulance had to be called. "You had to be ready to kill him," notes biographer Donald Goddard in *Joey*. "But if you were ready to love him and serve him, he would make you one of his people. You would belong. And on the streets of Brooklyn, to be one of his people conferred a respect—an identity, almost—that some could find nowhere else."[9]

Born April 6, 1929, to Neapolitan parents, Joey grew up in the Red Hook section of the South Brooklyn waterfront, where the infamous Al Capone had started as a petty criminal and suffered the wound that earned him the alias

"Scarface." From the moment they were old enough to fight, Joey and his brothers, Lawrence "Larry" and Albert "Kid Blast" Gallo, ran with the street gangs. As a teen Joey became a mini-mobster in the crime family headed by Joe Profaci, the old guard Sicilian don who ruled his territory with the might of a feudal lord. Under Profaci's watchful eye, Joey and his "Mod Squad," as he later dubbed them, strong-armed their way into the jukebox, numbers, and protection rackets, acquired a chain of restaurants and small bars that doubled as gambling fronts, and rapidly gained notoriety for the violence and crime plotted from their headquarters at 51 President Street.

Unlike Jerry, Joey never trained professionally as an actor, but as a teen he discovered an exclusive method for crafting a character calculated to intimidate. Drawing on big-screen heroes James Cagney, George Raft, Edward G. Robinson, and Humphrey Bogart—all short in stature like him—he honed the classic hard-boiled, shoot-'em-up, Prohibition-era gangster to perfection. But in 1947, while watching the film noir flick *Kiss of Death*, he had an epiphany. In that instant he found the capstone of his hoodlum persona in Richard Widmark's portrayal of Tommy Udo, a leering, murderous psychopath with a maniacal laugh who shamelessly shoved a wheelchair-bound old lady down a steep flight of stairs. Donning Widmark's black suit, black shirt, white tie, wide-brimmed pearl-gray hat, menacing grin, and eerie giggle, he packed a gun and took to the streets. No wonder NYPD Chief of Detectives Albert Seedman remarked, "He should have been in show business."[10]

Young Joey was as fair as Jerry was swarthy, blue-eyed with a full head of blond hair like Widmark; hence the nickname "Joey the Blond." In 1950, following his arrest for burglary just before his twenty-first birthday, he strode into court displaying full Tommy Udo gear, erratic conduct, and a defiant stare for the judge who promptly packed him off to Kings County Hospital for psychiatric evaluation. "The psychiatrists who checked him out," notes Paul S. Meskil in *The Luparelli Tapes*, "concluded he was fairly intelligent but 'incapable of understanding the charges against him.' They considered him a dangerous psychotic, a paranoid schizophrenic with homicidal tendencies. Their conclusion: 'Joseph Gallo is presently insane.'"[11] Overnight he acquired a new alias, and although no one would ever dare use it to his face, he never hesitated to phone reporters when they neglected to print it: "Crazy Joey."

Through the fifties he gained prominence in the underworld as a hired gun purportedly responsible for the barbershop slaying of gangland kingpin Albert Anastasia at Manhattan's Park Sheraton Hotel on October 25, 1957. (To this day the Anastasia killing remains unsolved, but it is commonly held that the contract was given to mob boss Profaci, who gave it to Joey, who then carried it out with his gang members.) His growing manipulation of local labor unions drew national attention on February 17, 1959, when he and Larry were summoned to Washington to appear before the McClellan Committee — the Senate Select Committee on Investigation of Improper Activities in the Labor or Management Field — for questioning by Chief Counsel Robert F. Kennedy. "When he first strode into my office, dressed like a Hollywood Grade B gangster..." Kennedy later wrote, "he felt the rug and said: 'It would be nice for a crap game.'"[12] Ultimately the interrogation would prove futile as Joey invoked the Fifth Amendment forty-eight times.

As his power and influence intensified, so did his expectation of an invite into Profaci's inner circle, but the tight-fisted, tribute-demanding don kept him at a distance. Seizing on the rising discontent among the boss's own men, Joey and his brothers ignited the Gallo-Profaci War, the bloodiest Mafia combat since the Castellammarese War of 1931. It ceased only after Joey's conviction for extortion and subsequent maximum sentence of seven and a quarter to fourteen and a half years on December 21, 1961. The Joey Gallo who emerged from prison on March 10, 1971, was a bona fide paradox of criminality and reformation. Behind bars he had drawn the wrath of fellow Italians when he crossed racial lines and befriended African-Americans whom he enlisted in a massive effort to overhaul the organized crime chain of command set to commence upon his release. On June 28, 1971, the Gallo-Profaci War picked up where it had left off ten years before when an African-American gunman named Jerome Johnson mortally wounded Profaci successor Joseph Colombo during a rally of the boss's Italian-American Civil Rights League at Columbus Circle. Seconds later, Johnson was shot dead by Colombo's bodyguards. Word on the street was that the assassin was a Gallo collaborator. At once suspicion shifted to Joey, who ultimately would pay the price during a pre-dawn surprise shootout in a Little Italy eatery.

In prison, Joey underwent an intellectual transformation that was nothing short of spectacular. There he acquired an astonishing command of words, literature, philosophy, politics, and art through rigorous self-education and voracious reading. After nine years and three months he could match discourse on Sartre, Kafka, Camus, Dumas, Hugo, Tolstoy, Van Gogh, Hemingway, and his revered muse Machiavelli, with the most erudite intellectual, for by then he was one himself. And that was precisely what impressed Jerry the evening they first met over dinner: "Breslin's book had portrayed Joey as a clown. Then when I met Joey, I was absolutely amazed to find out that maybe he had been a wild kind of nut before he went to prison, but something had happened to him inside. He'd done nothing but read there, and it was startling to talk with him."[13] Bright, well read, and colorful, the most charismatic gangster since Legs Diamond was about to become the "Pal Joey" of the showbiz set.

From the moment Lambert mentioned that Jerry was "a nice guy, not like an actor,"[14] Joey was intrigued. Yet his "curiosity" was more about admonition than admiration for he was seething over the film's portrayal of him and his gang as imbeciles. He checked out Jerry and Marta with his wife, Jeffie Lee Boyd, who knew the couple indirectly through mutual friends whose children attended PS 41 with their daughter Joie and Tony Orbach. A call to the friends assured him of the sincerity of the Orbachs, who had recently taken all the children to the circus and backstage at *Promises, Promises*. With that, Joey phoned Jerry personally, congratulated him on the part he'd played in the film, and straightaway invited him and Marta to dinner. But Jerry's response to Joey's bonhomie was guarded. "There was a long pause,"[15] Joey later told his top bodyguard, Pete "the Greek" Diapoulos. At length, Jerry dismissed his misgivings and acquiesced, convincing himself that this was just a dinner — nothing more. But it soon became a voyage into uncharted territory, entailing an unsettling rite of passage for which he and Marta were unprepared.

By the evening of the dinner, as Goddard reports,[16] the host's mood had shifted radically. He nearly reneged on his offer, especially when he answered the door of his Fourteenth Street apartment to find Jerry and Marta towering above him. Tension further escalated as the couples descended in the elevator, entered their cars, and made their way to the Queen Restaurant in Brooklyn Heights, tailed by police. Once inside, Joey strategically positioned all guests — both newly arrived and those already awaiting him — so as to have command of the event as it unfolded. When the food and wine had warmed everyone sufficiently, he launched into Marta, inquiring in a slightly mocking yet congenial tone, "Okay, you finally got to meet me. You wanted to meet the star, the star gangster of America, and now you've got your chance. So where are you from, big Italian girl? You're an Italian girl, right? Where are you from?"[17]

While Marta assessed his mood and weighed her comeback, Jerry remained silent, laughing only when jokes hit punch lines and then revealing a wall of white plaster between his teeth—evidence of dental work in progress. Joey was now pointing to him and inquiring of associate Frank "Punchy" Illiano, "Hey, Punchy—you see the one over there? With the white? That's the guy that played me in the movie. You know what, we should have broke his legs, just to teach him to be a better actor." Jerry laughed expansively, then took a large draw of his Dewar's. Pleased with the response, the interrogator continued, "And you know what else pissed me off?" All fell silent. "About you doing me?" Jerry nodded. "You ain't good-looking enough." The table exploded with laughter as Jerry assented amiably, took another belt of his drink and settled back into his seat. Quickly Marta steered the conversation to the less controversial subject of Italian cuisine.

"Mmm-mm! Is this good food! And *I* know. I'm a cook. My grandmother taught me how to cook like a good Sicilian girl."

"Hey, are you from Sicily?" inquired Joey, as if stumbling upon a cousin just off the boat.

"I'm Sicilian, Joey," Marta answered brightly. "You betcha."

"Yeah?" he replied, nudging one of his comrades. "Well, I'm from Naples." Again the table roared.

Despite ancient rivalries, Sicilians and Neapolitans understand each other. In time, Marta and Joey would reach that kind of appreciation, but for now the Sicilian chef continued her discourse on the art of pasta preparation, unfazed by the Neapolitan wiseguy who kept applying the art of scrutiny to both guests.

"He stinks," interjected one newly arrived Gallo man upon learning that the woman speaking was the wife of the guy who'd played Joey in the movie. "He stinks. You—hey, you!" he gestured to Jerry. "I didn't enjoy that movie. You weren't so hot in that." Once more Jerry just laughed it up and downed another gulp of his drink.

"You stir and you stir," continued Marta. "You got to do it with feeling. You're making it for your man." A pause. Then Joey looked her in the eye and asked, "Do you prefer Camus or Sartre?" The question hit her like a thunderbolt.

Sitting within earshot at a table between the front and rear entrances in case of a Columbo attack was Pete the Greek, who watched as a dumbfounded Marta slowly dropped her fork to her plate. Now "Marta was looking at Joey differently," wrote the Greek in *The Sixth Family*. "You naturally did when he started talking that way. Papa Gallo said, 'One smart boy I got.'"[18] Likewise dumbstruck, Jerry stared incredulously at Joey. Marta rebounded by stating a preference for Camus. In turn, Joey championed Sartre, because he considered Camus to be suicidal, and he favored survivors. "I challenged him on Camus being suicidal," she later explained. "He referred to the auto accident in which Camus was killed and said that anybody who went in a car with somebody driving that fast was suicidal."[19] The tenor of the evening shifted dramatically as the three, now on a first-name basis, dropped their guard and chatted easily while exploring common ground. At last, Joey came to his point, asking Jerry what exactly had made him take on such an asinine role as Kid Sally. "Well, the part came along, bit low on funds, and the bread was good,"[20] replied Jerry matter-of-factly. Joey liked the answer. Jerry asked if Joey had actually kept a lion in his basement. The lion had lived in the cellar of friend Armando the dwarf, Joey explained. Guys who had defaulted on loans quickly paid up once confronted with the lion (actually a fairly tame ocelot named Cleo that gang members raised in an apartment at their headquarters until she grew too big to handle.[21])

Marta mentioned that she was a freelance writer, and the Greek noticed that Joey "began rapping heavy"[22] with her. A lively exchange on deception in the works of Camus and Hemingway immediately gave way to an even livelier one when Marta asked Joey if he had ever thought of writing his memoirs.

"My what?"

"Your memoirs."

"Is there money in it?"

Indeed there was. With Mario Puzo's novel *The Godfather* electrifying the public and its film version on the brink of release, publishers like Viking Press magnate Thomas H. Guinzburg, whom the Orbachs knew personally, were ready to jump at the idea, and Marta was poised to set it in motion at Joey's word. While he might take her up on stopping by some time to try her spaghetti, the matter of his memoirs required some reflection.

On January 24, Marta wrote to thank Joey for "the most exciting evening she and Jerry had ever spent" offering to reciprocate any way he chose: "dinner in or out, with or without other people, some Sunday with the kids or another day without them—whatever Joey would like best."[23] A growing social register also awaited his review: actor Ben Gazzara wanted to meet him, singer Buddy Greco had asked Marta to bring him to his opening at the St. Regis, and the fabled Elaine's, which she described as "a haven for movie stars, writers and other major celebrities," would give them the best table and VIP treatment any time Joey wanted to go *there*."[24] Just set a date and give a call, she said.

No response. Clearly Joey didn't take to multiple options, so a few days later Marta tried a different tack—she phoned Jeffie Gallo personally with a direct invitation to a dinner party at the Ben Gazzaras'. (When the Orbachs asked if they could bring their new friend to dinner, Gazzara, who knew exactly who Joey was, approved with a rhetorical "He served his time, didn't he?"[25]) Joey told Jeffie to accept, and then—just like his initial encounter with the Orbachs—had second thoughts when the time arrived. "Call them up and say we can't come,"[26] he told her. Jeffie's unease at the thought of socializing with major celebrities was compounded by Joey's unpredictable social behavior. There was a heated exchange and several false starts before they finally left for the Gazzaras'.

Whether chastising his host for serving roast beef instead of Italian fare, hurling epithets about the black maid, mocking Buddy Greco for wearing knickers, or confiding to actress Janice Rule, Gazarra's wife, how much the boys in the slammer loved her films, Joey's performance was a crowd-pleaser. Intense but never cruel, he thoroughly charmed his audience fulfilling their every expectation. "It was fascinating to watch how he handled them all, and kept them interested," Jeffie later told Goddard. "He would come out with a dese, dem and dose line, and then follow up with some esoteric, erudite reference that would throw them completely. He played in and out. He was marvelous at verbal games."[27] The games lasted well into the wee hours as Joey, unaided on unfamiliar turf, completely won over each guest. Gradually, everyone drifted onto the terrace to watch the falling snow. It was the last social occasion Jeffie would share with her husband, whom she had remarried shortly after his release just ten months before. She had no idea that in less than eight weeks they would divorce and he would marry someone else at once. At five A.M. the guests departed. Unlike Eliza Doolittle's tryout at Ascot, Joey's was a smash, serving as his initiation into café society—one that contrasted markedly with the Orbachs' entry into his circle. That first encounter was now a thing of the past, for by the party's end Joey had bonded irrevocably with Jerry and Marta, who were dazzled to extremes by the brilliant celebrity keeping his dark alter ego from their sight.

The bonding soon included family and friends. "There's a corner of Italian background in me," Marta told *Time*, "that was ready to be activated. The first day I laid eyes on Joey, it was like being with my father. Joey sensed it, and my family sensed it."[28] It was time to revive an old Italian custom she'd enjoyed as a girl—the made-from-scratch spaghetti supper her grandmother served on Sundays. The ritual officially took root in her own home on Sunday, February 6, at five P.M., when Joey came by as promised—bodyguards and all—to taste her spaghetti and meet family and friends. But there was another motive. Now that his marriage to Jeffie was heading toward divorce, he needed a new official Manhattan address. By the end of the evening, Jerry and Marta had agreed to let him use theirs. The Sunday gatherings caught on fast with the Orbachs' friends who, in Marta's words, "were tired of the dressing up and the sitting down, with the servants waiting on you and the Baccarat crystal."[29] Hence, the gatherings were informal, family-type get-togethers with casually dressed guests sipping red wine or cocktails and children darting about pursuing or being pursued by the family cats or rambunctious dog, Spot. ("We should take that dog for a ride," Joey once quipped.) Upstairs, Jerry, or "the Actor," as Joey called him, welcomed guests. One of them was comedian David Steinberg, whom Jerry greeted *sotto voce* one particular Sunday:

"David, Joey Gallo's out and Marta and I think he's totally rehabbed."

"Bullshit," replied Steinberg.

"Sssh. He'll hear you," cautioned the host.

"Joey Gallo's here?"

"Yeah, and there's only one person he's really interested in meeting."

"Good, because I'm not interested in meeting him."

Too late. The Greek was already ushering him toward the gangster, who rose to meet him.

"Oh, I've been looking forward to this," he stated with delight.

"How do you know me?" inquired Steinberg

"Are you kidding? We used to fight to get to watch you on the tube in the joint....

You know, you'd do really well there."

"In prison?"

"Yeah, baby, you'd be a star."

"Well, it's good to always have something to fall back on,"[30] countered the comic, preferring the Plaza to the penitentiary.

Downstairs in the kitchen, Marta, dressed in jeans and an old sweater, frequently chatted with Joey, who "would sit around...with sad, sad eyes" while she tended to the details of dinner. He called her "Momma" or "the Big Job," and he was concerned about all the trouble the Orbachs were going to for him.

"People like me are a plague on you, Momma," he said.

"No, Joey. The reverse is true." Marta assured him.[31]

But Marta's nod to Italian tradition for Joey's sake only went as far as the kitchen. "He once told me to shut up," she said. "I'm Italian and I understand that. We had to make it very clear that in our family and our world women are bright and they talk, too, and he began to understand."[32] Marta's wit and straightforward, unapologetic way of speaking her mind stunned Joey every bit as much as his first discourse on Sartre and Camus had stunned her. "She was so entertaining, so irreverent," says Tony of his mother. "I mean she didn't care that this guy had been in jail. She would say, 'You're full of shit, Joey.' Whereas a guy would worry about what might happen if he said stuff like that. She had no qualms about saying anything to anybody. Joey just thought that that was the best. This was this outspoken woman. I think that was more of the attraction after they had met—'let's see what Marta is going to say about this'—and I wonder how that worked for Jerry."[33]

Adds Chris,

She was this intelligent, very engaging, very passionate and volatile, magnetic woman. And she would outshine Jerry in a lot of social situations. He was sort of the fulcrum whom everybody knew. People were sort of like, "Well, let's go here, because it's Jerry's place." Then all of a sudden they're talking to Marta for three hours and laughing their asses off. Like, "Who's this insane woman?" But that was a very good combination as far as entertaining, because you had the name to sort of attract people and then there was this cohost who just, once you were there, was like, "Oh, my God! This food and the drinks and the conversation!"[34]

Besides Joey, others were drawn to Marta and her kitchen retreat. Chris remembers his mother's description of an occasion when Mary Gallo, Joey's mother, and a portly elderly gentleman with a mustache sat side-by-side on the wooden radiator cover beneath the left window, smoking Pall Malls and conversing nonstop for nearly two hours as she sipped a Dewar's and he a Ramos Fizz. When the conversation concluded, the man rose, kissed Mary on the cheek, and politely departed.

"Mary, do you know whom you were just talking with?" Marta asked.

"Who?"

"Tennessee Williams!"

"What? I thought he was just a nice old man."[35]

When dinner was ready, Marta gave the signal and Jerry gathered the guests. Then everyone congregated in the dining room around the huge, dark oak, country-style table where heaping bowls of crisp Italian salad, steaming spaghetti, and Marta's exceptional sauce lay before them. Following dinner, a few lingered in the kitchen while the rest withdrew to the second floor, where Munich 1944 had been transformed into a stylish parlor–game room combination.

Entering from the hall, visitors were instantly impressed by the vast space with its high ceilings framed by crown molding, gleaming hardwood floors, and two huge fireplaces, one at either end. The entrance off the hall opened onto a common area where, along the opposite wall, a grand carved armoire housing stereo components and the family's extensive record collection rested on a zebra-patterned rug. To its right was a large color console TV; to the left, an upright piano. Contrasting with the white walls was a sleek black leather sofa that ran the width of the area and was complemented by a black leather recliner facing it on the opposite side — décor by Marta.

The parlor area on the extreme left continued her black and white motif with several conversation areas perfect for entertaining. Along the wall opposite the entry, two white bookcases with built-in stereo speakers rose to the ceiling, framing a marble fireplace over which hung a poster of the musical *Follies* in a gilded frame. Centered along the Twenty-Second Street side of the room were two elegant white brocade sofas that faced each other. Between them was a large, low, stained glass table, above which hung a crystal chandelier. Along the wall opposite the fireplace was another white sofa flanked by two end tables.

To the far right, two black metal lamps illuminated the centerpiece of Jerry's chocolate-brown game room—his newly refurbished 1920s Brunswick Arcade pool table that spanned the area in front of the doors leading to an enclosed porch that overlooked the garden below. Along the entry wall was a black tile fireplace over which hung a neon palm tree. It was flanked on either side by racks for the pool cues and a variety of chairs. In the left corner was a poker table, over which hung three pendant lights of varying height. On the opposite side, a well-stocked bar complete with ice machine, a small refrigerator, and two old-fashioned rotating bar stools awaited guests.

Generally the men were drawn to the game room and the women to the parlor. "If you wanted to chew cigars and gab about sports or theatre with the guys," says Chris, "that was the game room. But all the women who didn't want to inhale cigar smoke or watch the poker and the pool games could go to the parlor and talk to their hearts' content. It was almost Edwardian in a way. But, of course, there was no law against going from one place to the other."[36] But there was a "standard of particulars," as Marta termed it, to be observed by guests when socializing with Joey—a necessity given his unique circumstances. No sensationalism, exploitation, or judgments allowed. The Orbachs intentionally protected Joey in the belief that he was putting his gangster days behind him. "We knew his background, and he knew we knew and nobody pretended it didn't exist,"[37] Marta explained to Charlotte Curtis of *Harper's Bazaar*. As far as they were concerned, the fact that "he'd read in prison" was sufficient proof of just how well Joey was "rehabilitated" and how determined he was to achieve the goal he had discussed with them, namely that "he wanted to go straight."[38] To that end, Jerry and Marta would do everything they could. "We saw in him something that was different, and we tried to help him achieve that goal he wanted," Jerry told *Women's Wear Daily*. "We were completely above board with him and we introduced him to everyone we knew."[39] The introductions that began with Ben Gazzara, Janice Rule, and Buddy Greco prepared Joey well for the wider circle he would charm during Sundays at the Orbachs'.

After dinner, Joey would go up to the game room, where he sat at the poker table with his back to the wall. There he absorbed the conversations in progress while discerning which group to join among the guests scattered in twos and threes around the pool table, at the bar, on the white or black sofas, and by the piano. They were truly a distinguished lot: auto scion Edsel B. Ford II; banking heir John Barry Ryan III and his fashionable wife, D. D.; comedian David Steinberg; producer-director Hal Prince and his wife, Judy; playwright Neil Simon; *Scuba Duba* author Bruce Jay Friedman and his family; *Scuba Duba* director Jacques Levy; librettist Peter Stone and his wife; actress Joan Hackett and her actor-husband Richard Mulligan; and, of course, Viking Press President Thomas H. Guinzburg and his wife. After a while, Joey might head for the white sofas, where D. D. Ryan and company were discussing the value of life. But no matter where he landed he was soon the center of attention, attracting all kinds of people whether expounding on politics, literature, philosophy, or how tragic it was that Van Gogh had not been recognized during his lifetime.

The ever-vigilant Pete the Greek looked on in astonishment:

[Y]ou'd find yourself giving him a double take and a third.... Nobody could be a bad guy, a wiseguy, twenty-four hours a day, and there he'd be: smooth, articulate, a charming bastard.... I could never understand what kind of charge anyone got out of it. Maybe they liked being around a guy who was up for the shot, or maybe they had the stupid idea that they were immune from it and, like most people, thought that wiseguys only kill wiseguys.... But he never overheard the crap of how small he was, how hard it was to imagine him a gangster murdering anyone, or how he was like Lucifer holding court.[40]

One person remained steadfastly unimpressed with the mobster — Emily, despite his giving her a lift home one evening. "The adoration of him just astounded me. Jerry wouldn't talk to me very much about it, ... and I wasn't there very much, but when I was it just upset me terribly. Not only that, but everything that was in the papers."[41]

Despite strict observance of the Orbachs' standard of particulars, their Sunday soirées were soon fodder for the press. Forget Forty-Second Street. Where the underworld could meet the elite was Twenty-Second

Street — Number 232 West — and in no time it was the talk of the town. The media feeding frenzy was aided and abetted by Joey's high-profile struggle to surmount the social divide between President Street and Park Avenue. He quickly became the darling of the literati, constantly in the limelight, whether dining at Sardi's or Elaine's, attending opening night theatre parties, or being entertained in the posh homes of polite society. "Everyone talked about it," remarked socialite Mrs. Richard Clurman. "It was the thing to do. You'd go somewhere and people would say, 'Have you met Joey Gallo?', and it was like Stravinsky or Yevtushenko. If you hadn't met him, you weren't in."[42] Mobster hobnobbing was *très chic*. Jerry explained why the socializing was so intense: "Joey compressed time with us because he knew in the back of his head that he might not have much time, that he could go at any minute. Consequently, a minute spent talking to Joey was like an hour spent with someone else. There was no 'how's the weather?' or small talk. He was somebody who had to catch a train and get it all in now."[43] Added Marta, "Everyone who met him wound up committed in some way. You either loved him or hated him."[44] Of course, that choice depended on which side of Joey one encountered.

To the people who loved him, like those habitués of the Orbachs' Sunday socials, Joey was a self-designed philosopher extraordinaire who provided, in the words of one guest, "a refreshing insight and intelligence in a world of clichés."[45] Actress Joan Hackett, who adored his calling her "a broad," found him captivating long before she learned of his links to the Mafia. Mrs. Peter Stone was thrilled to have him come to her rescue when a dognapping ring stole her pooch. After dinner at the Orbachs', Joey cleared the dishes from the table and emptied the ashtrays. In the game room he patiently played pool with the Friedmans' young sons. Though conceding "I'll never make it in the straight world,"[46] Joey was nevertheless every inch the model guest.

On the flip side, there were many who despised the ex-convict and questioned his transformation. In *The Killing of Joey Gallo*, Harvey Aronson mentions a member of the city's Knapp Commission — the Commission to Investigate Alleged Police Corruption — who was livid over having to share a table with the gangster when the Orbachs took him to the Plaza's Persian Room one evening to see David Steinberg perform. Moreover, the federal and city officials responsible for investigating criminal organizations never once believed that Joey was going straight. Even eminent authors on organized crime, such as Gay Talese (*Honor Thy Father*) and Nicholas Pileggi (*Wiseguys*), went out of their way to avoid him. "You can't shop both sides of the street in the Mafia," Talese told reporter Denis Sheahan. "For my own welfare I didn't hang around with Gallo."[47] Neither did *The Godfather* author Mario Puzo. When friend Bruce Jay Friedman told him he was attending the Orbachs' weekly parties with his family, Puzo advised: "That's not intelligent."[48] Columbo's men were gunning for Joey.

Just when he should have been keeping a low profile, Joey not only continued living life in the fast lane but even accelerated the speed. The Orbachs were with him almost every day, and "if we didn't see him," said Marta, "he'd call up and ask where the hell we were."[49] Late nights over coffee laced with brandy or anisette, Jerry would discuss with Joey how "our lives cut across all kinds of circles, show business, literature, the arts."[50] Almost daily, Marta was collaborating with him on a dark comedy with the working title *A-Block*, intended to do for prison life what *M*A*S*H* had done for war. But their primary project was his memoirs—a potential page-turner for which Thomas Guinzberg's Viking Press was willing to pay handsomely. Goddard reports that by mid-February Marta had successfully negotiated a contract with the publisher, even avoiding the usual ten percent literary agent's fee by personally assuming those duties herself. But before the contract could be activated, there first had to be an agreement officially binding the Orbachs and Joey together as collaborators. For this reason, Jerry called on Joey one evening and laid out specifics for a proposed fifty-fifty, three-year exclusive collaboration. Essentially, the agreement would bind Joey to the Orbachs "in the preparation of various literary properties based on his life, assign them the exclusive right, and an irrevocable power of attorney to negotiate and act on his behalf, and also forbear [him] from speaking to reporters or other media representatives without first obtaining their permission. In return for these undertakings, Joey would receive fifty percent of the net proceeds of their collaboration, after the deduction of all expenses, but excluding any share in the money that Jerry … might earn from performing in any of these properties."[51]

Through it all, Joey remained poker-faced until after Jerry's departure, when he erupted in a fit of anger over the terms. Sensing his discontent, both Orbachs returned a few nights later for a second session, during which Marta, to the astonishment of Joey's attractive twenty-nine-year old girlfriend Sina Marie Essary and his father, Umberto, addressed every one of his objections so effectively that he allowed her to take the tapes he had recorded so far. Despite this, he demanded further proof of her ability to deliver the goods before signing on. He wanted a movie contract with an advance on the rights to the book he was to coauthor. So Marta prevailed upon a friend at MGM to engage one of the studio's chief production managers to discuss the matter. With the take from President Street down to a trickle since his neglect of things there, Joey was virtually penniless, and the news from the MGM executive that no immediate advance would be forthcoming only compounded his frustration. With assurances from the Orbachs that they had his best interests at heart, he reconsidered their offer.

One morning in early March, he had Pete the Greek take him on a special trip—first to the office of a publishing attorney, and then to the headquarters of Viking Press itself, where he, Marta, and Thomas Guinzberg finalized the deal on his memoirs. The Greek had a bad feeling about it all: "Marta...started Joey on the whole dumb idea of writing his memoirs, saying she would write them. It made wiseguys nervous. Ubatz, the crazy one, they said, was ubatz for sure. Walsh, the FBI guy on the block, said he thought it would make interesting reading. Very interesting."[52] On March 13, Joey signed the collaboration agreement forming Mingoya (Marta's middle name) Productions with the Orbachs. He was riding high. Nevertheless, he understood the Greek's apprehension and assured him this would be no Mafia exposé. "You know," he said mockingly, "there is something suicidal about publishers paying a lot of greens for the big nothing."[53] By now, Marta's approach to the book had also solidified. If people were expecting a Mafia tell-all like *The Valachi Papers*, they would be disappointed. As she later explained, "Joey absolutely wouldn't talk about his past. I hope that is understood. The book is only about the relationship between my family and his."[54] And Jerry was equally insistent about the content steering clear of the mob: "It's nothing like that at all. The book is a recollection of our experiences with Joey since we met him...and it also takes in something about his prison experiences...but it has nothing to do with the Mafia."[55] Even so, wiseguys' nerves were becoming frayed more and more, especially with news of Joey's wedding to Sina Essary, held in the Orbachs' home on March 16.

Jerry and Marta had met Sina in early February, when she and Joey joined them and the Gazzaras for Buddy Greco's opening at the St. Regis. Right from the start, Sina was comfortable with the Orbachs and their showbiz friends with good reason—her ten-year-old daughter Lisa was a Broadway actress. Sina was further impressed with Jerry and Marta's devotion to Joey and how they had even included his bodyguards (and the cops) in the table reservations. Like them, she knew about Joey's past but dismissed it, believing that he was no longer in the rackets. "It didn't bother me much that he had been in the Mafia," she recalls. "He told me he was through with the mob. I thought, so what, this is New York, so he's in the mob, big deal. I didn't realize who he actually was until I married him and had my picture in the newspaper!"[56] The day after the wedding, the *Daily News* ran a photo of "ex-mobster" Joey and his bride cutting the cake following the ceremony. Although the society page of the *New York Times* failed to announce the Gallo nuptials, the event was publicized in a special "Notes on People" piece that touched on the high points. The license arrived forty-five minutes late. The Reverend William Glenesk, who had famously officiated at the wedding of Tiny Tim and "Miss Vicky" on Johnny Carson's *Tonight Show*, did the honors since, as Marta observed, "No judge would touch the wedding with a ten-foot pole."[57] At the start of the service, the clergyman had trouble with the bride's name. "Not *Nina! Sina!*" the congregation chided. Tenor Allan Jones sang the Lord's Prayer and stirred Joey to tears. "You made a Christian out of me. I got religious hearing you sing that,"[58] he told him. And through it all, Jerry and Marta beamed with approval, convinced that this was yet another step Joey was taking in his quest for a normal life. At the end of the day, as the festivities concluded and he and Sina prepared to leave, the Orbachs were touched by his thanks. "Nobody ever gave me a day like that," he said. "I'll always be grateful."[59]

But days after the wedding Joey suddenly withdrew from his social routine, absenting himself from the Orbachs' Sunday suppers and his work sessions with Marta just as he had from President Street. He was immobile—unable to step back into his former status with the underworld or forward into the position of latest sensation to captivate the glitterati. Either way meant compromising his autonomy. No matter. The worlds he straddled were about to collide. He braced himself for the impact. Late on the night of April 6, Jerry and Marta went to comedian Don Rickles's opening at the Copacabana, where they shared a table with columnist Earl Wilson and his wife, David Steinberg and his date, and Gallo associate Frankie Illiano and his date. They were unaware that on the other side of the room Joey was celebrating his forty-third birthday with Sina; Lisa; his sister Carmella; Pete the Greek and his date, Edie Russo; and a second bodyguard, Robert "Bobby Darrow" Bongiovi. The Orbachs only realized Joey was in the house when Rickles acknowledged him and his crowd from the stage. They sent a bottle of champagne to his table. After the show Marta came by to congratulate him.

"You should have told us it was your birthday. We would have thrown you a party."

"My boys are right here. They're taking good care of me."[60]

Marta thought it strange for him to be out of touch for so long. Something was wrong. He seemed too happy and relaxed, and he laughed much more than usual. But the distance he had imposed was no laughing matter. It was undermining their friendship and their work, despite his insistence to the press that "I'm a writer"[61] when asked what his livelihood was. Jerry skipped the birthday revelry and waited in the lobby until Marta joined him. They were about to leave when Joey ran into them on his way to the men's room. There was little to say, especially after his failure to show that morning for a meeting to review the Viking Press contract with their lawyer—a meeting he had missed for the fourth time. Turning away in disappointment, Jerry and Marta left for home as Joey returned to the party, declaring to his guests, "Guess I took care of them."[62] The partying continued until the Copa's closing at four a.m., when Joey and company, minus Bobby Darrow, went hunting for a sunrise snack in Little Italy, finally stopping at Umberto's Clam House on the corner of Hester and Mulberry Streets.

At 5:23, just as the group was enjoying a second serving of shrimp and scungilli, three men burst through the restaurant's side entrance and opened fire on Joey and Pete. Joey took a fatal hit to the chest as he sprang up, flung his arms wide, and overturned the table to shield the women. While the Greek returned fire, Joey was struck two more times before careening from table to table through the front door and out into the intersection of the street, where he dropped to his knees, rolled onto his back, and died. "A supreme New York moment,"[63] Pete Hamill called it, and one that supremely shocked New York society, especially the Orbachs. Shortly after they received the news, Jimmy Breslin phoned and spoke with Jerry directly. "[He] said to me … 'We didn't understand him,' saying how good a person Joey was. He was shocked. He couldn't believe it."[64] Marta was hysterical with grief. Only weeks later could she reflect, "Joey had an intense sense of destiny. If he were truly marked for dying, this old-fashioned way — in style — would have been a point of honor to him.... In a terrible way, Joey's death would have appealed to his sense of drama."[65]

That drama was clearly not the stage or screen kind with vicarious thrills. Those who acted in Joey's real-life drama, whether pal or opponent, did so at their own peril. "Society took to Gallo," noted Nicholas Pileggi. "What could be more exciting than a Mafia boss? But these guys ... are not pets; they are just amused by these people.... Personally, I think Gallo was nutty for being exposed to that scene. Orbach and his wife could have been the ones exposed to being shot."[66] That was precisely Emily's worst fear and why she pleaded with her son not to attend Joey's funeral. But Jerry was determined to remain loyal to Joey and his family regardless of the risk. "When Joey died," Marta said, "Jerry's mother was very upset about him being seen at the funeral. But Jerry had very clear ethics, and there was no way in the world that he would not have gone to that funeral."[67] On April 10, Jerry and Marta attended the funeral without incident. The following evening, however, was a different story. Around ten P.M., police came to their door with word that a caller had reported seeing two men tampering with their 1969 Dodge station wagon in the lot across the street. Although police bomb squad experts examined the vehicle and found nothing dangerous, they impounded it with the Orbachs' permission so that a complete laboratory analysis and fingerprint examination could be done. As a further precaution, two detectives were assigned to remain with the family around the clock because, as the *Post* reported, "There had been strong speculation among local and federal mob experts ... that the execution might have been ordered by organized crime chiefs concerned with what Gallo might have been telling Mrs. Orbach."[68]

Early the next morning, as the detectives made their rounds about the house, Jerry sat alone in the kitchen at the big oak table, sipping coffee, uncertain as to how all this would affect his family and career. Yet one thing was certain — never would he let his curiosity get the better of him again.

Chapter 6

RAZZLE-DAZZLER, 1972–1977

. . . .

"SOMEBODY ASKED ME ONCE WHY I BECAME AN ACTOR, and I said I was too lazy to work and too scared to steal."[1] In point of fact, Jerry, now with twenty years in the business, was more diligent and daring than ever, especially after bringing *Promises, Promises* to a close on January 1, 1972. There was only one thing he regretted: "I always wanted to work in London, but I never made it."[2] London productions of *Carnival* and *Promises* were launched soon after their New York openings, but, at the request of producer David Merrick, Jerry stayed behind to be the anchor of the originals. Even so, he hoped one day to perform in Shakespeare's fair city. Merrick's decision to have Jerry anchor his long runs was a wise one. As with *Carnival*, Jerry never missed a performance during his long-term association with *Promises*. Even when sick, his resolve went beyond "if you don't show up, you don't get paid . . . I have to think of the audience and the cast. It's better and easier for both if I'm doing my own part, rather than have an understudy fill in. The cast is used to me; they react more smoothly when I'm in it, even if I'm not at my best."[3] The poor actors who understudied his roles never had a chance, for Jerry was the bane of an understudy's life. As long as he could stand, walk, and speak, he would perform, because there was nothing he loved more. So what if London was out of reach? There were bold moves yet to be made at home on the New York stage.

By spring he was deep into preparations for a new play due for September tryouts in Boston and Philadelphia before a mid-October Broadway bow.

Drawing on the shorthand used by realtors in classified advertisements, *6 Rms Riv Vu* centered upon a six-room Manhattan apartment with a Hudson River view on Riverside Drive where the action unfolded. Playwright Bob Randall's romantic comedy concerned two married thirtysomethings—advertising copywriter Paul Friedman and disenchanted housewife Anne Miller—competing to be the next tenant of the spacious, rent-controlled unit they are simultaneously inspecting. When the door is inadvertently locked, and they find themselves trapped inside, their brief encounter takes a sudden turn as they gradually lower their defenses, share details of their lives, and recognize their mutual attraction. When the play first came to his attention in fall 1971, Jerry was immediately impressed with its universality, candor, and charming yet substantial characters. He did have certain ideas about changes, however, which first-time author Randall willingly accommodated. But this "comedy of recognition," as Jerry termed it, also needed a top-notch Broadway producer. Ultimately, director Ed Sherin, later executive producer of NBC's *Law & Order*, had Jerry and costar Jane Alexander, fresh from reprising her Tony award-winning role of Eleanor Backman for the film version of *The Great White Hope*, do a reading for Alexander H. Cohen (1920–2000). This prolific showman and producer of the Annual Tony Awards had a remarkable aptitude for finding and presenting entertainment that was original and fresh. Among his productions were *Angel Street, Little Murderers, At the Drop of a Hat, 84 Charing Cross Road*, and *A Day in Hollywood / A Night in the Ukraine*. Cohen coproduced *6 Rms* with Bernard Delfont. Rehearsals began soon after Ron Harper, F. Murray Abraham, and Jennifer Warren joined the cast.

In rehearsal, Sherin remembers Jerry exuding "the same winning quality I saw in his previous roles—a feeling that he was at home on the stage, an ease in his voice that just kind of flowed out of him.... His response to the text was fresh, personal and believable."[4] A bit of comic business with an inflatable chair was a case in point. After he finished blowing it up, he sat in it, got comfortable, and then fell backward head over heels. His battle with the chair raged on until in frustration he tossed it out the window. "Everything about Jerry was natural," adds Sherin, "which was what was so good about his acting. And a lot of that was *acting* because Jerry was not all at ease in life. I noticed that he bit his nails, I mean rather shockingly, almost to the quick. He later grew nails. Eventually he just got a hold of himself, I guess. But the beautiful thing about him was when he hit the stage that was home."[5]

Jerry found *6 Rms* to be different from anything he had previously done—"a terrific, terrific experience ... [and] an amazing feat of staging; it's almost a two-character play, with no furniture on the stage."[6] But the characters of Paul and Anne were what intrigued him most for at age thirty-seven, he understood their issues well.

> They're marrieds in their middle 30s ... [with] all the vestiges of the old morality. Yet they feel this terrible restlessness. They belong to the in-between generation ... too young to be in the club of the World War II generation ... too old to be part of the new sexual revolution, or hippies. They're very straight, very moral, got married very young and now they see all this new sexual freedom around them.... And when they find themselves trapped away from their homes, they feel a tremendous attraction for one another.[7]

Following the debut in Boston, and the generally complimentary reviews, improvements continued to be made. To shorten running time, Sherin reduced the three-act format to two, cut dialogue, and sped up the pace. The excellent notices in Philadelphia presaged the hit that arrived on Broadway at the Helen Hayes Theatre on October 17, 1972, and was hailed by critics as a "perfectly charming entertainment—sexy, romantic and funny," abounding with "humor, freshness and charm."[8] But principally, it was the work of the leading players that impressed. "Miss Alexander, hiding behind dark glasses and beneath floppy hats on her way to an unlooked-for middle age, is sensitive, vulnerable and oddly realistic,"[9] wrote Clive Barnes. As for her teammate, "Mr. Orbach," observed Walter Kerr, "has such a happy openness as a performer that you could probably cast him as Iago and come to resent Othello's rude behavior."[10] Jane Alexander later recalled the constant pleasure Jerry's "happy openness" provided onstage and off:

> Jerry was unique among actors. I mean, there was nobody like him, and he was that way as a human being. I was very excited to work with him because Jerry didn't do too much outside of musical theater. He was a consummate professional. No matter what was going on in his personal life, and he had a complicated personal life particularly at that time, Jerry was always on time, off book, very present, and rarely

frustrated or upset. It was just a joy to perform with him. Every single performance was fun. He was a person who had fun and wanted to make sure we were all having a good time.... He was also a consummate poker player, and he would have a game once a week that would be an all-nighter.... The next day he'd come in and I'd just look at him and say, "Okay, what did you get this time?" And he would always put it in these terms: "A Cadillac car." That would translate to $25,000 in those days. I tried playing poker with him once just for fun, and you just didn't play with Jerry, because he was too good. So even though that was going on [together with] the *sturm und drang* in his family life, he was always there, always ready, always had a smile.[11]

For seven months, Jane Alexander's class and Jerry's humor richly furnished *6 Rms* until closing at the Lunt-Fontanne Theatre on May 19, 1973. After the letdown of two films that had gone nowhere, the play was just the thing Jerry needed. For the present, it seemed the stage suited him best, a medium that relied mostly on him and his actor's instinct. "Once the curtain goes up, it's all up to me," he explained. "In a movie you do something you think was good and the director picks a different version. Movies are the director's medium. Theatre is the actor's."[12] What he cherished most about the theatre was its immediacy with the audience and unique demand of actors.

You have a discipline in the theatre that doesn't exist any place else in the arts. You have to *be there*.... The point is the audience is sitting there.... They've not only paid to see a show, but they've paid to see you if you're one of the leads in the show. You've got to do your best and bring that sense of the opening night, the illusion of first-time, and you've got to do it every night. The minute you start to let down, the whole company lets down, even the person with one line. They see you screwing around and losing energy and just walking through it, and everybody starts to go. So you have a responsibility, a discipline in the theater. You walk in and you're going to work.... You have to bring one hundred percent with you every night.[13]

As for future stage challenges, he was searching for something with depth and a new form, like Stephen Sondheim's *Follies*, which he considered a milestone in theater. He also yearned to see a vast theatergoing public that would fill the theatres to capacity as in London. "[Here] people with the theatergoing habit pay for expensive seats — conventioneers, benefit ladies, and so on — [while] the cheaper seats go empty [because] TV watchers stay home unless it's a hit." Still he was pleased "that shows such as *Jesus Christ Superstar* and *Godspell* have brought younger audiences through the doors at least to know there is something interesting."[14]

Monitoring the theatre scene was one thing, monitoring the fallout from the Gallo fiasco another. The press continued to hound him about his relationship with Joey. "It was a personal tragedy, a very sad thing," he told the *Philadelphia Inquirer*'s Barbara Wilson. "Marta is still doing the book. It's a personal, memoir kind of thing. We haven't had any pressure about it, except for newspapers. I didn't know what newspapers could be like until I was involved personally. What certain people will do to sell newspapers. The sensationalism. Not even trying to check facts. I don't mean to side with Spiro Agnew, but in moments like that you think 'Maybe he's saying something.'"[15]

In the aftermath of Joey's murder, Jerry, a strict Democrat, curbed his political activism considerably. As a staunch opponent of the Vietnam War, he frequently participated in peace marches. But by fall 1972, his protesting, which had landed him on President Nixon's Watch List alongside other notables like Jane Fonda, was a thing of the past. "I'm not terribly involved in politics now," he said. "I've become disillusioned with a lot of aspects. I'm changing to the adage that the only difference between Republicans and Democrats is that the Democrats feel the poor have a right to be corrupt."[16] With the Watergate scandal now capturing the headlines, the Gallo controversy gradually receded into the background, leaving Jerry's career virtually intact. At home, he doubled his attention to family while continuing to enjoy pastimes like reading, poker, pool, and crossword puzzles. Sundays were now devoted to family, visiting friends, playing tennis, or going to the beach. Regular workouts at the gym kept him in shape and reduced stress. There also were travels to Europe aboard the *SS Leonardo da Vinci*, *SS France*, and *RMS Queen Elizabeth 2* with Tony, Chris, and Marta, now immersed in her book about their relationship with Joey, entitled *Winter Friend*.

In fall 1973, a staging of Tennessee Williams's *The Rose Tattoo* (1951) for the Philadelphia Drama Guild found Jerry costarring as Alvaro Mangiacavallo opposite Maureen Stapleton, reprising her Tony-winning role as Serafina Delle Rose. "Tennessee Williams came in one night, and said that I was the best Mangiacavallo he had ever seen. Later, Maureen told me, 'He says that to everybody.'"[17] Around this time, David Merrick and Gower Champion also offered Jerry the lead opposite Bernadette Peters in *Mack & Mabel*, their new musical about the ill-fated romance between silent film director Mack Sennett and actress Mabel Normand. The role of the hard-edged Mack, whose work-fixation inhibits his love for the feisty Mabel, starved for his affection, suited Jerry superbly. As with *Carnival*, the agreement with the producer and director was a verbal one, with the contract to be signed May 6, 1974, the first day of rehearsal. Then all of a sudden "it fell through at the last minute after Mr. Merrick and Gower had told me I was all set."[18] They had signed a bigger name—stage and screen star Robert Preston. Though justifiably indignant, Jerry wasted no time brooding over the matter, but immersed himself in the project at hand—directing and reprising his role as Paul Friedman in a summer production of *6 Rms Riv Vu* in Ohio, costarring Sally Field.

In time, another offer came along, but the terms were unsatisfactory. The salary was less than Jerry had been promised for *Mack & Mabel*, and the billing would reduce him to third place behind two other stars—an unappealing position after commanding a top spot for so long. When he dithered over taking it—just like fourteen years before with *The Fantasticks*—Marta did what she had done then: she pushed him to accept. "This show is amazing, the songs unbelievable and the role terrific. You'd be stupid not to do it,"[19] she told him. Reluctantly, he took it. On June 3, 1975, when he opened at Broadway's 46th Street Theatre (now the Richard Rodgers) as Billy Flynn, the flashy, fast-talking spin master of a lawyer who specializes in defending murderous chorines in Bob Fosse's *Chicago*, he was glad he had. "You know I love a show that leaves an audience happy and cheering," he told William Raidy of the *Chicago Daily News*. "We're a big hit now but somehow a gloom hung around the show before it ever got to New York. It was a very strange thing. People on Broadway were whispering the show was a bomb and there we were in Philly, selling out to standing ovations and breaking house records...."[20] *Chicago* gave Jerry his third Tony nomination and another long run—two and a half years to *Mack & Mabel*'s sixty-six performances.

With songs by *Cabaret*'s John Kander and Fred Ebb, the musical drew upon the 1926 play of the same name by journalist Maurine Dallas Watkins.

Her work was inspired by the actual case of a married woman charged with the homicide of her lover and later acquitted — though guilty — thanks to a deluge of media hype and disingenuous lawyering. Despite the Roaring Twenties setting, *Chicago*, with its satirical indictment of the justice system as well as the legal and journalism professions, could not have been timelier, coming as it did on the heels of the Watergate scandal's fetid finale. With the demise of the Nixon presidency, the country's mood had shifted perceptibly from the idealism of the sixties to disillusionment. Like Jerry, many Americans were dropping out of the political activism that had defined their lives for over a decade and taking a skeptical view of leadership, governmental or otherwise. So when the Windy City musical cannily tooted the message that people will inevitably get away with murder as long as they are well connected, the scandal at its gangster-driven Prohibition Era core seemed analogous to the capital's during the nadir of the Nixon presidency. Not surprising then, that its message, presented in the guise of a vaudeville pastiche, clicked spectacularly with audiences (as indeed it still does today), especially with Gwen Verdon's Roxie Hart and Chita Rivera's Velma Kelly as the killer-diller heroines who literally danced their way to acquittal via Jerry's razzle-dazzler of a shyster lawyer with the public and the press in his pocket. As Jerry commented, "In its own very American way, *Chicago* has a lot to say about the sickness of our culture, and people are responding to its sharp critique."[21]

But for some, like Walter Kerr, the critique was too sharp, the humor too dark. In that respect *Chicago* was perhaps ahead of its time. It was a hit, but not a phenomenon like *A Chorus Line*, which had opened off-Broadway only two weeks before and was aiming for a July 25 Broadway transfer to the Shubert Theatre, where it would reap unanimous critical acclaim and sweep all the awards for the 1975–76 season. Still *Chicago* had its allure — one that soon swayed Jerry as rehearsal began. Near the end of the first week, however, acclaimed director-choreographer Bob Fosse (1927–1987), who had revolutionized Broadway dancing with his sleek, jazzy, burlesque-inspired style and won the Oscar for *Cabaret*, Tony for *Pippin*, and Emmy for *Liza with a Z* in a single year (1972), suffered a heart attack, and the show went into a holding pattern until he recuperated. Weeks later, he returned, far less upbeat than at the start. "My impression is that after the operation and recuperation, Bobby had a lot more dark moments than he had before," recalls composer John Kander.

Initially, the actual writing of the show had been quite joyful. After we came back and got started on it [again], it was much more complicated.... The show was going through so many changes and Bobby's illness affected him. And the one thing you could always count on as being steady as a rock was Jerry. I loved working with him. Whenever you're working with somebody who is superbly talented, completely disciplined in terms of their craft, and completely professional in terms of their working habits, you want to work with them forever.... Jerry was just a gift — and I know Fred [Ebb] would back this up, too.[22]

When Fosse resumed work, he "realized that the money-hungry attorney must be the pivotal figure of the story,"[23] as Jerry put it. That breakthrough considerably eased whatever reservations about role size and billing he may have had. (Ultimately the billing issue was resolved by placing his name in the center, one line below Verdon's on the right and Rivera's on the left.) In the end, Fosse's brilliant staging showcased Jerry every bit as fabulously as Verdon and Rivera with three of Kander and Ebb's best — "All I Care About Is Love," "We Both Reached for the Gun," and "Razzle-Dazzle."

For "All I Care About Is Love," Jerry's silhouetted profile, sporting a fedora and puffing a cigar, signaled his entrance as a bevy of chorines pined, "We want Billy." Once the spotlight hit him, mustachioed flimflammer Billy Flynn emerged in all his double-breasted pinstripe-suited glory, asking, "Is everybody here? Is everybody ready?" in the manner of "Is everybody happy?" jazz bandleader Ted Lewis. With that, his facetious declaration of doing everything for love was set in motion as he spoofed Al Jolson, Bing Crosby, and Rudy Vallee and stripteased his way to the climax encircled by girls dancing about him with feathered fans à la burlesque queen Sally Rand. "When I did the striptease with the girls and the feathers, I walked out of that [number] in shorts and a T-shirt — into my office, where a tailor is fitting me for a new suit. The original [as opposed to the 1997 revival] had a lot of values like the costumes and the movie-dissolve changes from one scene to another. It was filled with that kind of stuff."[24]

"We Both Reached for the Gun" was a press conference to end all press conferences, as the celebrity lawyer became a ventriloquist literally putting his words into the mouth of defendant Roxy, as a dummy astride his lap

Emily Olexy, Jerry's mother, 1926. (EMILY OLEXY ORBACH COLLECTION)

Leon (Leo) Orbach, Jerry's father, 1921. (EMILY OLEXY ORBACH COLLECTION)

BOTTOM LEFT: Jerome Bernard Orbach, born October 20, 1935, Bronx, New York, pictured here at six months. (EMILY OLEXY ORBACH COLLECTION)

BOTTOM RIGHT: Leo, Jerry, and Emily, Mt. Vernon, New York, 1937. (EMILY OLEXY ORBACH COLLECTION)

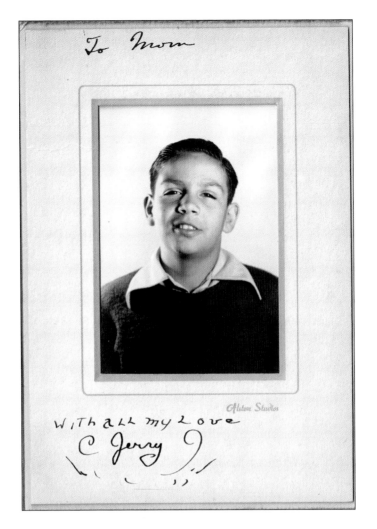

To Mom

With all my Love

Jerry

TOP: By the time his family moved to Springfield, Massachusetts, in 1946, Jerry, age ten, IQ 163, had skipped two grades. (EMILY OLEXY ORBACH COLLECTION)

LEFT: With Leo and Emily, graduation day, Waukegan Township High School, June 1952. (EMILY OLEXY ORBACH COLLECTION)

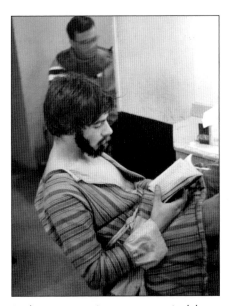

LEFT: In 1952, during his senior year at Waukegan Township High School, Jerry landed the starring role in the play *Mr. Barry's Etchings*; the experience set the course of his life. (EMILY OLEXY ORBACH COLLECTION)

BOTTOM RIGHT: Jerry's New York stage career began off-Broadway in 1955 at the age of twenty, when he scored as the Street Singer in *The Threepenny Opera*. (FLICKR)

Backstage preparing to enter as Azdak in Northwestern University Theatre's production of Bertolt Brecht's *The Caucasian Chalk Circle*, 1954. (EMILY OLEXY ORBACH COLLECTION)

LEFT: Jerry (Paul Berthalet) and Anna Maria Alberghetti (the waif, Lili) in *Carnival*, 1961. It was Jerry's first Broadway role. (PHOTOFEST)

BOTTOM: Early on, Jerry tried to ignite a film career via supporting roles in "B" films like *Mad Dog Coll* (1961) with Brooke Hayward, but was told by producers that he was too swarthy. (NEW YORK PUBLIC LIBRARY)

LEFT: In 1960, as El Gallo, the gallant storyteller in *The Fantasticks*. (PHOTOFEST)

BOTTOM: July 1962, at the age of twenty-six, with arranger-conductor Norman Paris during the recording of *Jerry Orbach Off Broadway*, his one and only solo album. (PHOTOFEST)

LEFT: In *Guys and Dolls* (1965), with Alan King (Nathan Detroit), Shelia MacRae (Miss Adelaide), and Anita Gillette (Sarah Brown). (PHOTOFEST)

RIGHT: His breakout role as the antihero of the off-Broadway satire *Scuba Duba* (1967), with Brenda Smiley, landed him back on Broadway a year later in *Promises, Promises*. (TIME & LIFE PICTURES/GETTY IMAGES)

BOTTOM: For his performance as Chuck Baxter, the schnook hero of *Promises, Promises* (1968), Jerry received the 1969 Tony for Best Actor in a Musical. (NEW YORK PUBLIC LIBRARY)

LEFT: Jerry and Chris at home, 1969. (EMILY OLEXY ORBACH COLLECTION)

BOTTOM: Marta, Jerry, and Tony in the kitchen of their home at 232 West Twenty-Second Street, 1969. (© BETTMAN/CORBIS)

With fellow Tony winners James Earl Jones, Julie Harris, and Angela Lansbury, 1969.

(PHOTOFEST)

attempting to explain her story to a swarm of scoop-hungry reporters. "Bobby [Fosse] wanted Gwen's mouth just to go up and down, but she couldn't help mouthing the words. My sort of scratchy falsetto sounded a lot like Gwen and people thought *she* was singing. I had to explain it to them later. I'm there—not moving my lips, being very proud of how I'm doing—and people said, 'Oh, really; you were doing that?'"[25] Nevertheless, the number keenly tested his vocal virtuosity as he alternated impressively between the jazzy patter of Verdon's mouthpiece and a mock operatic duet with M. O'Haughey's Mary Sunshine, a "sob sister" reporter. By the climax the press was eating out of his hand. The second-act "Razzle-Dazzle" took a lighter approach, one that gave Jerry a final memorable turn. Declaring to his client, "It's all show business, kid," he perched a pair of wire-framed eyeglasses on the bridge of his nose. The gesture initiated an effortless transformation into the slouched, rumpled, tousle-haired essence of renowned "Scopes Monkey Trial" lawyer Clarence Darrow—with a touch of Jimmy Durante. As Flynn sang, danced, and juggled his way through a courtroom that literally became a circus, an array of acrobats, clowns, tightrope walkers, and unicyclists joined his spectacular hoodwinking of judge and jury before an audience wise to his tricks.

Despite distinct approaches to the material—Verdon and Rivera's as dancers as opposed to Jerry's as an actor—the three stars made a splendid team. "Those ladies have a different feeling than I do about the show," he explained. "They're all movement. All body and dance. They come off the stage and are busy talking to me about turns and timing. 'You went this way when I went that way.' It's incredible, they're perfectionists. Meanwhile, I'm involved with the script and listening to the audience react to the lines. I'm having a marvelous time."[26] So was Chita Rivera:

> I had to laugh because even though that character [Billy Flynn] was a ruthless guy, there was still something about him that was very funny. Not just funny because Jerry was doing funny business, but also because he was making a statement about that kind of person which really made the role palatable.... Jerry was gifted and smart. He shared the stage with you. He listened. He was a fabulous singer, fabulous actor, totally musical and so professional. He really put himself into the role. I never saw him walk through anything. He was there at all

times and gave you everything that you needed when you worked with him.… You want a rock. You do want a rock. Jerry was that guy, that rock of Gibraltar. I remember being in awe of him hitting the show on the nose because he was so perfect for the role.[27]

All the same, Jerry was not above the occasional prank, as Rivera learned one evening.

I swear it wasn't like him to clown around. Jerry was always the perfect professional person. But I had a scene with him that lead into a number I did with a chair ("When Velma Takes the Stand"). I would say to him, "Hey Billy, can I show you what I would do on the stand?" and he was supposed to say, "Yeah, kid." But this one night, he pulled up the chair, straddled it, looked me straight in the eye, and said, "No, you can't do it." I'm looking at him with egg on my face and then we both just got hysterical. [*Laughing*] The show was over for Velma. Then I finally said, "But I gotta," and he shouted, "Gotcha!" That was one of the fun times with him because he was [usually] so straight and narrow.[28]

Just two months after *Chicago* arrived on Broadway, Verdon had to undergo surgery. From August 8 to September 13, 1975, Liza Minnelli took over the role of Roxie Hart, requiring Jerry to "totally adjust my performance and my relationship. I couldn't beat up on her, the way I did on Gwen, because Liza was more like a wounded bird. I had to play it more big-brotherly," he chuckled, "or the audience would have booed me off the stage."[29] Deep into the run, when Ann Reinking and Lenore Metetz took over for Verdon and Rivera, he adapted the role once more. "We now have two *young* girls," he said with a respectful tone. "Now I'm suddenly not a lawyer the same age as the girls—I'm an older lawyer."[30] Being in a long run was no excuse to cease growing in a role.

Offstage, Jerry was mastering other media, enjoying super-success as a regular in TV commercials (like the one for the 1977 Chevrolet in which he touted its five extra cubic feet of interior space) and guest starring on episodes of *Love, American Style* (in 1973 with Bernadette Peters prior to their *Mack & Mabel* near-pairing), *Diana* with Diana Rigg (1973), the hospital drama *Medical Center* (1975), and the New York City-based police thriller *Kojak*, with Telly

Savalas (1975). He also did two films that, like his previous efforts, quickly came and went. *Foreplay* (1975) was a sex comedy in which he portrayed an author whose writer's block is cured when his Speedo-clad muse, played by George S. Irving, conjures his girlfriends past for new and improved conquests. For *The Sentinel* (1977), Universal's star-studded (Ava Gardner, Burgess Meredith, José Ferrer, Eli Wallach, Martin Balsam, et al.) amalgam of *Rosemary's Baby* and *The Exorcist*, he played a TV commercial director trying to focus the attention of fashion model Allison Parker (Christina Raines), traumatized by the hellish goings-on inside her stately Brooklyn Heights apartment house.

Occasional as they were, these television and film experiences were schooling Jerry in the essential differences between working before the camera and working on the stage—differences actors must negotiate well if they are to succeed in all three venues. As Jerry realized early on, mistakes are edited out in television and film, but sometimes they appear in a final cut if appropriate for the characters and story.

> There's a wonderful moment in the movie *State of the Union*, with Spencer Tracy and Katharine Hepburn, when he's running for president. Katherine Hepburn had a brother named Richard Hepburn who was a playwright, and he was kind of an anarchist wild man. In the scene, this waiter comes into their hotel suite and rants, "Comes the revolution, you know, people like you won't be doing this," and storms out. Tracy [then] says to Hepburn, "He reminds me of your brother, Dick." And she kicks him. Well, they left that in. But it's very rare that they leave stuff like that in a movie or a television show. And those are the moments that you see on stage. It's not as naturalistic, [but] onstage the acting has to be bigger because you've got to fill a theatre. Every gesture, every word is bigger than life. But occasionally, you can see reality creep in.[31]

Other differences caught Jerry's attention. In television and film, a confluence of artists—director, technicians, cinematographers, etc.—calculate the specifics of a scene long before the actor enters.

> On the stage [however], once the curtain goes up, you're not only the actor, you're the director. You are directing the audience's attention

83

where you want it from moment to moment. You're telling them where to look, when to look. They don't know who is going to talk next.... The whole thing is what we call a *master shot*. It's a big shot of the whole stage and everybody on it. There are no cuts, no over-the-shoulders, and no close-ups. As an actor, you have to learn to direct the audience's attention where you want it. So naturalistic behavior is, "Here, I'm in a movie and I'm about to drink the poisoned coffee, and as I'm talking I start to bring it to my lips, and ... Mr. Hitchcock now does a big zoom-in on the coffee." In the theater there is no zoom-in, no close-up, so instead of me just behaving naturalistically with the coffee, all of a sudden, I bring the coffee up slowly, unrealistically, but I create a close-up for the audience. That's the difference. You're the director at the same time as you're the actor. That's why actors who love the theater say, "I love working on stage live." Maybe they don't even know why they love it so much, but that's one of the reasons.[32]

For all his devotion to the theatre, Jerry couldn't deny that film acting had its advantages. "Yes, I like making movies," he admitted. "They only take six weeks and you can make enough money to live for a year."[33] Joviality aside, he was as earnest as ever about expanding into film. As for the profession of acting itself, when a reporter asked whether he'd still choose it if given the chance to start over again, he answered directly, "Yes. I never get bored with the part I am playing [because] each day is different. However, after a while, when the role becomes old news, there is a need for career mobility — to start looking for something else."[34] Solid as his career was, he was increasingly conscious of the younger actors around him struggling to make their mark. Recalling his post-*Carnival* doldrums, he advised them never to get discouraged: "The greatest prerequisite for an actor is physical and emotional strength. An actor must love his career so much that he does not think about doing something else when the going gets rough."[35]

Outside the theatre, a growing interest in ecology motivated Jerry to make numerous personal appearances for environmental causes while Marta "went around practically ripping fur coats off women in the city"[36] as she campaigned for the protection of endangered animals. Asked about how his celebrity affected his children, he replied that their lives were not hampered, but intensified by it. Admitting that they had to deal with a little more pressure than other children, he was especially proud of their achievements, like Tony's recent admission to Stuyvesant High School, one of the most competitive public high schools in the country. Most of all, he enjoyed his free time with Tony and Chris—the result of a work schedule that usually kept him in or close to New York.

Jerry's love affair with the city and its people had deepened with time. The Big Apple's cultural diversity impressed him greatly, especially as it played out in his own neighborhood of Chelsea, with its tenements and privately owned brownstones. "One day one of my cats ran out, and when I rushed to look for it, suddenly everyone began helping me—there is a tremendous sense of neighborhood there."[37] It made him optimistic about the city's future, especially as he watched Tony and Chris form friendships with children whose backgrounds differed from theirs. Maybe it was a sign that people were beginning to feel unified, even though he knew that it probably "won't really pull together for quite a while. [But] there is hope for New York.... I think there is a future for it. New York is the talent pool for the whole country, whether it's in the arts, advertising, or marketing."[38] This optimism did not blind him to the city's problems, however, like the inequities of the tax structure, the lack of meaningful employment for all, and welfare which "should be federalized so that New York would not be the only place where one can stand on a street corner and make 95 bucks a week."[39]

In June 1976, as he began his final year with *Chicago*, there was little fretting over what he would do after it closed. "One thing follows another inevitably, no matter what,"[40] he reflected sanguinely. Still, in an essentially insecure business he longed for security, "the freedom from the concern of what I have to do next—how long the show will run."[41] With that kind of security he could pay off the mortgage on the house and fund great educations for Tony and Chris. But what if all his plans were suddenly dashed, and he found himself with only one more day to live? "What would you do?" asked a reporter. He paused, collected his thoughts, and replied, "I would probably lie down outdoors on a sun deck and think about what I had done—recall everything and try to evaluate it, see if I made peace with myself, and look to where I was going next. I wouldn't buy a case of champagne or eat a huge chocolate sundae or something like that."[42]

Placid as he was on the surface, inside a mounting unease was consuming him, and Marta, too. Despite their best efforts, their marriage was crumbling.

By July 1976 they had agreed to separate romantically, though not literally. "We have a house ... that's sort of a Noel Coward set-up," Jerry told columnist Earl Wilson. "We have a separate apartment in it.... We're not living together, but we're not apart, either."[43] Marta occupied the fourth-floor apartment of their brownstone while Jerry lived with Tony and Chris on the three floors below. Increasingly frustrated with the role of stay-at-home housewife, Marta had hoped to establish a career as a writer to ease the strain. But by the time she finished *Winter Friend*, the Joey Gallo story had been thoroughly mined by several authors, and her memoir, despite its unique perspective, was old news. Her unhappiness and resentment were difficult for Jerry to bear. "I became angry and disappointed," she later recalled, "and he just shut down. When I look back on it, it makes me very sad, because he never asked what ... made me angry."[44]

To Marta, it seemed that Jerry was investing his passion more in his work than in their relationship, with the result that home had become a place where he merely ate and slept. Reflecting on marriage once during an interview, he prophetically observed, "There has to be a romantic, emotional quotient in married life to carry over the years. If not, you're dead."[45] He was now at that point. Notes Chris,

> There are a lot of guys of that fifties generation who can just absolutely kill it in their professional lives, but when they come home they don't want any waves at all. That's what he expected when he came through the door. So that was some of it, too. Doing any show eight times a week is very draining, and being a father and husband as well. But then if the dynamic of the relationship itself becomes difficult, there are a lot of people who don't stand up under that pressure. I know he was willing to try, but it was my mom who said — and again without any ill will, because she always loved Jerry — that she just felt him kind of closing up and distancing himself, making it feel like it was half a relationship, and she didn't want that.[46]

For Chris and Tony, life grew difficult with parents who had been virtually inseparable and were now giving each other the silent treatment. At age seven, Chris was too young to notice the change, but Tony, then fourteen, remembers the palpable tension in the house that resulted from behavior too deeply rooted for his parents to change. "Marta was always a very outspoken and entertaining person. For the most part she would upstage Jerry in any situation other than when he was on stage. She was the one who was the life of the party. Jerry would sort of have a quiet conversation with you or would rise to the occasion every so often. But she always was on and always the one everyone wanted. More than anything that was what came between them."[47] Not that Marta deliberately plotted to steal the limelight from Jerry. It was just that in social settings her extroverted nature soared while Jerry's tended to be quieter and more circumspect. As a rule, their relationship had been respectful, supportive, and protective, so much so that they approached everything as one, including controversies like their friendship with Joey Gallo. "In her way, Marta had lived for Jerry," says Tony, "but she always had something to get out there and do. She didn't intend for it to be at odds with what he wanted, but sometimes it wound up being so by accident or unbeknownst to her. They'd work something out. Jerry was always a dutiful husband, too. He would stand by her. He would never say, 'Well, that's my wife, don't listen to her.' If Marta were saying something, he'd back her absolutely. To his credit, he did that whenever she was part of something he might prefer not to happen."[48] But now, after eighteen years of marriage, the constant effort it took to reach that accord was draining them both.

In terms of personality, both Jerry and Marta reflected classic archetypes. Jerry was what is known in Yiddish as a *mensch* — a decent, upright, mature, and respectful man who makes an ideal neighbor or friend. Apart from his considerable talent, these traits earned him the esteem of people in the business and also won him numerous friends, to whom he remained ever loyal. This same degree of loyalty was likewise characteristic of Marta (which may explain why both she and Jerry stood by Joey Gallo and continued their relationship with his family long after his death). But Marta was also a *virago* in the sense of the ancient Latin term — a woman of great stature, strength, and courage, ever ready to protect, defend, and fight for what is precious to her. Where one stands with a virago is never in doubt, because she never shrinks from speaking her mind, as *Daily News* columnist Rex Reed experienced firsthand one evening at Sardi's — right in the midst of his interview with Pearl Bailey! Before it ended, the *Hello, Dolly!* star, who was innocently drawn into an altercation between the virago and the journalist, was out-shouting them both. As Earl Wilson reported in the *Post* the morning of November 17, 1975, "Mrs. Orbach went to a table where Reed was interviewing Miss Bailey, to reopen an old feud. Pearlie Mae protested that Mrs. Orbach was interfering with her interview and demanded that the waiters remove Mrs. Orbach within ten seconds. It was considerably later that Mrs. Orbach and her husband, one of the brilliant performers in *Chicago*, but a non-participant in the evening's hostilities, departed."[49] Reportedly Marta took issue with "Reed's characterization of the Orbachs in relation to their friendship with...Joey Gallo."[50] As the clash peaked, the two adversaries stridently demanded satisfaction from proprietor Vincent Sardi, fortunately out of earshot in London.

During Jerry's post-*Carnival* slump, Marta had scored big for a time as a television talk show guest and became the breadwinner, even to the point of purchasing the family home on Twenty-Second Street. But in 1967, as Jerry's star ascended with *Scuba Duba*, she felt it necessary to tone down her career ambitions and personality to be the ideal wife, mother, and hostess. "I remember her telling me things about Dad being pretty envious of the attention she was getting," recalls Chris.

> To make the relationship work better she would do everything she could to try and put a lid on that. Years later, I think she had a lot of regrets about it. That is probably why she threw herself into the hostess aspect of things.... [Although] they were very much a sixties and seventies couple, they had internalized a lot of fifties values, because that was when they grew up. They were a little too old for the "hippie" mind-set. They were about ten years older than that. So there was this sense of trying to hang in there to work it out. They really gave the marriage a real try.[51]

By summer 1976, Jerry and Marta had agreed to divorce. "I think he was a little bit at sea when it came to breaking up his marriage,"[52] Marta later reflected. For Jerry, it was a difficult but necessary decision: "I knew how tough it was...for Chris and Tony—harder on them than it was on me, certainly. But it was the right thing for me at the time and for them."[53] Yet to Tony the divorce seemed to come out of nowhere, because the separation—with both parents continuing to live under the same roof—was never truly one in the first place. "They would have some arguments, but for the most part it was a shock to me that they were splitting up. I was not thinking, 'Well, finally.' But again, with the benefit of time, I could see why it happened, and it certainly makes sense. Of course, I'm sure that at the inciting time it was difficult, but beyond that, there was no animosity between them. They didn't hate each other or anything like that."[54]

With *Chicago*'s closing to take place on August 27, 1977, Jerry, now with alimony and child support to pay and no Broadway job in the offing, signed on for the first six months of the show's national tour. A nine-month tour followed as the lead in the national company of the Neil Simon comedy *Chapter Two*. He would be on the road for nearly a year and a half—the longest he had ever been separated from his sons. "I have a lot of guilt about being on the road, especially when the boys were young. I knew I had to do certain things because that was the job and where it took me to support them. But, God knows, if I listened to 'Cat's in the Cradle,' the Harry Chapin song—'We'll get together then, we'll have a good time then'—I would just break down in tears when I'd hear that song...about the lack of time with the son. Sure it was tough. Tough on them, and tough on me."[55] Just how tough it was Tony remembers well:

> It was difficult for me because I was getting to be a teenager and I was already starting to do my own thing. When they were divorced, Marta was drinking a lot.... They were coming out of the sort of stereotypical drinking society years of the fifties and cocktails. They both drank a ton. Jerry drank a lot, and he may have been a functioning alcoholic—a very high-functioning alcoholic. I think you could say that about him, but you wouldn't be able to tell.... Of course, with Marta, you'd know it a little bit sooner. She was drinking a lot in those years and with the age difference between my brother and me, I wound up being a caretaker for him and for Marta, too.[56]

As for Chris, in an effort to shield him from the trauma of the divorce, neither Jerry nor Marta told him about it. "The really messed-up thing was that I didn't find out that my parents were divorced until I was nine. They, in their 'wisdom,' decided to keep it from me. I found out almost two years after it had actually happened, when I overheard my father refer to my mother as his ex-wife during a phone conversation in the other room. So, for a good decade after that, in a very animal, visceral way, I just said, 'I'm not going to trust a thing that comes out of the mouths of these people ever again.'"[57]

But things were different the evening of August 27, 1977, when Emily and Tony took Chris to see Jerry in *Chicago*'s final Broadway performance. It was the first time the seven-year-old saw his father on stage:

> The thing that happens to you is so very weird. You see your dad and you know your dad around the house. You know him trying to kill rats, taking out the garbage, reading the paper and "Quiet, the game is on," or whatever. Then you see him with a house of three thousand people, all these lights on him and all these girls around and doing a striptease act, and again killing it, putting it away. You're seven years old and you see somebody elevated like that almost to the level of a god, and he really does a number on you, because you admire him for a lot of very strange reasons. It's funny, because there's this dichotomy that exists. It's like, "Okay, he's gone for this amount of time; he doesn't show up for this, he doesn't do that." Then you see him in this elevated, heightened atmosphere. It's very hard not to admire him and love him almost like a half-fan, really.[58]

The boy gazed up in awe at his father, who perfectly nailed the climax and stopped the show cold with a booming baritone that ironically yet resolutely proclaimed, "All I care about is love."

Chapter 7

CROOKED COP/ INDOMITABLE DIRECTOR, 1977–1985

· ·

IT WAS A THANKLESS JOB, ONE PERFORMERS SHUNNED with good reason. Unlike the understudy who goes on for the disabled star before the curtain rises, the standby literally stands in the wings throughout the entire show ready to enter at a moment's notice should the star have a mishap. That takes an extraordinary talent who can fill the star's shoes and propel the show forward without missing a beat. Not exactly an enviable position, especially for a standby covering a star the caliber of Chita Rivera, who, in January 1977, was returning to the role of *Chicago*'s Velma Kelly. As far as Bob Fosse was concerned, there was only one person with the timing and talent crucial to stepping in for Rivera on the spot—a lively, congenial redhead and veteran of *Sweet Charity, Here's Love, Flora, the Red Menace, How to Succeed in Business Without Really Trying*, and *Fiorello!*. Elaine Cancilla had it all—the spunk of a Molly Brown and the cockeyed optimism of a Nellie Forbush, roles she had played to high praise in touring productions of *The Unsinkable Molly Brown* and *South Pacific*. She could meet the challenge estimably. The question was: would she? That was what Fosse wanted to know when he asked her to be Rivera's standby. But the five-foot-two, thirty-six-year-old dancer from Pittsfield, Massachusetts, who had studied with George Balanchine, cofounder and ballet master of the *New York City Ballet*, and danced for Fosse (*Sweet Charity, How to Succeed*), Peter Gennaro (*Fiorello!*), and Michael Kidd (*Here's Love*), was less than enthused. Performers want to perform, not hover in the wings awaiting some misfortune. Besides, Elaine could receive greater recognition and have a better time continuing to star in local theatres across the nation, where she had many fans. That was the reply her agent conveyed to Fosse who, in the end, acquired his standby of choice despite her misgivings.

Elaine joined the cast, and regretted it almost immediately. When not standing by for Rivera, there was no place backstage where she could get off her feet, and elbowing her way into overcrowded dressing rooms with a tightly knit company that had been together since the first day of rehearsal was simply too daunting. So the standby opted to remain in the wings when the star was offstage. "Hiya, kid," said Jerry with an affable smile as he breezed past her on exiting the stage. For years, Elaine had admired his work. During rehearsal breaks for *How to Succeed*, she and some of the other dancers had rushed from the 46th Street Theatre and through a secret passageway leading to the Imperial, to catch glimpses of him and the cast of *Carnival*. Now, nightly, as he went by her on the way to make his entrance, he politely inquired, "Hi, how are you doing?" He could sense her discomfort even in the heat of his customary backstage poker games. "You know I'm always downstairs playing poker between entrances," he told her. "Why don't you just sit in my dressing room? My dresser's there—a very nice young man."[1] Elaine accepted Jerry's offer; soon small talk passed easily between them.

One night after the show, she and friend Alice Evans entered Joe Allen's for drinks. The bar was mobbed. Just as they were about to leave, Jerry motioned for them to join him and his crowd. Jerry told Elaine that his legs were tired and he needed his seat—but she could share it with him, if she liked. By the evening's end, she was sitting in his lap. "Jerry took me home in his car," she later wrote, "and we necked a little bit. I said good night, and as I went inside, something inside me was already saying, 'Whoa! What is this?'"[2]

Despite some mutual flirting—on winter nights when Elaine arrived at the theatre in her rabbit fur jacket, Jerry teased, "Here comes the wabbit"—no one thought the two were heading into a serious romance. On dinner dates they split the bill. The relationship was decidedly circumspect. It had to be. "He was barely divorced," said Elaine. "I thought, 'I'm not putting my eggs in that basket.'"[3] The new divorcé was shuttling between the theatre and the Twenty-Second Street brownstone where he was still living, checking on Tony and Chris between shows and preparing their dinner while Marta was in England visiting friends. Furthermore, Elaine herself had a very successful career in full swing. All the same, neither she nor Jerry could deny the nascent attraction that steadily deepened between them as the weeks progressed. "We became friends little by little," she remembered. "I had no inkling that this whole thing was going to become serious. He didn't, and I didn't. It's not the way it usually plays out. It was just a very nice relationship. Little by little I was falling in love with him,"[4] as Jerry was with her.

Jerry introduced Elaine to his family starting with Tony and Chris, who became acquainted with her on matinee days, when they would dine out with their father between performances. Even at fifteen, Tony could see the positive aspects of the relationship.

> Elaine was perfect for Jerry because she lived for him. She really did. I mean she was absolutely her own person and she had her own career. And not to put her down, but what Jerry wanted—whether [or not] he said he wanted it—was someone who would take care of him. What he really needed was someone who would work everything around his schedule and make sure that he could go and play golf, go to the gym and get his nap. And Elaine loved that, so it wasn't like she was just doing it to be the dutiful wife. It was a mutual thing they both loved. And the time they spent together—apart from tending to chores and his things—was a great time for them.[5]

For Chris at age eight, the impact of the relationship was different than it was for his brother.

> [By then] Tony just wasn't around as much. He was older and had girlfriends, a successful band, and was headed for college. He was doing things, but I was little. I was this sort of walking, talking, vulgar kid. I really had quite a potty mouth, between a Sicilian mom and a lot of public school friends. I took some adjusting to. I was like this feral child almost in a way.... And, to her credit, Elaine would say, "You can't say that at the table." And she gave me a lot of structure that I never had because I grew up with none essentially.[6]

By spring 1977, Jerry decided it was time for his sixty-six-year-old mother to meet Elaine. "Jerry called me one day," recalls Emily, "and said, 'I think you should meet Elaine.' We met for lunch at this coffee shop on the corner of Sixty-Second Street and Broadway, near the nonprofit organization where I was working. When I came in, the two of them were sitting there wearing black leather jackets. I thought, 'Good heavens, they look like a motorcycle gang; I expected their bikes to be parked outside.'"[7] Her initial response notwithstanding, Emily soon came to appreciate that this indeed was a serious romance. Jerry and Elaine had much in common and were good for each other.

After the closing of *Chicago* on August 27, 1977, and through preparations for its road trip, the two continued to see each other. In February 1978, they reluctantly parted: Jerry to Boston to launch the national tour, Elaine to Baltimore for an industrial show. When she returned to New York, he would drop by on weekends when visiting Tony and Chris. At length, afraid that their romance might perish in his absence, he asked her to come back with him to Boston: "We talked about it and I said, 'Do you want to go with me?' And she said, 'Yeah!' But I really meant go with me and be on my arm. She'd be unavailable for work which she'd been doing for twenty years on her own."[8] Elaine understood exactly what he meant and accepted at once: "I knew I didn't want to be separated, so I just thought, 'Put your career away for now.' I'd rather take care of my man than take care of me. And it was beautiful."[9]

The bond between them was soon apparent to everyone, including Chita Rivera: "I came out to see them while they were doing *Chicago* at the Chicago Theatre in Chicago, Illinois. I was talking to them about coming back in the company to take it to L.A. and San Francisco. And I came down to the basement, and there he was playing cards with the guys, and just over his right shoulder, there was this cute little redhead. From that day on, I don't remember them being separated. It was the kind of relationship you envy."[10] With Elaine at his side, the dreaded loneliness so endemic to life on the road soon dissipated for Jerry, freeing him to focus on the work at hand.

Even in the final days of the tour, he was still perfecting Billy Flynn. "I think we were in our last week in San Francisco, and I'd been doing the show for three and a half years. I came offstage and I said to Gwen Verdon, 'Tonight, I did it perfect,' and she said, 'You mean in three years you never had a night when you thought it was perfect?' And I had to say to her, 'No—maybe ninety-nine-point-nine percent, but tonight I got it right.' For those three years I had been looking and changing and trying things to make it perfect.... It's your job to go out there and refine the work and make it as perfect as you can."[11] When the tour concluded in San Francisco in August 1978, Jerry and Elaine returned to New York City, setting up housekeeping in her tiny apartment on Fifth-Fifth Street off Eighth Avenue. After six months on the road, they had earned the respite, but it had to be brief by necessity. With no Broadway prospects in the offing and no indication when there would be, the break could quickly develop into an unemployment phase for Jerry. To wait for something was risky, so he signed on as the lead in the national tour of Neil Simon's autobiographical comedy *Chapter Two*. Though they soon would be on the road again, this time their trip would begin on a different note. After rehearsal one day, he entered Elaine's apartment and pulled a small box from his pocket. "I have to do this right," he explained to her, going down on bended knee. "What's in the box?" she asked curiously. "It's a car," he teased, quoting a line from *Chapter Two*. The engagement ring had the elegant simplicity of the man who knelt before her. To her surprise and delight, Elaine was going to be married and embraced his proposal as he rose to embrace her.

By late fall, Jerry and Elaine were back on the road—this time for nine months. In the role of writer George Schneider, Jerry portrayed a newly remarried man trying to resume life while still mourning the death of his first wife. Elaine also auditioned and landed standby for the two female leads, filled by Marilyn Redfield and Jane A. Johnston. Jerry's other costar was Herb Edelman, in the role of George's brother, Leo. Edelman, later ex-husband Stanley to Bea Arthur's Dorothy Zbornak of *The Golden Girls*, quickly became a close friend of Jerry's and a favorite target of his backstage pranks. Behind the scenes, Jerry had a reputation as a mischief-maker. As far back as *Carnival*—and likely beyond—he'd been playing practical jokes on people backstage. Charlie Blackwell, *Carnival*'s stage manager, knew who the prankster was and found the perfect way to deal with him. Instead of a direct confrontation, he assembled the entire company, went up to the person next to Jerry, and said, "How could you do that? How could you do something as unprofessional as that? I am shocked that you would conduct yourself in that way. Now someone like Jerry Orbach would *never* engage in such ridiculous, unprofessional behavior."[12] Jerry got the point, but it never really altered his behavior.

Chris was eleven when Emily took him to Los Angeles to visit Jerry and take in *Chapter Two*. While spending time backstage with his father and observing him on site, Chris received his first lessons in the art of acting—and in the lesser art of high jinks.

It really was *Chapter Two* where I began to get this education about him as an actor and respect for him both as a person and as an actor that is undiminished to this day. But what I remember most fondly about *Chapter Two* was that he would often have me assist him in the jokes he'd play on Herb Edelman. We would constantly try to find things that would mess up Herb during his last exit. This was relatively safe because Herb delivered his last line and then exited through an upstage center set door. Technically, he was invisible onstage and his reaction not seen by the audience, so it wasn't as if they would know. But after exiting, he had to walk half the length of the stage to get off at stage left. Dad would always have some insane prank rigged up—at least two or three times a week—just to screw up Herb. Two stand out. One of them involved a sheet of bubble wrap that we stretched along the back of the set. Herb came through the door looking toward stage left, expecting some kind of onslaught to try to screw him up. Dad and I both put our fingers over our lips and went, "Shhh. Quiet." Herb sort of shrugged his shoulders and went, "What?" Dad and I were all very secretive and shushing, so Herb tiptoed, and as soon as he hit the bubble wrap it went *pop, pop, pop, pop*, like firecrackers. "Whoa!" he shouted; then he walked around it and came up to us like he was going to strangle us. We were just on the floor laughing.

But the other one was even more ingenious—a sight gag that happened spontaneously one day when I coincidentally came to the theater dressed almost exactly the way Dad's character was dressed in the second act—red-and-white checkered shirt and beige pants. Of course, I was his son, so I looked like him. Dad had gotten a clear glass and he had this weird-looking, iridescent concoction in it—sort of half orange juice and half Scope mouthwash. Off of stage left, there was a flat that he had me hide behind with an empty glass identical to his. As Herb came off the stage, Dad lifted his drink to toast him, knocked it down, started contorting and grabbing his throat, and then threw

TOP: Would-be don "Kid Sally" Palumbo crashes the dinner of Lionel Stander, Robert DeNiro, and Harry Davis in *The Gang That Couldn't Shoot Straight* (1971). (PHOTOFEST)

LEFT: In *6 Rms Riv Vu*, 1972, sharing a comic moment with Jane Alexander. (PHOTOFEST)

Giving 'em the old "Razzle Dazzle" in *Chicago*, 1975. (PHOTOFEST)

42nd Street (1980) marked another long run for Jerry—1,929 performances over nearly five years. It was his last stage role. (PHOTOFEST)

LEFT: Producer David Merrick announces the death of director Gower Champion on the opening night of *42nd Street*, August 25, 1980. (PHOTOFEST)

BOTTOM: With Gus Levy, the steadfast friend of Treat Williams' Danny Ciello in Sidney Lumet's *Prince of the City* (1981), Hollywood finally took the actor seriously. (WARNER BROS./ PHOTOFEST)

One of his celebrated roles—Jake, the protective father of Jennifer Grey's Frances "Baby" Houseman in *Dirty Dancing*, 1987. (ARTISAN PICTURES/ PHOTOFEST)

Jerry as Martin Laudau's corrupt brother, Jack, in Woody Allen's *Crimes and Misdemeanors*, 1989. (PHOTOFEST)

TOP LEFT: The keepers of the castle in Walt Disney's *Beauty and the Beast*, 1991—Cogsworth (voice David Ogden Stiers), Mrs. Potts (voice Angela Lansbury), and Lumière (voice Jerry Orbach). (©THE WALT DISNEY COMPANY. ALL RIGHTS RESERVED. PHOTOFEST)

BOTTOM LEFT: A 1990 appearance on *The Golden Girls* reunited him with *Threepenny Opera* castmate Bea Arthur and earned him the first of three Emmy nominations. (ABC STUDIOS/GETTY IMAGES)

Receiving the Crystal Apple award from Mayor Rudolph W. Giuliani for his film and TV work in New York City, June 11, 1997. (RITA CANCILLA HUBBARD COLLECTION)

Briscoe and Logan, *Law & Order*, 1992–1995. (NBC/PHOTOFEST)

"I had the good fortune to know Jerry as a friend, brother, and at times, a surrogate father," comments Benjamin Bratt. A lifelong friendship developed as a result of their four-year partnership as Briscoe and Curtis. (NBC/PHOTOFEST)

The New Dramatists 48th Annual Luncheon honoring songwriters Kander and Ebb. From left to right, Kaye Ballard, Gwen Verdon, Jerry, Liza Minnelli, Fred Ebb, Liliane Montevecchi, John Kander, Joel Grey, and Chita Rivera, May 20, 1997. (RITA CANCILLA HUBBARD COLLECTION)

Jerry and Elaine enjoying the sea in Nova Scotia, 1999. (RITA CANCILLA HUBBARD COLLECTION)

With Al Pacino in Greenwich Village during filming for *Chinese Coffee*, 2000. (PHOTOFEST)

Celebrating the 300th episode of *Law & Order*, April 8, 2003, with Fred D. Thompson, Jesse L. Martin, Sam Waterston, Elisabeth Rohm, S. Epatha Merkerson, and Dick Wolf. (GETTY IMAGES)

himself behind the flat. Two seconds later, I came out from the flat, the consequence of the potion he had drunk. And it killed Herb![13]

Los Angeles also was the last stop for Jerry's stint with *Chapter Two*. After closing there in late summer 1979, he and Elaine remained in hopes of igniting his long-sought film career. But generally, Hollywood agents were still cool to Broadway actors—even Tony award–winning ones—so Jerry turned to penning a couple of TV scripts with actor Ronnie Graham and buddy Tom Poston, but the effort was fruitless. Entirely out of options, Jerry and Elaine were glumly basking in the California sun when suddenly noted film director Sidney Lumet called to offer Jerry the role of a lifetime—crooked narcotics detective Gus Levy in his police drama *Prince of the City*—shooting to begin early January 1980; location: New York City! The inveterate Gothamite was ecstatic, and his fiancée no less so. Their anticipated homecoming was marked by a special celebration. On October 7, 1979, at the historic Little Brown Church on Coldwater Canyon Avenue in Studio City where Ronald and Nancy Reagan married, Jerry and Elaine also wed. Surrounding them in the sanctuary during the nonsectarian service that day were best man Herb Edelman, maid of honor Katherine Doby (Elaine's friend and cast member from *Sweet Charity*), Elaine's relatives from Los Angeles, and the couple's friends from *Chapter Two*. Afterward, Jerry's longtime pal Ed Asner hosted a festive, casual reception in his home. Late that night, the newlyweds arrived home so tired they nodded off in the midst of *The Tonight Show*—the groom perfectly content that his life at last had begun its own chapter two.

Post-wedding plans included a trip to Hawaii with Tony and Chris, who by now were better acquainted with Elaine and had vacationed with her and Jerry while in Los Angeles. "Jerry was as close as he could be with his sons while being away from them in the theatre," Elaine observed. "Of course, he wasn't there at night; he wasn't there when they got home, because he was doing a matinee or whatever. But he was there for them when they needed him. I was there when they needed me. There was tension, of course … [but] we would do what was necessary at the time. When we were on the road, it was hard…. I was as close to them as distance would allow. [When we returned to New York,] we didn't have room to have Tony and Chris there, and they didn't want to be there, and I can understand that. So it was as comfortable as it can be comfortable. It was hard. Jerry felt guilt. He had to get on with his life."[14] In early January 1980, following the lengthy flight from Honolulu, all four arrived safely back in New York, but disaster confronted Jerry and Elaine when they entered their home. While out of town, their apartment had been burglarized. Now they needed to find a place that was not only larger, but also safer — a task Jerry took up immediately.

On the set for *Prince of the City*, he joined Lumet and the cast for rehearsals prior to filming. Treat Williams starred as Danny Ciello, an edgy narcotics detective who reluctantly consents to expose police corruption as an informer for the Feds only to find that he must betray partners and friends, like Jerry's Gus Levy, to insure concealment of his own wrongdoing. The screenplay was based on Robert Daley's 1978 bestseller of the same name. It chronicled the actual story of detective Robert Leuci, whose testimony and covert tape recordings led to the indictment and conviction of fifty-two members of the New York Police Department's Special Investigation Unit for income tax evasion. Provocative and complex, the content was perfectly suited to Lumet's talents and his fascination with "the human cost involved in following passions and commitments, and the cost those passions and commitments inflict on others."[15] The theme was central to his works — classics like *12 Angry Men*, *Long Day's Journey into Night*, *Failsafe*, *Serpico*, *Murder on the Orient Express*, *Dog Day Afternoon*, *Network*, and *Equus*. Another incentive for the director was the setting, the inspiration behind many of his films — New York City, the multiplicity of its ethnic neighborhoods, and the striking contrasts between its art and corruption, urbanity and baseness, splendor and squalor. A legend in New York moviemaking, Lumet also held high regard for New York actors grounded in the candid, pensive style of "the Method." He and Jerry were well matched.

With *Prince*, Jerry finally realized his goal of working with Lumet, noted for eliciting powerhouse performances from actors. The two had known each other since 1968, when the director tested him for *Bye, Bye, Braverman* but decided he was too young for the part that eventually went to Jack Warden. Now, at age forty-four, Jerry was perfect for Ciello's partner and buddy, Gus Levy. Based on real-life former narcotics detective Leslie Wolff, Levy is the one cop who will not be coerced by the Feds and whose trademark western outfits Jerry sported right down to the leather jackets and cowboy boots. As for the role itself, "I wanted it as soon as I read it," he said. "There's something about a cop that is inherently bigger than life and heroic, like in the old westerns.

He's dealing with life and death. Every day he puts a gun on in the morning and doesn't know if he'll come home at night. Whether he's a crooked cop or a hero cop, there's a kind of grandeur there."[16]

Jerry figured that his combination of "toughness and intelligence"[17] was what influenced Lumet to cast him as Levi. His preparation for the part actually required very little research, because he had done it over the years: "I've known some detectives, and I have sat and talked with them for many hours. I felt close to them, and I could empathize with them, so I didn't feel that I had to immerse myself in what they are like.... [Also] knowing Joey [Gallo] ... made my background pretty complete."[18] He still kept in touch with Joey's mother and his family. "That's family with a capital F. They are very nice people,"[19] he said evenly to *New York Times* reporter Judy Klemesrud. "I've been friendly with astronauts, politicians, scientists, artists," he added. "Actors have an entrée into every stratum of society. They cross many social lines. There are no social barriers."[20]

Shooting began, and with their similar backgrounds, Jerry and Treat Williams quickly built a camaraderie that would prove lifelong. "I came from musicals myself," Williams later commented. "I did *Hair*—and we had a kinship; we both worked in all three mediums—theatre, TV, and movies. I felt a real kinship with Jerry because very few people are able to bridge that gap."[21] The friends had their share of lighthearted moments.

> We were taking a break before shooting a scene for *Prince*. We went to lunch at an Italian restaurant, one of those joints on the Upper West Side, and we might have had a glass of wine. And we get back and we had one of those lines like 'I won't tell if you don't tell, because you know that I know what you know.' And we just couldn't get our tongues around it. Jerry had the giggles, and it went from the sublime to the ridiculous. Sidney loved to finish by four-thirty, five, and there we were, on the floor. It was just one of those things.[22]

It was during this time that David Merrick and Gower Champion offered Jerry the role of indomitable director Julian Marsh in their song-and-dance extravaganza *42nd Street*. Originally intended as a straight acting role for Kirk Douglas or Richard Harris, it had been reworked (probably to avoid comparison with the role of director Zach in *A Chorus Line*) for the impresarios' number one choice. But Jerry was still miffed at them over *Mack & Mabel*: "Though I liked the whole idea of it, I wasn't counting on anything high with *42nd Street* because of my experience with *Mack & Mabel*, among other things. I just said, 'Well, it sounds fine. Let me know when you're going to start. When I see the contract, then I'll know I'm doing it.'"[23] Days later, the contract arrived, and after weighing the matter Jerry decided to team with them once more. But with the release of *Prince* still a year away, he wisely had an out-clause inserted into his contract as a precaution. That way he could accept any film deals that might be offered.

As rehearsals for *42nd Street* got under way, Jerry and Champion discussed the role of Julian Marsh and decided that there should be nothing campy about it. Playing it straight with deadpan earnestness would get maximum laughs out of theatrical clichés like, "You're going out there a youngster, but you've got to come back a star!" The fact that the two of them were actually *discussing* the character told Jerry that this was not the same person he'd worked with in *Carnival* nearly twenty years before. Having matured as a director, Champion was now more collaborative with performers and open to their input. But no one in the company knew that the director-choreographer was suffering from Waldenstrom's Syndrome, a rare disease that was daily sapping his vitality and forcing him to undergo periodic blood cleansing treatments to reduce the viscosity of his white blood cells. Jerry recalled,

> One day Gower was out sick. He went to the doctor…. We had had hardly any time to rehearse certain scenes and we had a scene that … had some traffic problems getting around chairs and things like that. So I came up with something that we all agreed was going to work. Well, the next day we got into a kind of run-through. When we hit that scene and did this new piece of blocking, Gower went through the ceiling. I mean he just went nuts, screamed and said, "Who's been directing around here while I was away?" I said, "Well, I'm sorry, Gower, but you weren't here and we had this problem and I fixed it by doing this." He just fumed like he was going to storm out of the place or fire me. He pulled a cigarette out and fumbled around for a match. I gave him one, lit it for him, and then he laughed. We both broke up. He said, "Next time, ask me first."[24]

Jerry could see how the strain of creating the show was affecting the director's health. Like the other members of the cast, he thought Champion had pernicious anemia — something they expected him to recover from once he returned to California and rested after the opening.

A six-week tryout in Washington, DC was followed by a score of canceled Broadway previews and postponed openings — work of the mad mastermind that was producer David Merrick. Explained Jerry,

David Merrick was a kind of Jekyll and Hyde character who was a genius, and a genius at publicity. I did my first Broadway show for him, and my last. When critics started to come to previews, he was paranoid and decided to keep them out until opening night. So we literally had previews that were just like rehearsals, with an empty theatre. He wouldn't let anybody in because he didn't want the critics to sneak in. Actually, sometimes he made a lot of sense. And, God knows, his track record spoke for itself. He was the biggest thing in the theatre for many, many years.[25]

Finally, on August 25, 1980, *42nd Street* opened grand and glorious at the Winter Garden Theatre. After the finale, first-nighters leapt to their feet roaring their approval through a dozen curtain calls. On the last, the cast was breathless with elation as Merrick took the stage and raised a hand to silence the applause. Then he announced that Champion had died earlier that day, plunging the euphoric assembly into utter grief. Seconds passed until Jerry finally glared into the wings shouting, "Bring it in! Bring it in!" With that, the curtain fell on one of the most incredible nights in Broadway history.

With the obvious impasse between cast and audience, bringing down the curtain was instinctive for the forty-four-year-old actor then in his twenty-eighth year in the business. "It was kind of like a bad movie," he later explained to film director Rick McKay.

I think Neil Simon said, "If you brought this script in to a movie producer, he'd throw you out." ... It was an unbelievably dramatic situation. I think Merrick helped to make it that way. But the funny thing for me was the craziness of it. After all the curtain calls, Merrick came out and made this announcement.... The audience stopped, we stopped, and we're all standing there frozen on the stage. And, playing the producer/director, I said, "Curtain, Bring it in." … And everybody said, "My God, what presence of mind! How did you think to take over and do that?" I said, "It was because we were standing there with egg on our face. You've got to save yourself some way, you know." … [But] it was the front page of every newspaper in the world the next day.[26]

Sterling reviews and international publicity boded long-run status for *42nd Street* and also for Jerry, whose performance was toasted by the press. As Jerry Tallmer wrote in the *New York Post*, "Jerry Orbach has always been a strong, virile song and dance man.… Halfway through the show I wondered when the hell Orbach was going to sing. Gower Champion was a shrewd strategist. … *Now listen, Sawyer, and listen hard. Don't give a damn about me. Think of all those kids there!* —THAT's when Jerry Orbach, turning on the line, strides forward, opens his mouth and sings, not sings, rockets our emotional readiness into 'Lullaby of Broadway.' Between the tar and nicotine ratings on the back page of my program, I scribbled one word: 'Thrilling.'"[27]

In what would be the crowning role of his theatrical career, Jerry supplied a genuine edge to showman Julian Marsh, one *Newsweek*'s Jack Kroll described as "an oddly effective, eerily amusing abstract style. After all the big numbers, he takes the finale alone. As he sings a reprise of the title song, chanting of 'naughty, bawdy, gawdy, sporty Forty-Second Street,' he seems really to be evoking its successor—the crummy, scummy, bummy, slummy 42nd Street of today, the reality that lurks inside the showbiz fantasy we can't surrender."[28] Through four and a half years and 1,929 performances, Jerry would help keep that fantasy going until his departure in April 1985. His attraction to long runs "was a matter of survival," he explained to writer Don Shewey.

Why leave something where you're making money to go and take a chance on something else? I envy people who have what I call a British career, where they go from film to television to stage without much trouble. Here you have to make a commitment to living either in Los Angeles or New York. The travel is not the problem; it's the attitudes. If you're an actor from New York, they still say, "If you're willing to relocate, we feel we can give you more work. [Do] you want to become part of this community or are you going to stay in New York and be a foreigner?"[29]

If remaining in New York meant being branded a foreigner in the film industry, so be it. New York was home for Jerry and Elaine. Now, with his combined income from *42nd Street* and commercial voice-overs, they could at last afford to escape the confines and risks of Elaine's apartment and move into a more spacious and safer home of their own. One day, during a rehearsal break in spring 1980, Jerry found just the thing in a brand-new building going up on the northwest corner of Eighth Avenue and Fifty-Third Street. With one look at the sample apartment, Elaine concurred. That August, when Champion's memorial fell on the same day as their moving date, Elaine managed the changeover with an assist from friends so Jerry could attend. Apartment 20A was just the thing the Orbachs needed—a spacious living and dining area decked out in salmon-colored paint with lime accents, a kitchen with room for two, two bedrooms and, as Emily recalls, "the most spectacular view of the Hudson and beyond you ever have seen."[30]

A year later, shortly after the Orbachs returned from a week in the south of France and their first real vacation, *Prince of the City* opened to outstanding notices. And when Gus Levi pushed a desk over on a federal prosecutor pressuring him to rat on his buddies, audiences cheered. Why? "Because he's the one guy who strikes out against the grinding, overbearing system," Jerry explained. "The system is really the villain in the film, the overbearing system that adds on layer and layer of pressure, just like Kafka."[31] So powerful was the scene that one critic asked, "Why has Orbach been wasting his time in dumb Broadway shows all of these years?" The absurdity of the question was not lost on Jerry, who by now was receiving three screenplays per week—signs that his TV and film work would soon be on the rise. Television called first, with leading roles in the Cable Network Presentation of Neil Simon's *Plaza Suite* with Lee Grant (1982) and the CBS movie *An Invasion of Privacy* (1983). There were also appearances on episodes of *Buck Rogers in the 25th Century* (1981), *Trapper John, MD* (1982), *Ryan's Hope* (1983), *The Streets* (1984), and *Our Family Honor* (1985). And as the voice of King Thorn in *The Special Magic of Herself the Elf* (1983), Jerry added a new dimension to his career doing voices for animated characters.

He liked his new audience: "When you're on television, you're in people's living room, and they feel they know you; there's a familiarity in the greeting. If they've seen you on the stage, there's a little bit of being on a pedestal, a kind of respect. If your face is familiar through moves, they're awed and overwhelmed because they've seen you on the screen, forty times bigger than life."[32] The public response to his brooding Gus Levy filled him with roguish delight. Following the release of *Prince*, he was more widely recognized — and not just by cinema cognoscenti. "More cops and robbers know me now," he laughed, adding gleefully, "I can hardly walk in Times Square without being stopped by muggers and junkies and every sort of thug wanting to know, 'Hey, weren't you in that movie?'" The most prized tributes, however, came from police. "When a cop tells you, 'Man, you really nailed it,' that's the highest compliment of all."[33] Compliments aside, film roles continued to evade him despite his powerhouse performance in *Prince*. Following it and *Underground Aces* (1981), four years would pass before he landed the role of minor league baseball manager Charlie Pegler in the Richard Pryor film *Brewster's Millions* (1985). Although he was receiving screenplays weekly by the dozens, "Judging from the scripts," he said with a smile, "I think I'm going to be playing a lot of Jewish detectives."[34] More than he realized, *Prince of the City* was determining his future course.

Chapter 8

BABY'S FATHER/ DEBONAIR LUMIÈRE, 1985–1994

. . . .

"WHAT'S THE SILLIEST THING ABOUT BEING AN ACTOR?" Jerry once was asked. "The feeling that one is still not a grown-up at fifty," he answered. "I'm reasonably intelligent, I work hard, and if I'd been thirty-five years in the shoe business, I'd be president of the corporation or chairman of the board and making my own decisions. As an actor, I'm still waiting for phone calls."[1] Following his departure from *42nd Street* on April 27, 1985, phone calls were few and far between. His career was in another slump, but this one differed from his sixties revival/survival period or seventies post-*Chicago* phase. Professionally, he was at a crossroads: he could play it safe sticking with long-runs that brought financial security but little recognition beyond Broadway, or gamble everything on a nascent television and film career that might win him nationwide fame or fold completely. Day after day, as he passed time at the gym or on the golf course or investigating promising projects, the direction to take became clear: "Right now instead of getting into another show, I'd like to concentrate more on films and television. One needs the national exposure."[2] Yet the stakes were high: if his plan succeeded, he and Elaine could be set for life; if not, they could be ruined. Elaine totally supported his pursuit of movie and TV prospects, but, in the interim, how were they to get by?

Jerry passed the intervals between jobs playing poker at the Lone Star Boat Club, where he made the "unemployment money" that kept Elaine and him afloat. Two or three nights a week he was there with the "big boys," as

Elaine called them. The big boys were club regulars who eventually became Jerry's "outside-of-show-business" friends. Every Wednesday night, and on weekends from eleven A.M. to closing, Jerry was with them at the atypical health club on West Fifty-Fourth Street between Broadway and Eighth with its green tiled walls, scuffed linoleum floors, and dated patio furniture. There, he mixed exercising with socializing and — in the "pinochle room," with its early-sixties fluorescent lighting and police precinct color scheme — card playing. The décor was of no importance because the facilities, friendly atmosphere, and location — a block and a half from home — suited him fine. The Lone Star and Jerry bonded the moment he first walked through the door and took in its workout rooms, Olympic-size swimming pool, sauna, and party room, where, as Elaine observed, "wives could come — the only room where women were allowed. Otherwise, it was all bellies, cigars, and men in towels."[3]

Founded in 1887 by two young Jewish men — sculling team members from the Lone Star State of Texas — the club was an alternative for those who, like them, were excluded from the major New York clubs of the day. Over time, boating was abandoned and the Lone Star became more gym-oriented, drawing prestigious clientele like Ed Sullivan and Walter Matthau. Jerry, one of the club's biggest advocates, was constantly recruiting new members. "Jerry would always try to bring Al Pacino and those guys in," recalled president Douglas W. Romoff. "They'd take one look and run out the door."[4] Some years later, his *Law & Order* costar Chris Noth joined, but as a non-card-playing member. "I would see Jerry there three or four times a week," said Noth. "He would play double-deck pinochle, and I would play basketball. It is a run-down old place that was our sanctuary."[5] (Noth once brought *Sex and the City*'s Sarah Jessica Parker by, when, as he expressed it, "there weren't too many sagging bellies hanging out. She seemed impressed, but you know, she's a good actress."[6]) On the poker table in the club's pinochle room was a bowl of fruit. Whether he won or lost, Jerry always departed with two bananas for Elaine's breakfast. When he arrived home at two A.M., she was already asleep, and when she awoke in the morning, he was still asleep. He devised a sweet solution to the problem of not being able to kiss her goodnight or good morning: In the morning, when Elaine came into the kitchen, she found two bananas — and a poem Jerry had written to her when he got home. Over the next twenty years, his verses — humorous, charming, and affectionate—formed a time capsule of their romance, almost like a diary. But during these "lean days," as Jerry called them, they mostly disclosed the status of their "unemployment money"—his wins, losses and those ubiquitous two bananas:

Holy mackerel
sweet Rosy O'Grady
I won two bananas
and 1580!

Har! Har!

Jerry[7]

All the same, there were a few times when Jerry lost and, to make matters worse, there were no bananas to bring home for Elaine. But the losses were temporary. Always the optimist, he was soon winning again and bringing home bucks and bananas.

He was having less luck with his foray into television, and it frustrated him greatly. Landing a role in a major series depended upon how well he was known, rather than on how well he fit the part. "They now have this insidious computer system called the Q-Rating," he complained, "which, when they punch your name in, gives a rating of how many people in this country know who you are."[8] He cited the example of Lucille Ball, who would score a hundred on it, as opposed to his twenty. With the success of *Murder, She Wrote*, Angela Lansbury jumped from twenty to ninety-five. One time in particular, Jerry said, when he was on the verge of landing the perfect role in a television movie, "the network punched up my name on the computer and said, 'No, get somebody else who has a more visible name in television.'"[9] Despite his low Q rating, some TV work finally came his way in early 1986—a featured role in the CBS mini-series *Dream West*, and the voice of Captain Zachary Foxx in the futuristic animated series *Adventures of the Galaxy Rangers*. But neither was enough to land him a steady role—and salary—in a weekly prime-time series. As for film, he appeared as Michael Nouri's business partner in *The Imagemaker* (1986), a less-than-thrilling political thriller that quickly came and went. Two other offers were on the table: one as a mafioso who enters a witness protection plan after turning state's evidence, and the other a doctor in a dance-themed teen romance. Though he accepted both, he almost lost the first.

His breakthrough performance in *Prince of the City* had a down side. After being typed for years as a Broadway song-and-dance man, Hollywood now saddled Jerry with a new label — street tough — and his frustration with it nearly cost him his key role as the perfectly coiffed and pressed gangster Nicholas DeFranco in the top notch *F/X*.

> The director [Robert Mandel, later of *School Ties* and TV's *Lost, Nash Bridges*, and *The Practice*], a young guy who didn't know my work, said, "Would you mind reading a scene for me?" So I did a real tough Brooklyn street gangster. A few days later, they asked me to come in again. They said, "We feel he shouldn't be so street tough; we want him a little better educated. Would you mind reading it again with that in mind?" I said, "Yes, I would. I don't see any point in reading it again. If you want him better educated, more well-spoken, I can do that. If you want a Norwegian sailor or an Alabama sharecropper or what ever the hell you want, I'm an actor. I can do all that." I thought I blew it. Two days later, they called to say I had the job.[10]

An action-packed thriller, *F/X* concerned a New York City special-effects whiz (Bryan Brown) engaged by a Department of Justice agent (Mason Adams) to fake the murder of a mobster about to enter the Witness Protection Program. Betrayal and deception spiral as an NYPD detective (Brian Dennehy) gets suspicious about the mobster's demise. *F/X* quickly achieved hit status, connecting Jerry's face with moviegoers across the country.

As for the other film role, his expectations were not high; neither were the studio's. The low-budget flick, bankrolled at a paltry four million dollars at a time when the average was twelve, would clearly not pay him much and probably disappear into oblivion shortly after release. Despite the odds, Jerry signed on for *Dirty Dancing* because the role of Jake Houseman "was a nice straight father — a doctor from Brooklyn with two daughters. Not a gangster, not a cop."[11] By showing a softer, more vulnerable side, the role might help register Jerry's versatility with directors who otherwise might continue to typecast him. But there was more. With the salary such as it was, he managed to strike a deal with the studio, Vestron Pictures, for a "point," or one percent of the gross. "Nobody knew how big that movie was going to be," he confided with a sly smile to a reporter, "or they wouldn't have given us a little piece of it."[12]

Dirty Dancing was the little film that could — a phenomenal 1987 box office smash that became the paradigm for films of its kind. It instantly connected with audiences worldwide, especially young women. Set in the summer of 1963, its coming-of-age theme centered on seventeen-year-old Frances "Baby" Houseman (Jennifer Grey), who is less than thrilled to be at Kellerman's Resort in New York's Catskills, where she is vacationing with her father, mother (Kelly Bishop), and sister (Jane Bruckner). But Baby's ennui quickly fades under the instruction of the resort's dance coach, Johnny Castle (Patrick Swayze), as he teaches her to dance dirty during his off-hours. Gradually, she becomes enmeshed in his world, much to the consternation of her protective father, Jake, whose line "When I'm wrong, I say I'm wrong" was suggested by Jerry. He was particularly proud of the way it resonated with young women.[13] But Castle outdid the uptight Jake when he declared, "Nobody puts Baby in a corner," and led his daughter from the dining table to the dance floor for the film's climax.

Though Jake Houseman was a choice role for Jerry — one that would define him as "Baby's father" for a generation — it felt nothing like that during the film's forty-four-day shooting in early September 1986. In a matter of days, the weather on the film's Appalachian Mountain locations — the Mountain Lake Resort in Pembroke, Virginia, and Lake Lure, North Carolina — plunged from a sizzling 105 degrees to a frigid 40. The sudden change triggered the onset of fall foliage, jeopardizing the summer setting essential to the story.[14] As set designers literally spray-painted tree leaves green to keep the film season-appropriate, Jerry was suffering from cabin fever off-location in a hotel that boasted a single TV with two channels. "I had so little to do," he remarked, "that I picked up a stick and carved a bird's head cane out of it, which was like outpatient therapy for me."[15] On long weekends, the patient had a visitor who immediately understood the need for the therapy. "Believe me," said Elaine, "the accommodations were rustic."[16] Jerry was living in a dorm-like setting with a common living area and TV. Worse was his austere bedroom — a bed, chair, sink, and bare light bulb operated by a pull-chain suspended from the ceiling.

Whether off or on the set, Jerry made the best of things and worked to encourage the cast and crew. One who profited from his support was leading man Patrick Swayze: "When I was shooting *Dirty Dancing*, I think probably the eyes I trusted [to be sure] I was real, and it worked, and I had nailed it, were Jerry Orbach's eyes. I would go over to him and under my breath go, 'What do you think?' And he'd go, 'No, go there further. I think there's more you can get out of that.' He would say little things like 'courage.' It gives me goose bumps to say that, because I really, really respected that man. I watched his career from the time I was little."[17]

Like many young actors, Swayze, who later played the role of Billy Flynn in the Broadway revival of *Chicago*, felt an affinity with Jerry from the start:

[Doing] Billy Flynn in *Chicago*, which Jerry Orbach originated, felt like a legacy to me.... His life has in many ways paralleled mine. We were almost on a certain level born into musical theatre, ... the presentational school of acting. When I was going to transition into film, all of a sudden I had to learn what organic looked like. Jerry Orbach has been one of the most successful actors who ever lived to make that transition from musical theatre into real, organic, break-your-heart kinds of reality in his work as a film actor. [He could] transition back and forth seamlessly.[18]

But in late fall 1986, after a month and a half on *Dirty Dancing*, Jerry was still mastering the ability to transition. Back in New York, he went before cameras in the supporting role of Lt. Garber in the cop thriller *Someone to Watch Over Me*, starring Tom Berenger, Mimi Rogers, and Lorraine Bracco. While shooting the film, he continued scouting prospects. Then, just like with *Prince of the City*, from out of the blue came a call from television producer Peter Fischer in Los Angeles, asking if he would be interested in doing a recurring role as a partner to Angela Lansbury in the new CBS series *Murder, She Wrote*. Within days, he was on location in L.A. as a fellow detective to Lansbury's celebrated sleuth Jessica Fletcher. Recalled Lansbury,

We tried to lure as many Broadway stars out to the coast to be on the show, because Peter knew, and I knew, that we needed that zing, that wonderful kind of expert quality that only Broadway actors have. I was lucky enough to get Jerry Orbach to come out to the coast, and Peter Fischer devised this wonderful character [for him] by the name of Harry McGraw. Well, let me tell you, to have Jerry on the set with me, it was like a breath of Broadway. Suddenly, I was alive, I was enthusiastic, and I loved doing what I was doing. I thought, "This is fantastic! God, I wish I had him on the show every week."[19]

Their two characters had very different approaches to matters criminal. Even so, Jerry's blundering Boston private eye with a heart of gold and a touch of larceny complimented Lansbury's refined and resourceful widow of Maine's Cabot Cove so well that Fischer soon considered a spin-off, *The Law and Harry McGraw*. Confident that Jerry was the "real deal," Fischer and CBS forged ahead with plans for a sixteen-episode commitment. However, a Q rating–obsessed programming chief bent on replacing Jerry with some better-known actor attempted to sidetrack progress by categorically insisting that "Jerry was not and never would be, a television star."[20] In the end, Fischer got his actor of choice, and Jerry his own TV series.

"First of all, this is really what I've always wanted to do," Jerry stressed. "I don't feel I'm done with theater, but I don't feel I've done enough of this to make me happy. I haven't gotten worn out here yet. The big consideration is that even if *The Law and Harry McGraw* has a lousy rating of say 13 million, that's more people than have seen *The Fantasticks* in the past 28 years. I'm able to now get known by more people which helps me in every way."[21] Whether the show succeeded or not, Jerry's Q rating was sure to get a boost. The plot centered on the rough-edged private investigator whose Boston office is across the hall from that of attorney Ellie Maginnis, his new colleague and his dead partner's refined wife, played by Barbara Babcock. Though she finds Harry's crime-solving methods objectionable, Maginnis continues to employ him, all the while keeping tabs on his tendency to overstep boundaries and also to play the ponies. The contrast between the two characters generated an interesting tension in their relationship that would have been lost if they had become romantically involved. As Jerry observed, "I don't ever want the two of them to get together because that'll be the end of whatever suspense there is. [Like her character in the series,] Barbara Babcock really is a Wellesley graduate, daughter of an ambassador. She and I really are from different sides of the track. We are almost like our characters."[22]

Because Fischer and the writers encouraged his input, Jerry contributed greatly to the formation and definition of Harry's persona. "Harry's very softhearted," he explained, "but he's a street guy. Where I feel akin to him is that Harry knows the grays of humanity. He doesn't see it in black and white. There are street people and hustlers and gamblers who are very nice people, and there are doctors and lawyers who are no-good rats. It's not good guys and bad guys to Harry."[23] Between takes, Jerry found a comrade in Fischer, who enjoyed the challenges of Scrabble and other mind-bending games as much as he did. But marking time at work was one thing; after hours, it was another. After a month's shooting, the three-thousand-mile separation from Elaine in New York was taking a toll on them both. Ever resourceful, Jerry found an ingenious way to cope. In an upcoming episode, there was a featured role for a lively waitress in the subplot. Jerry went to Fischer and ever so diplomatically asked if he might consider casting his wife.

"Can she act?" asked Fischer.

"Absolutely," Jerry assured him. With the straightest of straight shooters certifying her ability, how could the producer refuse? Days later, Elaine was on set and all set to go as Shirley, the waitress with the talent, looks, and humor that easily could have made her a regular on the series had it not been on the brink of cancellation. Much as Fischer and his colleagues fought to save *The Law and Harry McGraw*, the show fell victim to network apathy evidenced by poor time slot it was assigned. And although Jerry would continue making guest appearances as Harry on *Murder, She Wrote* until 1991, the loss of his own show was hard: "It's an amazing thing to be lifted so high, to have your own series, your own parking space on the Universal lot, be on the cover of *TV Guide*. And then, one day they cancel it and it's like you've been thrown out of the business, because a week later you go to the front gate at Universal and they say, 'Excuse me, do you have a pass? Who are you seeing?' ... [The show's success] ... would have changed my life. Everything would have been different. It would have meant living in L.A."[24] Even so, he had squeezed the maximum out of his time there with featured roles in the TV film *Out on a Limb* with Shirley MacLaine and guest appearances on *Love Among Thieves*, *Tales from the Darkside*, and *Simon and Simon*. As the summer of 1988 began, he headed back to New York and to Elaine.

"He was making his name bit by bit," she reflected.

When he'd come back, he had to get incidental work [doing commercials]. At that time, he was a very big voice-over person; we made major money from his voiceovers. But that was beginning to wane as the business changed and new people were coming up.... We had to be careful financially. Thank God, neither of us were big spenders. We didn't own a house; we only had one car.... We did have two cats that we adopted as kittens from Bideawee [the animal welfare organization]. I never had animals because I was working all the time. But Jerry always did—lots of cats and a dog. He loved animals. Later on, I was giving donations to animal organizations all over the country. We even adopted a wolf—"Rogue." Rogue the Wolf. I told everybody we had two cats—and a wolf.[25]

In 1989, Jerry and Elaine celebrated their tenth wedding anniversary. Emily, at seventy-nine, moved from her East Seventy-Sixth Street residence into an apartment by Lincoln Center to be closer to them. Chris was a twenty-year-old college theatre student, and Tony, now twenty-seven, was married and had his own contracting business. Although they had blended as a family over the past decade, initially it had not been easy and required some adjustment, especially for Chris and Tony. "The relationship with Elaine was a tough one for a stint," Tony remembered,

just as it would be for anybody. But the most difficult thing for me, and I think probably for Chris, was the caretaker aspect of Elaine for Jerry. That included sheltering him from us in her mind. So we found that as much as we got along with Elaine—and I came to a real fondness for Elaine—it was one thing to go for the holidays when everyone would be together. But the best way to get to Jerry was to go and see him at work or see him at the gym where we'd have just us—me, Chris, and him—and play pool and have a sandwich. And that's when we could let the guard down because we were past the first line of defense in Elaine. And Elaine thought she was doing the best thing for Jerry. That was really her main concern. It wasn't because we were doing anything to disrupt him. But there was a misunderstanding at times with Elaine. She never had kids of her own. Not to generalize about people who don't have kids, but now that I'm a father and have big kids, I see there's a big difference in people who've never had a kid.... That was a thing that Elaine didn't quite get. She was looking at the main thing—Jerry—and it's his time, and he shouldn't be disturbed. So I didn't take that personally, like "who are you to tell me that?" I just thought, "Well, I'll have to call him later. I'll see him later," rather than draw a line in the sand about it.[26]

Every Saturday, while at the Lone Star, Jerry would phone Marta and catch up with her. "They would talk often when he went to his men's club," Chris recalls. "He and my mom always stayed very good friends."[27] Marta, a recovering alcoholic, now had several years' sobriety, thanks to the intervention of Tony and his wife, Martha. She also had become a wonderful mentor to many other people struggling with addiction. Her social life had begun anew as well; she was dating.

By now, Jerry's films were becoming more home-based with *I Love N.Y.* (1988) and *Last Exit to Brooklyn* (1989). In his next, however, he would join forces with a major film director whose works, like Lumet's, were rooted in New York City—Woody Allen. As Allen biographer John Baxter rightly observes, the filmmaker's works "offer characters and situations that could have sprung from the pages of the *New Yorker* itself."[28] Indeed, the list is impressive: *Annie Hall*, *Hannah and her Sisters*, *Alice*, *Manhattan*, *Everyone Says I Love You*, *Deconstructing Harry*, *Celebrity* and—*Crimes and Misdemeanors* (1989).

Though the film depicted the moral dilemmas of two sets of brothers, it focused primarily on the ethical angst of ophthalmologist Judah Rosenthal (Martin Landau), respected family elder and community pillar. His mistress, Dolores (Angelica Houston), is bent on wrecking his life by exposing their clandestine affair to his wife, Miriam (Claire Bloom). In desperation, Judah turns to his shady, underworld younger brother, Jack (Jerry), who arranges her murder. In the aftermath, Judah becomes more and more guilt-ridden, knowing he is a partner in the crime. The other pair of brothers includes Judah's patient Ben (Sam Waterston, later of *Law & Order*), a rabbi coping with the imminent loss of his sight, and his brother, Lester (Alan Alda), an egotistical and narrow-minded wealthy TV producer. Another character ensnared by his own moral choices is Ben and Lester's brother-in-law, Clifford Stern (Woody Allen), who is married to their sister, Wendy (Joanna Gleason). While filming a documentary about Lester, Cliff becomes involved with Halley Reed (Mia Farrow), his brother-in-law's associate producer.

Appropriately, Allen's original title for the film was *Brothers*, but he changed it to *Crimes and Misdemeanors* after learning that a TV series called *Brothers* was in the works. Additional adjustments followed, notably in the role of Judah's corrupt brother, Jack. Initially, Allen had assigned it to Laudau, but as filming progressed, he was taken with the actor's astoundingly nuanced style and gave him the role of Judah, and Jerry the role of Jack. "The result," notes Baxter, "would be a moving and truthful dual performance from both men. It reveals the strengths of the brother we'd assumed to be weak [Jack], and the weakness of the apparently stronger Judah, who whines and agonizes in guilt over his connivance in a murder. Jack unexpectedly emerges as undeluded and dignified, not pleased with his ability to arrange a killing, but sufficiently in control of his inner demons to accept the moral price: in short, the *mensch* he advises his brother to be."[29] The Laudau-Orbach pairing is most tantalizing in the winter scene at Judah's vacant summerhouse—the perfect spot for planning a murder. As the brothers tensely discuss the idea, they circle around the desolate house—its tarpaulin-covered pool and shuttered windows "under wraps" like their conversation. The combination of the metaphorical setting, the direction, and the actors' performances is brilliant. No wonder Jerry remarked that the film was "a personal favorite" and the role of Jack Rosenthal "something you could get your teeth into."[30]

In television, he was also gaining ground with two guest appearances on *Perry Mason*: one aptly entitled "The Case of the Musical Murder" (1989), and the other "The Case of the Ruthless Reporter" (1991). Others included *The Flamingo Kid* (1989), *Kojak* ("None So Blind" — 1990), *The Golden Girls* (1990), *Hunter* (1990), *In Defense of a Married Man* (1990), Neil Simon's *Broadway Bound* (1992), *Quiet Killer* (1992), and *Mastergate* (1992). Of these, two were Emmy-nominated performances. The first he gave on the NBC *Golden Girls* episode "Cheaters," which aired March 24, 1990, and reunited him with *Threepenny Opera* cast member Bea Arthur. He played Glen O'Brien, a man with whom Arthur's Dorothy Zbornak once had an affair—until she discovered he was married. Some years later, when Glen reappears, divorced and seeking to renew their relationship, he wins Dorothy over for a time, until she realizes that he only wants to be with her because he loathes being divorced and alone. For his performance, Jerry was nominated for Outstanding Guest Actor in a Comedy Series. In 1992, he was honored with another Emmy nomination in the category of Outstanding Supporting Actor in a Miniseries or Special for the role of paterfamilias Jack Jerome, opposite Anne Bancroft, in Neil Simon's *Broadway Bound*. He also brought his mellow baritone to documentaries like *Coney Island* (1991) and continued to raise it in song on TV specials like *Showstoppers: The Best of Broadway* (1985), *Night of 100 Stars* (1985), and *Irving Berlin's 100th Birthday Celebration* (1988). (When a production associate for the Berlin gala called to inquire when he wanted the limo to pick him up, he replied, "Limo? … Nah, I'll walk."[31]) Before President and Mrs. Reagan at the White House, he joined Pearl Bailey, Marvin Hamlisch, Larry Kert, and Jerry Herman for *A Salute to Broadway* (1988). At his invitation, the First Lady even came to the stage when he serenaded her with "Lullaby of Broadway"—quite an honor for a man who had once been on Nixon's Watch List.

His screen credits were mounting up, too. Remarkably, in 1991 he appeared in a total of seven films—*Dead Women in Lingerie, California Casanova, Out for Justice, Toy Soldiers, Delusion, Delirious*, and, most memorably, as the French-accented voice of the candelabrum, Lumière, in the Walt Disney Oscar-nominated animated feature, *Beauty and the Beast*. Asked what had triggered his inspiration for the saucy-voiced candlestick with *joie de vivre*, he replied, "I played him halfway between Maurice Chevalier and Pepe Le Pew."[32] Everyone from tykes to old-timers delighted in his rendition of the Alan Mencken–Howard Ashman, Oscar-nominated showstopper "Be Our Guest," which "reminded people that I could sing."[33] For Angela Lansbury, the voice of teapot Mrs. Potts, Jerry's recording of the number was "a very special occasion which we shared together. … Jerry singing that song is one of the funniest, most wonderfully thought out, carefully prepared performances I've ever seen. It's one of the great animated performances, and Jerry was responsible for it. I think he is loved and will be remembered by every kid who has ever heard the soundtrack of *Beauty and the Beast*."[34]

Jerry was amazed by the way Disney animators endowed Lumière with the facial expressions and gestures he'd projected in the recording studio. "As I saw the animation develop, I found it fascinating that they were putting in some of my facial characteristics and some of my takes and faces that I made when I was doing the voice. I think the nose is there, and all kinds of things on me, which was a lot of fun for me to see."[35] Months after the opening, his career came full circle when he donned tux and tails to join a high-kicking chorus opening the 1992 Oscars with "Be Our Guest." "They told me 2 billion people were watching," he said anxiously. "That's a little nerve-racking."[36] Lumière became so popular with children that Jerry reprised the role several times—in the Disney direct-to-video sequels *Beauty and the Beast: The Enchanted Christmas* (1997) and *Belle's Magical World* (1998), as well as on the Disney Channel's *House of Mouse* series (2001–2002).

Once more, Jerry's career was on the rise, and thanks to his vigilance, he was no longer pigeonholed. But even though he was popping up all over screens large and small, there was a new problem: he now was emblematic of can't-recall-his-name-but-know-his-face syndrome. He explained his cockeyed celebrity this way: "It breaks down demographically. If a teenage girl comes over to me, she's going to say, '*Dirty Dancing.*' If it's an older couple, '*Murder, She Wrote.*' Any cop comes over, '*Prince of the City.*' Families will say, 'You were the candlestick in *Beauty and the Beast.*' And 90 percent of the black people that come up to me say '*F/X.*' I don't know why, but *F/X* must have gotten a tremendous black audience."[37] Asked if he had any regrets about turning down a role, he replied, "Yes, the Sid Caesar type in *My Favorite Year* (1982), which went to Joe Bologna. Who knew?"[38] During 1992 he made four more film appearances, including *A Gnome Named Gnorm*, *Straight Talk* with Dolly Parton and James Woods, *Universal Soldier* with Jean-Claude Van Damme, and as Billy Crystal's easily amused manager in *Mr. Saturday Night*. Summer 1992 marked his return to the stage in a production of *42nd Street* with Elaine and members of the Broadway cast, including Karen Ziemba, Tammy Grimes, and Lee Roy Reams at the Music Fair Theatres in Westbury, Long Island, and Valley Forge, Pennsylvania. That fall, he landed what would become his signature role—NYPD Detective Lennie Briscoe on NBC's *Law & Order*.

Set in the streets and courtrooms of New York, this provocative one-hour drama stressed timely, topical plots that were played out by a superior ensemble of the city's finest actors. Though critically acclaimed when it debuted in fall 1990, *Law & Order* did not fare well in the ratings up against the nightly serving of popular sitcoms then pervading network television. But gradually, audiences were drawn by its power to "go beyond the headlines to explore gray areas of ethics and procedure," as Matt Roush has written, and its challenge "to confront the limitations and consider the possibilities of our legal system while looking into the darkest abysses of human misbehavior."[39]

Jerry and *Law & Order* were superbly matched—an archetypal New York actor playing an archetypal New York character in an archetypal New York drama. A number of factors combined to make the match. The series was first brought to his attention by Elaine, who was a fan from the start of its opening season, 1990–1991. So much did Jerry like what he saw that he took on a guest role as defense attorney Frank Lehrman in a second season episode entitled "The Wages of Love." His performance deeply impressed creator-producer Dick Wolf, who would offer him the role of Briscoe less than a year later. "Jerry didn't audition for the show ever," says Wolf.

> We just offered him the role of Lennie Briscoe. When Paul [Sorvino, who played Detective Phil Cerreta] decided that he couldn't come back because another season outdoors would affect his voice as an opera singer, we were dealt a situation where we had to replace an actor halfway through the season. There were very few people that I could think of and I didn't have to think very hard. Jerry had done such a good job as the defense attorney that [it] was his audition. I just thought, "He's already been tried." There was a bit of controversy with NBC because Warren Littlefield had not been a fan of *The Law and Harry McGraw*. It hadn't worked. I said, "Sorry, that's who it is," and he said, "Okay, if that's who you want. I don't know. I'm not sure about that."[40]

But Wolf was. As *Murder, She Wrote* producer Peter Fischer had told him, "Working with Jerry would be the happiest relationship he could ever hope for."[41] That was all Wolf needed to hear. He had been a fan of the actor's since *The Fantasticks*.

During the course of its first three years, *Law & Order* had rough going, and part of the problem was retaining an actor in the role Jerry was about to play—the veteran cop. George Dzundza had played Detective Sergeant Max Greevey, a no-nonsense type whose deep religious convictions were often at odds with the ethical imprecision of the cases. Though he established the pattern for the role, he left at the end of the first season. At that time, Paul Sorvino was chosen to fill the spot as Detective Phil Cerreta. Sorvino's inscrutable, reflective, straight-talking cop contrasted neatly with partner Chris Noth's more quick-tempered and outgoing Mike Logan. But both actors were keenly competitive. According to executive producer Ed Sherin, "Not only would the pair keep track of how many lines of dialogue they'd each get, if one of them had their shoulder ahead of the other guy's in the doorway in one scene, you'd better make damn sure it was the other way around in the next freaking scene!"[42] Then, after nearly a year and a half with the series, Sorvino announced that *he* was leaving. "Jerry came on and killed them for twelve seasons," comments Wolf. "To me he was the essence of New York, an iconic stage actor in one of the greatest theater cities in the world for thirty years. It wasn't much of a casting challenge. That's whom I wanted—hook, line and sinker. There was nobody else. Fortunately, he said yes."[43] Even so, Jerry wouldn't sign on without a clear image of the character—something he pressed Wolf to convey the day they met for lunch at a New York deli to discuss his coming aboard: "Jerry said, 'I'm interested, but I'm not quite sure how you see this guy.' And I said, '*Prince of the City* would be fine,' and he looked at me and said, 'Got it.' And that's the last acting advice I ever gave him. When Lennie Briscoe walked onstage, it was a fully formed character—there were no tweaks, no agonizing over the back story, just a guy who knew all that was required was essentially him."[44]

Jerry was ecstatic: "When I'd gotten the job, I saw [Paul] Sorvino at Billy Crystal's roast at the Friars Club, and I hugged and kissed him and said, 'My whole family thanks you.'"[45] The fact that both Sorvino's and Dzundza's characters had exited the series by getting shot in the line of duty did not deter Jerry in the least. "As far as I'm concerned, they'll *really* have to shoot me to get me out of here," he told a reporter. Now, as a regular in a series that was rooted in excellence and in his hometown, he finally could do something about "that elusive thing they call a Q-rating"[46] which, to his surprise and delight, would soon climb into the ninety-point range. As he prepared for the role, the question of Briscoe's ethnicity was discussed at length in production meetings: "To me, the name Briscoe implies Sephardic Jews who were conscripted into the Spanish Armada during the Inquisition and jumped ship onto the south coast of Ireland and became known as the Black Irish," he explained. "Many were raised as Catholics and they all look like me."[47]

When Jerry came on board, *Law & Order* was almost halfway through its third season. The first day the fifty-seven-year-old actor, now a grandfather of two, arrived on the set, he found himself new kid on the block once more. And, as he had learned to do fifty years before as a boy adjusting from one new town to another, he applied humor to make friends of strangers. "A few actors had already moved on from the show," remembers Dann Florek, who played Captain Donald Cragen, "but Jerry walked in, smiled at us and said, 'Unlike my predecessors, I plan on being here a very long time.'"[48] He then introduced himself to Chris Noth: "When Jerry came on board, he was my third partner. The first day he came up to me and said, 'I may be your last partner, but you won't be mine.' I cracked up...of course, he was right."[49] The two worked together for almost three years until Noth was released from the series and moved on to HBO's *Sex and the City*.

Jerry's debut on November 25, 1992, in that season's ninth episode, "Point of View," introduced exactly that—a new point of view. From the moment he emerged from the fog as the hard-bitten Briscoe, Jerry was the consummate portrait of a seasoned city cop: gruff, sardonic, and streetwise, but also human, knowledgeable, and ever ready with a glib one-liner for each new crime scene—and partner—encountered. "Beeper not workin'?" asked Logan, irked at his partner's delay. "For what I was doin' I don't need a beeper," Briscoe shot back. Lennie was twice divorced ("Both my ex-wives are thrilled that I got this [job]. They're under the mistaken notion that I'm heavily insured"), politically incorrect ("Italians and Hispanics kill for love; Micks kill for money"), and not above accepting an occasional favor. After lunch at an Italian restaurant, when Logan asked why they never got a check, Lennie replied, "Ah, it's okay. The guy who runs the place is my snitch. He thinks I'm corrupt so he trusts me. All right?"

The character was more than all right with critics. "Viewers are in for a shock when Jerry Orbach blows into the scene in tonight's four-star episode," wrote Matt Roush in *USA Today*. "As Lennie Briscoe,...he has more personality than we've come to expect from *Order*.... Orbach's arrival signals a welcome new layer of grist to an already substantially entertaining mill."[50]

Key to that entertainment was a united ensemble effort by performers who understood that this drama was more about plot than it was about any one character. Chief among the contributions Jerry made to *Law & Order* was a deep regard for the kind of ensemble acting he had known in the theatre. A star uncorrupted by stardom, his work fit squarely alongside the work of his fellow actors. "There's...pleasure in doing real ensemble work, convincing everybody that you're just what you are, just a cop,"[51] he explained unpretentiously. Within days of his arrival, that focus was plain. "He's the most accessible actor I've worked with on the show," said Chris Noth of Jerry. "We're working together really tightly. There's no competition."[52] His sense of humor also endeared him to the cast by giving a lift to the waiting time between takes—something Steven Hill, who played District Attorney Adam Schiff, looked forward to daily. "We had a nice, warm relationship, because every day I would ask him to tell me the latest joke," said Hill. "Jerry had wonderful one-liners that would knock me off my seat."[53] For Noth, it was a factor that made this third partner the charmer: "When I first met him, I was just astounded by how many stories and jokes he knew. One time after lunch he hit me with about ten jokes in a row. I said, 'I can't believe this. I'm going to make a bet that you can't know a joke about everything. Tell me a joke about an Eskimo!' And in a nanosecond, he said, 'An Eskimo's pushing a snowmobile...'"[54]

Wednesday evenings, after *Law & Order* concluded, were special times for Jerry and his mother. "I was in the habit of calling Jerry after every show," said Emily, "and we'd discuss the show at eleven o'clock. He would go over it with me and tell me why things were as they were and clarify things I didn't understand because some of the episodes were so complicated. Truthfully, I thought it was a very good role to begin with.... And the jokes were his very own. They came very easily to him, which always amazed me. He had a brilliant mind."[55]

In January 1994, more than a year into his twelve-year run with the show, Jerry was hit with ominous news. Results of his yearly Prostate-Specific Antigen (PSA) Screening Test revealed a higher PSA level than normal—a four, instead of zero. Jerry then saw an urologist and underwent further tests, painful ones that confirmed what the PSA indicated: he had prostate cancer. But, given his age and early detection, the prognosis was good. With a choice of three treatments—radiation, chemotherapy, or prostatectomy—he opted for radiation because the side effects were least likely to interfere with his commitment to *Law & Order*. During his regimen of thirty-six "zaps," as he called them, he never missed a day's work. When the treatment concluded, the cancer was gone and his PSA normal. Doctors were so delighted that they told him to resume life as before. With his next PSA test six months away, he and Elaine celebrated. In June, they joined a shipful of celebrities on a fabulous cruise of the Eastern Mediterranean and had the time of their lives with friends Professor Richard Brown, in whose New York University film class Jerry had been a frequent guest, and his wife, Zora.

The Greek islands were Jerry and Elaine's favorite place. On one small island, as they dined with the Browns in a tavern overlooking a spectacular sunset, a small, elderly Greek man approached their table. "He said something in Greek to Jerry," said Brown,

> something with love in his eyes…. We didn't know what it was, but nobody in the area of this little port spoke English, so he wrote it out because we didn't know what he was talking about…. The following day, when we docked at Santorini, I pulled the paper out and spoke to the first person that could speak English and Greek. The man laughed and said, 'I don't know what it means, but in Greek it means "We love you, *Dirty Dancing* daddy." And Jerry said, "It's Jake. He follows me all over the world!"[56]

That fall, Jerry began his second season with *Law & Order*. In December, he took the PSA test again. In six months his level had jumped from zero to sixty. Not only had the cancer returned, it had left the prostate and was now coursing through his system, seeking a place to settle.

PART III:
DEEP IN DECEMBER

Chapter 9

TRENCHANT DETECTIVE/ LIVING LANDMARK, 1994–2004

· ·

"L'CHAIM!" DECLARED JERRY, RAISING A GLASS OF WATER in one hand and a small blue pill in the other. In a shot, he downed both. At this moment in his fifty-ninth year, the ancient Hebrew toast he had learned as a boy from Leo was extremely ironic—*to life!* Yet it also reflected his unruffled determination to make the most of the time hormone therapy could give him. With it, doctors said his life might be extended by as much as ten years. Sitting quietly across the table from him, Elaine carefully measured the moment: their remaining days together were numbered, and each had to be lived for all its worth. That would not be easy, given the insidious form of cancer Jerry was fighting and the demands it would make on them both.

Prostate cancer feeds on testosterone, the male hormone, which must be eliminated by ingesting a form of the female hormone, estrogen. Among the side effects, which include sweating, hot flashes, breast tenderness, bone thinning, memory loss, and increased risk of heart attack, impotence is the most mortifying. Fundamentally, the therapy kills the libido, no picnic for any man, especially a man's man like Jerry. He took it in stride and with his characteristic good humor. Each morning before heading off to the day's location for the *Law & Order* shoot, he penned a poem to Elaine, often assuring her that he had taken his "bluies."

I've had my yogurt and my pills.
I think they're curing all my ills.

Now I'll go face the icy chills,
'Cause that's the way
We pay the bills!
I love you to pieces!
XXXX's
Jer

To keep the treatment effective, his doctors at Memorial Sloan-Kettering Cancer Center would alter the prescription every two years. As his PSA numbers rose, so did the strength of the medicine. For nearly a decade, a succession of pills—blues, pinkies, greenies, brownies, and whities, as Jerry referred to them—would keep the cancer at bay and his face before cameras. "Daily," said Elaine, "he faced the cancer with a smile, with fortitude, with trust. He was a great patient. He would do everything the doctors told him to do. And we had a life; we had a happy life despite this terrible cloud over us at all times."[1] For a decade, Jerry's attitude and work ethic would help him endure the hardship with dignity and ease its effects on his loved ones.

He broke the news to his family with a matter-of-fact attitude that deflected the gravity of the disease. As Tony remembers,

Not long after the diagnosis, he told us about it, but it was a very 'oh well, it's not a big deal' type of thing. 'I'm going to have this radiation. I'm going to have to do this thing.' Around the same time, Mayor Giuliani had been diagnosed with prostate cancer, and he was having some procedure that Jerry was interested in doing. But it was about managing it, and from all accounts he was told that he'd probably die of something else. At his age, it was a very slow-acting thing, and they caught it at a time that was early…. So with the advances in medicine, he could be working and be having these treatments. He didn't want to say anything [public] for fear of having people treat him a different way…. And with the media, it wasn't as if he were Brad Pitt or Elaine was Angelina Jolie, but it would have become a thing and would have been a distraction, if not an annoyance. He didn't see the point in that.[2]

For Emily, it was difficult to watch her only child face serious illness.

In the beginning, I only hoped that he would get the best doctors that he could.... He had a contract he couldn't break by being out for months by having surgery or whatever. He had to make decisions all the time. That's pretty tough.... Elaine talked to me about it, and she went through the whole thing. Well, he thought he'd get the best doctors and so on — "Oh, the next time I get an exam things will be fine." He had a very good attitude about it and thought, "Well, it's just something I have to live with." ... He didn't want you to worry. Maybe he didn't even want you to talk about it.[3]

For Jerry, work was the best therapy, and as long as he could do it, he would return to *Law & Order* season after season. Chris, who started with the series as an extra before taking on bigger roles, saw firsthand how his father's work ethic sustained him throughout the decade:

[At the outset,] there's something with serious illness, like day-to-day you feel okay, it's just that there is this thing going on in you. For a few years, that generally was the case. And he would say as much, like "My numbers were up, so I had to do XYZ." But he took great lengths to ensure that nobody found out or that it was downplayed. He didn't want it to jeopardize his work situation. Even when he was losing his hair, ... he was always trying to give us the sense of "Oh, it's another setback." To acknowledge that kind of illness is also to acknowledge in a very real way your mortality, which is terrifying for anybody. By focusing on his work he was able to take some of the stress off of those thoughts and that possibility.... You can't fault any human being for doing that.[4]

Although *Law & Order* was a bicoastal operation — with Dick Wolf, the writers, and the editors on the West Coast and the non-writing producers, directors, and production crew on the East — it was New York producers Lewis Gould, Jeffrey Hayes, and Kati Johnston whom Jerry initially took into his confidence. Optimistic as he was about his condition, he was concerned about how it could affect his job. The three producers kept the matter among themselves and the assistant directors, who arranged to work the shooting schedule around his treatments. "That worked out fine," says Gould.

We were always able to accommodate him. For the longest time, we all felt that he was really beating the cancer. He still looked great and his energy was great. So there was no need for people to know. [Eventually,] Dick Wolf and the people at Universal learned about it, but they didn't know about it at first. As loved as Jerry was and as wonderful as he was in the role, I think there was a part of him that lives in every actor of "I don't want them to know I'm vulnerable; I don't want to be replaced." Believe me, that can happen. And some of us got questions from the top about how he was doing. I know they were thinking, "Is he going to finish the season?" We were always quick to tell everybody that he was absolutely fine. And he *was* fine up until the very end. So we kept it quiet and scheduled his things, and it went on like that for years.[5]

In fall 1995, as his first year on hormone therapy drew to a close, Jerry was also beginning his fourth season with *Law & Order*. More and more, he was becoming the mainstay of the series as his wisecracking Briscoe won fans with lines like "Subject Hagan had a blood alcohol level of .03; that's higher than when I gargle in the morning." When a bystander informed him that a murder was the work of the devil, he countered, "No, this was done by someone who knows the neighborhood; Satan's not a local." And while arresting a subject who was in the middle of a phone call, he grabbed the receiver, shouted, "He'll call you back in twenty-five years," and hung up. It was amazing how his comically feisty and fearlessly astute Briscoe connected with all kinds of people. The popularity of the character was such that viewers were saluting him in the streets. Police officers, impressed with how keenly he understood the realities and risks of their work, routinely thanked him. "He was Mr. New York," commented Chris Noth. "You walk down the street with Jerry and people are like, 'Hey! Jerry O!' Cops. Firemen. He really relished all of it."[6]

He equally relished the work. "You have to remember," he told one reporter, "*Law & Order* is a story-driven script and there's little interpersonal or personal information offered. No wives or girlfriends. Mercifully." Then, with a grin, he added, "I don't want to sound chauvinistic, but there's a lot of fun in that police precinct. All that male bonding!"[7] That was modified in fall 1993 when NBC mandated changes in the all-male principal roles: in the stationhouse, S. Epatha Merkerson's Lieutenant Anita Van Buren for

Dann Florek's Capt. Donald Cragen, and in the courtroom, Jill Hennessy's Assistant District Attorney Claire Kincaid for Richard Brooks' ADA Paul Robinette. Through the departures and arrivals, Jerry continued to foster a solid camaraderie and chemistry with cast and crew. Other changes followed: Sam Waterston's Executive ADA Jack McCoy for Michael Moriarty's Executive ADA Ben Stone (1994) and Benjamin Bratt's Det. Reynaldo "Rey" Curtis for Chris Noth's Det. Mike Logan (1995). "Chris Noth and I had one relationship," said Jerry, "and sometimes we almost sounded like we could say each other's lines. So we had to keep the writers working on arguments between us."[8] As Noth stepped into the role of Mr. Big on HBO's *Sex and the City*, a different dynamic would emerge between Jerry's Briscoe and Bratt's Curtis, a short-fused, staunchly Catholic, designer-suited technology whiz. With his bilingual skills and ardently religious, conservative views on social and political matters, Curtis was destined to collide with the politically incorrect and liberal Briscoe. Sizing up the newcomer, the veteran remarked, "I got ties older than him. And some shoes, too, I think."

Off-camera, a warm regard developed between the two performers from the moment Bratt first stepped onto the set anxious to prove his worth. The actor was a bundle of nerves as he prepared for his first shoot—rehearsing, then, while lights were set, racing to his trailer, where for the next twenty minutes he practiced lines and breathing exercises in an unsuccessful attempt to quell his anxiety. Back on set for a final rehearsal, his unease was apparent to Jerry, who empathized with a quick smile before averting his glance as if dodging an impending disaster. Bratt focused and took a final breath, his heart sinking. "Roll sound!" shouted the assistant director. "Action!" called director Ed Sherin. "All eyes were on the actors," says Bratt, "and Jerry O leaned into me and slyly said out of the side of his mouth, 'You're not really going to do it that way, are you?' I froze solid, then everybody fell out laughing, including me, and that was the start of a beautiful friendship.'"[9] Although the two remained crime-solving partners for four seasons until Bratt's departure in 1999, their friendship was lifelong.

Very much the *Law & Order* team player, Jerry was quick to emphasize the chief distinction that set the series apart from others in its class: "Actually shooting in New York makes a tremendous difference. Take a show, God love them, like *NYPD Blue*. They come to New York for a week or so, and they film what they call dry runs and walk-ins. But when they go inside the building, they are in Los Angeles. Filming in the streets of New York can be difficult."[10] Just how difficult, he knew full well. One day, he and Bratt were filming a sidewalk scene in front of a grocery store. They were less than an arm's length from each other when in the middle of their dialogue a passerby plowed right through them, undaunted and undeterred. As the man dashed on, the actors continued the scene without missing a beat, making his intrusion seem like it was planned.

Invariably, when shooting on the street, there would be a handful of fans eager to get an autograph or snapshot. Jerry always made time for them. That was part of the job; it went with the territory. As for celebrity, he took it in stride, accepting the occasional complimentary hot dog from street vendors or ride from police: "If it's raining and I can't get a cab, sometimes a squad car will come by and they'll say, 'Where are you going?' I say, 'I don't want to get you guys in trouble.' They say, 'Get in the back. We'll pretend you're under arrest.'"[11] He took great pride in his public, too. Once, as he sat in a restaurant lunching with Bratt and S. Epatha Merkerson, a succession of fans came to the table to greet him, and he warmly chatted with each. "Jerry would be in the middle of the fork from the plate to his mouth and he would stop if someone came over. And I remember whispering to him, 'Jerry, you're eating.' And he went, 'Kid, these are the people who keep us working. You know, it's a moment. It just takes a moment.' I think that some of the things I do now are literally in direct response to watching how gracious a man Jerry Orbach was."[12] That graciousness was precisely what was so unique about Jerry. As Sam Waterston puts it, "[H]e was so completely invested in daily life and in other people."[13] To illustrate the point, he tells of an occasion when a crew member, who was having friends from Florida visit the set, asked Jerry if he would say hello. He not only said hello, he sat them in his chair with his name on it, told them a couple of jokes and chatted with them at length about Florida and everyday matters like sports. Waterston notes,

> When it was all over and for years after, these people would say, "You know, it was like talking to a regular guy." Jerry would cross the street to accommodate an admirer or fan. He was so generous with himself and it was one of the lessons he taught me. He grew up in the musical theater and I grew up in the classical theater. And as a classical actor, I had a little bit of that snobbism that sometimes goes with that group

of people. Jerry was one of those people who knew he was doing what he was doing because people liked him and he was grateful to them for that. So it was no skin off his nose whatsoever to give them some of his time.… If I'm a nice guy when I run into fans on the street, it has a lot to do with Jerry.[14]

Jerry once described the plot structure of *Law & Order* as "a ritual, like a High Mass,"[15] much the way Tennessee Williams described his play, *The Rose Tattoo*. A discovery initiates the action—gunshots or a body found. The detectives enter with a score of technicians and medical personnel. From there, the plot moves from point to point to point, with that well-known "chung-chung" sound marking transitions between scenes. This format, Jerry noted, was "a comforting thing people can count on and, for good or for bad, that's what I think makes the series have that kind of longevity."[16] Apart from the ritual aspect, there was another factor that contributed to the show's staying power—the actors who played the six principal characters. Again, as Lewis Gould, a producer and director for thirteen seasons, notes, "Whether cops or DAs, the actors spent a lot of time asking questions, extracting information, and analyzing data. That requires great acting skill, because that stuff could easily become mundane and boring. To make that material interesting… is probably more difficult to do than a chew-up-the-scenery kind of thing."[17] Nevertheless, by the middle of his fourth season, Jerry was hinting at that very thing—an episode that would "give me one of those chew-up-the-scenery scenes where I can talk all about my personal stuff."[18] He yearned for just a slice of the kind of emoting Dennis Franz got to do as Andy Sipowicz on the character-centered *NYPD Blue*. But the plot-centered *Law & Order* was another thing entirely. Whether Dick Wolf and the writers took Jerry's hint seriously or decided for themselves to toy with the format to see how viewers would respond, the 1995–96 season finale was unlike anything the actors had previously done.

"Aftershock," which aired April 22, 1996, was purely experimental and veered radically from the ritual, opening with Briscoe, Curtis, McCoy, and Kincaid witnessing the lethal injection of murderer Mickey Scott (Chris Bauer), for whom they had sought the death penalty. The subject matter was timely, given the recent reinstatement of the death penalty in New York State (later overturned in 2004). The remainder of the episode showed how the execution impacted the personal lives of the four: the straitlaced, married Curtis falling for an attractive NYU coed (Jennifer Garner) and McCoy drowning his self-remorse with a bunch of barflies while awaiting the arrival of Kincaid, busy seeking advice from her stepfather/law professor (Len Cariou) and support from Van Buren. As for Briscoe, a recovering alcoholic with years of sobriety, he goes on a bender after badly bungling a surprise visit from Cathy, his estranged daughter (Jennifer Bill). By the time Kincaid arrives at the bar, McCoy has left, but she gives Briscoe a lift home. En route, a speeding car runs a stop sign and slams into Kincaid's side of the car. A dazed Briscoe stumbles out of the car, around to the driver's side, and peers in. Kincaid is dead and he is grief-stricken. Much as "Aftershock" brilliantly highlighted the range of the actors, it did not go down well with the faithful, whose "Wednesday night at ten" ritual, producers learned, was indeed sacred. "It was a mistake we never made again," notes Dick Wolf. Essentially, the experiment violated the procedural style of the show. Procedural television programs, like *Law & Order*, in which a problem is presented, probed, and resolved, usually within an hour-long episode, require a certain kind of acting skill. "Why actors like Jerry are so valuable in procedurals," explains Wolf, "is that they bring that unwritten, unstated backstory with them. They're people with a past and secrets. And Jerry managed to communicate that effortlessly and that is the essence of procedural acting."[19]

Still, there were ample opportunities for Jerry to expand on his role, like "Corruption" (October 30, 1996), in which a corrupt fellow officer (Kevin Conway), whom Briscoe is investigating for the murder of a drug dealer, accuses him of stealing evidence from a police lockup. Occasionally, there was also a story arc, a series of two or three episodes that highlighted a particular character. One of these included the threesome "Bad Girl" (April 29, 1998), "Damaged" (May 6, 1998), and "Monster" (May 20, 1998) that once more focused on Briscoe's relationship with daughter Cathy (Jennifer Bill), a nurse and recovering drug addict arrested for stealing drugs. Slated to testify against her drug-dealing ex-boyfriend — the real source of the crime — she rejects her father's offer of police protection. Much as Briscoe tries to convince Cathy that she is in danger, he cannot overcome the damage his alcoholism and desertion inflicted on her as a child. For Cathy, Lennie's expression of paternal concern is too little, too late. Ultimately, she is stalked and killed by her ex for testifying against him. Called to the murder scene of a Jane Doe, Briscoe arrives with Curtis and, to his horror, discovers that the corpse is Cathy's. At the cemetery, as Cathy's remains are interred, her mother stares despondently at her ex-husband, who stands before their daughter's grave utterly shaken. Not long afterward, when a snitch offers him a chance to avenge Cathy's death, Lennie finds the temptation hard to resist.

While at Trinity Cemetery in Washington Heights preparing to shoot the graveside scene in which Lennie decides to get even for Cathy's murder, Jerry cracked, "I just want someone to die in my arms so I can cry and get an Emmy nomination."[20] The barb, a reference to *NYPD Blue*'s four-time Emmy winner Dennis Franz and his recent tragic parting with partner Jimmy Smits, immediately drew peals of laughter from the crew. Though he never admitted it outright, that was precisely the kind of leave-taking Jerry would liked to have had with Chris Noth or Benjamin Bratt, who would soon be leaving the series. "So I could weep," he dryly stated. "Copiously."[21] But episodes like "Bad Girl," "Damaged," and "Monster" were precisely the reasons why Jerry received a third Emmy nomination in 2000: this time for Outstanding Lead Actor in a Drama Series. Reflecting on the honor, he told Jason Lynch of *People Magazine*, "*Law & Order* is about the case, not about the people. We don't get to agonize over the soap-opera elements of life. I've said that the only way I'll win an Emmy is if they let some partner die in my arms, and I get to be very dramatic and cry over it. That's okay. I don't think I ever aimed for awards, as evidenced by the fact I haven't won many."[22] James Gandolfini of *The Sopranos* won the Emmy.

Sam Waterston observes,

Jerry had a lot of [acting] chops to show, and the series didn't give him a whole world of opportunity to really show everything he had in him. I know he felt that way. It's one of the reasons that he didn't win a lot of prizes for his work on *Law & Order* even though he was a major part of its backbone. And it wasn't fair. He was as good as the ones winning prizes. He was a very versatile guy. He had his ambitions like anybody else in the business. You don't go into this to hide your talents under a bushel basket. But I don't think losing the Emmy was a heartbreaker. He was a realist and he liked to look at things as they were. It was a gyp, but I don't think he lost sleep over it.... It's just the nature of the business that they pick out winners and losers. They don't recognize that it's really about working in a company, a web in which everybody is holding everyone else up. And in Jerry's case, he was more than carrying his own weight. He was part of the spine of the show.[22]

As for his fans, they continued to relish those rare details of Briscoe's personal life sporadically dropped during conversations with colleagues or criminals. A pool shark and steady consumer of street vendor coffee and hot dogs, Lennie was a recovering alcoholic who once joked, "After I traded in the Chivas bottle for the Grecian Formula, I became a saint." He also was the father of two daughters (the second daughter, Julia, was mentioned, but never appeared as a character). After surviving two divorces ("Two priors, no convictions"), he had soured on marriage, and his bitterness was palpable. During a discussion about prostitution, when Curtis asked him, "You ever pay for it, Lennie?" he answered, "I was married, wasn't I?" Acrimony was his spiny shell. Beneath it was a compassion that could embrace a woman mourning a murdered husband or bolster a frazzled partner with a gentle pat on the shoulder. For viewers, that concern was probably Briscoe's most endearing quality, and it rang true because it was characteristic of the actor who portrayed him. How much of Jerry Orbach was invested in Lennie Briscoe? "A lot," he told *Newsday*'s Blake Green. "My character's very human, fallible; people seem to like his humor. I don't write the lines, but if the structure doesn't sound like Lennie, I get them to change it. But Lennie's tougher than I am, and he carries a gun. I'm not a recovering alcoholic, and both my children are alive. Lennie's into fast food; I'm very aware of nutrition."[23] Quite so. To maximize the effect of the medication he was taking, a healthy diet was essential, and, apart from the occasional vodka martini doctors permitted, he ate properly thanks to a daily assist from Elaine.

As the workday drew near quitting time—or went into overtime due to a delay—Jerry grew more and more anxious to get home to Elaine, calling her at intervals to let her know how soon he would join her for dinner. Elaine's good old-fashioned Italian peasant fare—different varieties of pasta served with tomato, vegetable, or garlic and oil sauces—was the center of a nourishing diet and always a hit with a good eater like Jerry. It pleased her greatly to see him enjoy what she prepared, even on those rare occasions when it didn't quite turn out as she'd planned. On his mornings off, Jerry was breakfast cook—omelets made to order or scrambled eggs blended with cottage cheese, bacon crisp not dry, and toast with just a "schmear" of butter like Leo had taught him.

Elaine described Jerry as "a good-bye kisser and a hello kisser," and, on evenings after dinner while cuddling on the couch watching *Jeopardy*, "a between-commercials kisser."[24] However, when standing to kiss, they were height-challenged, so Jerry devised a way to bridge the distance between his six-foot-two and her five-foot-two. The "kissing stool" was an old upholstered footstool, and when Elaine stepped to the top of it, she and her husband could be face-to-face. Their romance even made the humdrum weekend chores fun. Their choreographed routine for changing the bed sheets was something Bob Fosse would have admired — and picture Lennie Briscoe, in T-shirt and boxers, wielding a vacuum with the same deadly skill as his .38 Smith and Wesson. When Elaine was recovering from back surgery, Jerry did the laundry. In the laundry room of the apartment complex, wives who discovered him sorting and folding were soon asking their husbands why they couldn't do the same. "People used to say they didn't know couples like us," Elaine commented. "They didn't know anyone who had the love that we had for each other and the compassion. When I was late for something that I was to join him for, the people sitting with Jerry would [later] tell me that he just kept looking at his watch saying, 'Where is she? I think I ought to make a phone call.' And I was just stuck in traffic or one thing. Or if I disappeared out of the room for a second, he'd ask, 'Where's Elaine?' Not that it was crazy, but it was just that we were soul mates. But we weren't leaning on each other at all times. We both always quoted the Kahlil Gibran proverb about the two trees having roots that were strong but separate. Only their branches intertwined, so that they didn't strangle each other at the bottom. And not only was our love for each other strong [like that], but also our friendship."[25]

Elaine was not dazzled by diamonds or jewels — presents Jerry always wanted to buy her. Expensive gifts were unnecessary. Moreover, from the outset of their marriage, they both had agreed not to exchange presents. It was one reason why "he always called me the best wife in the world," she acknowledged with a laugh, "because I wasn't saying, 'Buy me, take me, give me.' He certainly was generous. I just didn't choose to take."[26] Both were savers, socking away as much of Jerry's income as they could to insure a secure retirement for themselves and a legacy for the family. Their one extravagance was the yearly cruise they took during Jerry's summer break from *Law & Order*, a time they always looked forward to because they could be together twenty-four/seven without interruption — to a point. Whether in the Caribbean, the Mediterranean, or the Aegean, invariably there would be a local who would shout, "Briscoe!" or "Lennie!" Whether the inflection was Spanish, Italian, or Greek, it meant that Jerry was known and loved around the world as much as he was in New York City.

At the onset of his illness, Elaine bent the rules and gave Jerry a gift that had great meaning for them both. Since they were raised Catholic, they were familiar with the belief that each person has a guardian angel, a God-given protector that watches over them and keeps them from harm. As a reminder of that, "I gave Jerry an angel [with an opal stone, his birthstone] for his lapel that you see on his tuxedo in many pictures," explained Elaine. "People would say, 'What is that?' And he'd say, 'It's an angel from my angel.' And he always wore it. It was his flag."[27] In 1999, as Jerry neared his fifth year on hormone therapy, the angels seemed to be working overtime as he and Elaine continued to weather the stress of his illness. "He was still taking the pills, and I was still asking, 'Honey, did you take? Did you take?' [Even] when we would go away, I'd have to pack how many bluies and how many greenies he'd have to take. It had to be done. Our whole life revolved around this. Absolutely. It never went out of our heads."[28] In the course of caring for Jerry, Elaine developed high blood pressure, a condition she hid from him. But keeping track of their health issues was not their only worry at the time.

Although neither Jerry nor Elaine was computer savvy or familiar with the Internet, they had a close call with online identity theft on March 15, 2000. At that time, they learned from a friend that eBay, the Internet auction site, had posted digital images of two of Jerry's contracts from 1958, one of which listed his Social Security number. A third document with his signature was also posted. Five days later, on March 20, Jerry laid down the law for the disorder. He filed a complaint in Manhattan U.S. District Court asserting that by posting the documents, eBay, on behalf of an auction dealer in Maine, had exposed him to "identity theft and credit card fraud" and could ultimately damage his credit rating and "personal and professional life" by causing his "name to be broadcast in conjunction with his Social Security number throughout the state of New York, the United States of America and internationally via the Internet."[29] For these reasons, he requested a judge to order eBay to remove the contracts from its web site. Within twenty-four hours of the posting, however, the company had already done so after a caller warned that the items might have been incorrectly placed there by one of its users. "His Social Security number was on eBay for everybody to see," Elaine confirmed. "Thank God, nothing ever happened."[30]

There also were changes at work that were challenging for Jerry. Benjamin Bratt's departure from the series at the end of the 1998–99 season hit him hard. Working daily together for four seasons, they had bonded strongly not only as colleagues, but as friends. Tough as it was to bid farewell, Jerry rose to the occasion during the wrap party at the season's end, serenading Bratt with a parody of Michael Jackson's "Ben." "He rewrote all the verses to fit our friendship," says Bratt. "It was brilliant, both moving and hysterical, and quite nearly wrecked me. The man is a prince."[31]

In fall 1999, Jerry started the new *Law & Order* season with a new partner and a fellow song-and-dance man—Jesse L. Martin. On Broadway, Martin had originated the role of Tom Collins, the gay, AIDS-afflicted PhD of the Jonathan Larsen musical *Rent*, and on television, he had starred as Dr. Greg Butters, Calista Flockhart's singing fiancé on *Ally McBeal*. As *Law & Order*'s Det. Ed Green, he was a gambling-addicted vegan who sported a Rolex and favored unconventional tactics over conventional procedures—a constant source of irritation to Briscoe. Their dynamic was shaped by a generation gap that, at first, neither the "old school" Briscoe nor hipster Green dared to bridge. As Jerry expressed it, "You have to have different points of view.... With Jesse, it's a new, younger generation. Also, he's an African-American, so there is a lot of clashing views there."[32] In time, however, the two detectives would adjust to each other, with Green a great straight man for Briscoe's one-liners:

GREEN: Did anyone find any type of weapon in Peter Rubin's home?
BRISCOE: Not unless you count the world's most boring record collection.

Ultimately, when Briscoe announced his retirement at the end of their five-year partnership, Green would be devastated by the news. Soon he would be the senior partner, showing the ropes to junior colleagues as Briscoe had done for him.

At the start, the rapport between the two actors was a bit strained. "Jerry Orbach had a very special relationship with Benjamin Bratt and was very upset that Ben had left the series," explains Martin. "When I showed up, he was sort of hesitant to get to know me and get close to someone new. He was gracious, but it took some time for us to work it out. By the fourth episode, I was at ease around him and loving it. It was the best time in my life."[33] What made it so, according to S. Epatha Merkerson, was "the people. They're all dear friends. But the coolest times were with Jerry Orbach and Jesse Martin. We'd all done musical theater, and Jerry and Jesse knew every Broadway song, so somebody would start singing a tune and we'd start singing three-part harmony. Nobody could be as cool as Jerry Orbach. He was the king of Broadway."[34] To keep the king current, Martin taught him all the new songs, and in exchange, Jerry taught him all the old ones. Singing their way through waits between scenes made the time pass more quickly. Soon Martin knew Jerry as a mentor and friend: "I got tips from him every day. He knew everything there was to know about everything. Not just acting on stage, in films or the small screen.… When my father was sick, Jerry was invaluable. He put me in a space where I could mourn but also could work and live. I'll love him forever for that."[35]

The king of Broadway also had a keen social conscience that Martin saw in action one day while shooting a scene in a Bowery mission. When the homeless people there flocked to him, Jerry was kind and attentive to each. "When we left," recalls Martin, "Jerry said, 'I have to make a couple of phone calls. Something's got to be done [about how they are living].' And I know he made those calls."[36] Much as he identified with New York — "I live it, love it and represent it" — he considered the plight of the homeless, among other things, a disgrace to the city. As he commented in a 1993 interview: "It's the decline of New York and all the major cities caused by the neglect of the last two [presidential] administrations. Federal funds were pulled, so hospitals had to release the mentally ill, creating a large homeless population. There has also been a lack of endowments in the arts — all modern civilizations have art endowments. That's a must! The mishandling of welfare programs … Don't give me that, "We don't have the money," stuff. We have plenty of money for a war in Iraq."[37]

Concern for people — be they down and out, rich and famous, or somewhere in between — ran deep in Jerry. On the *Law & Order* set, he would frequently put nervous guest stars at ease by introducing them to the cast and crew or serving them juice to moisten a dry mouth. While off-camera, he would run lines with actors—whether stars or day players—to help the scene work better during shooting. Actor Ted Sod fondly remembers such an occasion:

When I appeared on *Law & Order*, I didn't know what to expect when I got on the set. It was my second time on the series, having appeared on *L & O: Criminal Intent* in the past. Jerry immediately made me feel as if I were welcome. He introduced himself and we spoke for a bit about my hometown, Wilkes-Barre, Pennsylvania, where he had relatives. We talked about the theatre and then he asked me if I would like to run lines—I was so taken aback by his generosity. No television star has to encourage day players, and it's a small example of what a class act Jerry was. He understood that a day player needs the encouragement that he offered, and he also knew that the shoot would run more smoothly if I was on top of my game. The shoot went well, and, as it was late Friday afternoon, the end of the workweek for Jerry and Jesse Martin, it made a difference in the wrap time. As we left the set, Jerry thanked me for being prepared.[38]

A stalwart supporter of better pay for police, Jerry appeared at rallies of the Patrolmen's Benevolent Association and at benefits for slain officers' families. He was always welcomed because, for scores of officers, his Det. Briscoe was as close to their world as an actor could get. "He was never a caricature, like some of the people that play cops and detectives,"[39] said Joseph Pentangelo, an ex-police detective turned actor, who appeared with him on a number of episodes. Both on and off camera, Jerry was the real deal. When strolling through his neighborhood, he would often visit the Midtown North Precinct. "He'd be walking down the block, and he'd always stop by and say hello," said James Heaphy, a twenty-year veteran of the force, who was so impressed with Jerry's work that he too decided to study acting professionally: "Watching guys like Jerry Orbach making it look so natural, you think, 'I can do that.'"[40] And then there were those, like Michael J. Palladino, president of the Detectives Endowment Association, who thought the actor would have made a great cop: "Outside of the script, he seemed to have a good handle on investigative techniques. He probably would have been a damn good New York City detective."[41] Jerry's respect for the men and women in blue was as authentic as his portrait of a seasoned city cop was for them. On the frigid morning of January 12, 2001, as he stood with hundreds of officers rallying at City Hall for higher wages from Mayor Giuliani's administration, he stated, "All I can do is try and represent you guys on a TV screen and make you look as good as I can. I could never go out and not know if I'm coming home that night the way you do."[42]

The more New York gave to Jerry, the more Jerry gave to New York, hosting celebrity golf tournaments and benefits for Bideawee, North Shore Animal League, New York City Opera, Brooklyn Academy of Music, and other organizations. Generous a benefactor as he was, his fundraising acumen was really what charities sought. He had a remarkable ability to attract other celebrities and big contributors—a reason why he was tapped by Jacqueline Kennedy Onassis to assist the effort to save Grand Central Station. But more than anything, it was his association with *Law & Order* as Lennie Briscoe that identified him with New York: "It may sound a little off the wall to say this, but having the opportunity to do this in this long an arc has given me—and is continuing to give me—a feeling that I'm doing something for the city and for the people of it and for the cops. I see it every day in the street. The profile of *Law & Order* has gotten bigger and bigger. And the way the city feels about us … it's like we're part of the good things that happen in the city."[43] Following the tragic events of September 11, 2001, those "good things" included the time he volunteered on behalf of the Office of Emergency Management and its "Ready New York" service campaign doing public service announcements emphasizing the need for emergency preparedness among his fellow New Yorkers.[44]

By 2000, Det. Lennie Briscoe was a TV classic and Jerry a superstar. He played Briscoe not only weekly on *Law & Order*, but also in the TV film *Exiled: A Law & Order Movie* (1998), and on episodes of the series' spin-offs, *Law & Order: Special Victims Unit* (1999, in which son Chris played nephew Ken Briscoe) and *Law & Order: Criminal Intent* (2001). When he voice-acted the character for the *Law & Order* video games "Dead on the Money" (2002), "Double or Nothing" (2003), and "Justice Is Served" (2004), he conquered yet another entertainment medium. There were also crossover appearances on NBC's Baltimore-based *Homicide: Life on the Streets* (1996, 1997, 1999), in which he teamed with Richard Belzer's Det. John Munch. In the 1996 episode, "For God and Country," when Munch challenges Briscoe to a game of pool ("I think you shouldn't play unless your ego can handle defeat"), he nearly has to run to an ATM to cover his $500 loss when the New Yorker runs the table ("Just protecting my ego"). When Munch learns that Lennie once had an affair with one of his ex-wives, his loss is further compounded, and by the end of the game he is utterly dejected. The comic jousting between the two actors, who were also great friends, provides the perfect touch of comic relief in a powerful plot about a paramilitary terrorist (J. K. Simmons, later Dr. Emil Skoda) guilty of mass murder.

The third occasion of *Law & Order*'s crossover with *Homicide* provided a happy reunion for Jon Olexy with his Cousin Jerry and Elaine. Sunday morning, he drove them from the Harbour Court Hotel to his home in Lutherville for a family brunch his wife, Dorie, had prepared. Afterwards, Olexy played a recording of his favorite poet, Dylan Thomas, reading the poem "Fern Hill." "To my amazement, Jerry recited this long poem along with the recording," he remembers. "When I asked how he knew 'Fern Hill,' he said simply, 'Jon, when you're an actor, you have to learn everything.' He was very smart. The *New York Times* crossword puzzles were usually a breeze for him, and he even won the TV Celebrity *Jeopardy* tournament."[45] His excellent recall was due to his photographic memory—the reason why Sam Waterston fondly observed, "He always knew his lines—and yours, too."[46]

His work on the big screen, though, was less frequent and generally tended toward supporting roles: Diane Ladd's husband in *The Cemetery Club* (1993), a used car dealer in *To Wong Foo, Thanks for Everything! Julie Newmar* (1995), and the businessman who sings "Loch Lomond" to young Frankie Nasso in *Prince of Central Park* (1999). He was the voice of the villainous Sa'luk in the Disney animated feature *Aladdin and the King of Thieves* (1996) and, once again, Lumière in the 3D short subject *Mickey's PhilharMagic* (2003). He contributed voiceovers for the films *Temps* (1999) and *Manna from Heaven* (2002), and also did a cameo for *The Acting Class* (2000). As a legendary stage performer, he was interviewed in the documentaries *Broadway: The Golden Age, By the Legends Who Were There* (2003) and *Try to Remember: The Fantasticks* (2003). But his most noteworthy work from this period—perhaps of his entire film career—was his costarring role opposite Al Pacino in the drama *Chinese Coffee*. An independent film that played art houses when released in 2000, it was directed by Pacino and shot during Jerry's break from *Law & Order* in summer 1997. "It's from a play by Ira Lewis," explained Jerry, ". . . about a couple of intellectual losers in the Village, West Village types, who have never succeeded really.... One's a writer, the other's a photographer. It's basically a two-character play which has been expanded into a movie..."[47]

An intriguing study in character contrasts, *Chinese Coffee*, as Al Pacino explains, is about "the fragility of friendship ... how easy it can just sort of tip, [and] the things that make it go [that way]." In other words, it shows how certain factors can instantly turn friendship from benevolent to malevolent. That is the crux of this gripping and unsettling duet between writer Harry Levine (Al Pacino) and writer-turned-photographer Jake Manheim (Jerry), two aging, destitute "Beat-era" artists adrift in eighties-era Greenwich Village. Both are desperate for a measure of success that will ratify the artistic promise of their youth, the glory days when their friendship began and they were poised to become the next Allen Ginsberg or Jack Kerouac. That friendship is now about to implode as Harry pounds on Jake's door well past midnight, irate over being fired from his doorman's job for failing to fawn sufficiently over patrons. More than ever, he needs to collect an overdue loan he made to Jake, along with the manuscript of his novel that Jake has promised to critique—his sole hope for success. A high-strung insomniac with acute hypochondria, Harry obstinately and compulsively presses Jake for the money and, more importantly, the assessment of his work. The jaded, complacent Jake coolly informs his friend that he is broke. But what really irks Harry is not Jake's inability to pay so much as his reluctance to comment on the novel. Into the wee small hours, they vent their feelings about money, aesthetics, past girlfriends, and their friendship—Jake skirting the issue of the novel all the while. By the climax, however, the subject looms large again, and it is clear that the content of the novel is a sore point with Jake, who erupts in rage over Harry's audacious exploitation of his personal misfortunes and failed professional life. Feeling deeply deceived and jealous, Jake threatens to dash Harry's dream of success, ejecting him from his apartment and into the night—the manuscript's pages flying furiously behind him.

After seeing the initial staging of *Chinese Coffee* at the Actors Studio, Pacino took on the role of browbeaten writer Harry Levine and perfected it in productions presented off-off-Broadway, and later on Broadway. "I always wanted Jerry Orbach to play Jake," he explains. "Jerry is really a wonderful actor who really knows how to just get in there. And I have to respect the fact that he didn't have any time with this. I only had Jerry for a window of a few weeks because [of] ... *Law & Order*. He only had this creative time and it worked. I got him and we rehearsed together in this room. And he did this major role.... It's what they call a 'two-hander.' And I had the experience of having done it for years on the stage; he had three weeks."[48] Over the course of a twelve-day filming schedule, the pair covered eighty-four pages of continuous dialogue. The result is two virtuosos at their peak as archetypal washouts, on the skids and alienated from the successful whose aptitude they would easily have matched, even surpassed, had they had the same breaks. After two failed novels, Pacino's manic-depressive Harry is still as determined to succeed as Jerry's passive-aggressive Jake is resigned to flop, and therein rests the brilliance of writer Ira Lewis's ninety-minute, late-night tête-à-tête and the power the actors bring to it. But what is truly remarkable about the Pacino-Orbach match is the cunning way both play out Lewis's chess game and con the audience. By the evening's end, we are as horrified as Harry and Jake to learn that their camaraderie, for all its years and bonhomie, is bogus as they come face-to-face with the treachery they keep beneath it. Both actors pull this off superbly — one reason why *Chinese Coffee* should be mandatory viewing in every acting class.

Much to his surprise, Jerry was becoming a record breaker — on television as the longest-running character on the longest-running drama series, and in the theatre as a veteran who had appeared in more performances of American musicals than any other living actor. These were just a few reasons why he was honored with the Crystal Apple Award from the Mayor's Office of Film, Television and Broadcasting for his contribution to the arts (1997), the Edith Oliver Award for Sustained Excellence at the Lucille Lortel Awards (1999), a Friars Club "surprise roast" in recognition of lifetime achievement (2000), and the Drama League's star-studded gala at the Pierre Hotel honoring his contributions to the American musical theatre. As a long-standing New Yorker, loved by the city he loved, he was designated a Living Landmark by the New York Landmarks Conservancy (2002). "It means they can't tear me down,"[49] he joked when accepting the honor, one that his *Law & Order* costar, Sam Waterston, also received. And despite a long-term absence from Broadway, he still could deliver the goods to great acclaim, as he did at the Brooklyn Academy of Music the evening of February 10, 2000, when he opened the gala celebration of composer Kurt Weill's one-hundredth birthday with "Mack the Knife." "He moved slowly, almost stealthily, across the stage," noted critic William Wolf, "hauntingly interpreting the … song with the requisite edgy mix of menace and humor that most singers rarely get exactly right."[50] Forty-five years after his bow as the Street Singer in *The Threepenny Opera*, his interpretation of the song was flawless as ever. So was his bittersweet rendition of "I Won't Send Roses" in the concert version of *Mack & Mabel* at Lincoln Center on March 31, 2003, that conclusively proved what an excellent Mack Sennett he would have made. Such moments prompted *Playbill*'s Michael Buckley to ask what the odds were on Lennie Briscoe's breaking into song to "give 'em the old Razzle Dazzle" on a *Law & Order* episode. "We talked about Lennie falling off the wagon and getting drunk at a karaoke bar, but I think that'll be the point at which *Law & Order* 'jumps the shark!'"[51] said Jerry with a laugh. Nonetheless, he paid tribute to his musical roots by narrating the PBS TV documentary *Broadway: The American Musical* (2004).

Privately and professionally, his life at sixty-eight was rich. He found great pleasure celebrating Christmas 2003 with grandchildren Peter and Sarah Kate, daughter-in-law Martha, and Tony, now a successful contractor with his own business. Chris, now in demand as a commercial/voiceover artist, was launching a second career as a singer-songwriter after a stint as Briscoe nephew Ken on *Law & Order: Special Victims Unit*. As for Emily, she was still active at ninety-three, and determined to remain so. With his health holding steady, so many good friends and, most especially, the perfect soul mate in Elaine, Jerry considered himself blessed. Professionally, his work on *Law & Order* had brought him landmark recognition in the entertainment community, the nation, and beyond, as well as the financial security he had long desired: "It's kind of like a golden parachute. It means for the rest of my life, I'm in a position where I don't have to do anything I don't want to. I can pick and choose."[52] Four months later, in March 2004, as the end of his twelfth season with *Law & Order* approached, so did his time on hormone therapy. With the cancer now detected in his major organs, Jerry faced a grueling choice. "Up until then," explained Elaine, "he avoided chemotherapy and was doing quite well until there were no more greenies, pinkies, bluies, or brownies.… The bag was empty. His oncologist said, 'In order to save you or to keep it at bay, you have to do chemo.'"[53] One morning a few days later, Elaine arrived at the breakfast table to find these words:

I'm off for my "infusion";
I know things won't go badly.
And this is no illusion—
I'll always love you madly!

XXXXX's
Jer[54]

Doctors insisted that Jerry lessen his responsibilities while undergoing chemotherapy. Reluctantly, he asked Dick Wolf to lighten his workload. It was the toughest request he ever had made, and one just as tough to grant for the producer, who had always told the actor he could have anything he wanted. Though it was obvious that Jerry could no longer tolerate the daily rigors of the series, especially those bitter winter morning shoots he hated, Wolf asked him to consider a starring but less taxing appearance as Briscoe in a new spin-off beginning that fall, *Law & Order: Trial by Jury*. In it, the former detective would resurface as an investigator for the district attorney's office, an assignment frequently given to NYPD detectives near retirement or injured in the line of duty. Jerry's presence would also help anchor the fledging series. He accepted the offer gladly. On March 26, he announced that he would be departing *Law & Order* after completing a span of twelve seasons and a total of 272 episodes as Det. Lennie Briscoe. As the chemotherapy took hold, he was glad to find that he was losing only a minimal amount of hair—a common side effect. What he didn't know was that each morning before he could notice, Elaine was taking a lint brush to his pillow and removing the hair he had lost during the night. "He just made it to the last day of work," she said, "because his hair was falling out at that point. Of course, he was always saying, 'I'm going to beat it. I came this far, I'm going to beat it.' But ten years, from what I understand, is now the stopping point with how long you can live with metastasized prostate cancer."[55]

We'll miss you so much read the inscription on one of the cakes presented to Jerry by the *Law & Order* cast and crew at the party closing the '03–'04 season. By now, most of his coworkers knew he was battling cancer. "I knew of it early," recalls Epatha Merkerson.

> He took Ben [Bratt] and I to lunch and told us shortly after he found out. And honestly, and I know this may sound crazy, but he fought that crap so long. I just didn't think it would beat him ... because he

never would have left the show. He loved what he did.... [On] his last day [after] he finished the scene and the photographers and everybody were there, he had the biggest smile on his face. At that moment I realized that he was very ill. I remember just leaving the set quickly and crying because he had fought it so long.[56]

It was hard to imagine the show without him. One by one, as each person learned of his struggle, they had kept faith with him. From Tommy Seccamanie, the driver who had taken him to the hospital for his weekly dose of radiation to the producers, directors, cast and technicians who sang with him and laughed at his jokes, each made certain that Jerry's illness remained "top secret." "Nobody at work ever spilled the beans," said Elaine. "That shows how much he was loved and respected. The story could have been sold to the supermarket tabloids for a lot of money. The cast and crew loved him for all those years, and I loved them for loving him."[57] Determined to persevere, Jerry spoke enthusiastically about joining *Law & Order: Trial by Jury* come fall, but there were many who wondered if he would have sufficient strength to do it.

On May 19, "C.O.D.," the season finale, aired. On his final day at the 2-7, Lennie stood at his desk packing the memories of twenty-five years into a box. Van Buren and Green arrived with news that two suspects he helped bring to justice had been found guilty of murder. "It's good to go out with a win," he replied with a warm smile. Then, as they watched forlornly, he picked up the box and went his way.

Chapter 10

EXIT, 2004

· ·

EMILY OPENED THE DOOR EXPECTING TO FIND THE cleaning lady, but instead found Jerry, nattily dressed in casuals with a wide-brimmed straw hat and sunglasses to ward off the mid-September sun. "We're supposed to go for lunch," he said. Thursday was their day for lunch, not Wednesday. Something was amiss, and it was evident the moment he stepped inside and removed the hat and glasses—his face pallid, his manner deflated. Since April he had been receiving chemotherapy biweekly, but today he seemed unusually drained by the treatment. In place of his easygoing demeanor was an edginess that seemed to rise by the minute as they awaited the arrival of the cleaning lady. Sensing his irritation, Emily finally left the key to her apartment with the concierge so the cleaning lady could work while they were out. At lunch, Jerry ate little and was distracted and humorless. Afterwards, they wandered into a small neighborhood park and sat on a bench till mid-afternoon, hand in hand. At length, he told her what he had learned at the hospital that morning—nothing more could be done for him. She looked into the eyes of the boy she had rescued from the fire escape long ago, powerless to rescue him from this. The inevitable was unthinkable. She tried to rally his spirits, urging him to stay strong. But immediately after he left, the thought of losing him overwhelmed her and she was utterly devastated.

All summer long, Elaine had watched his decline, just as helpless. "He would take his chemo and go play golf. He was going to continue to live. He knew that this was not good [and] not like taking pinkies, bluies, and greenies. Chemo was killing his body, as was the cancer.… They found spots in his kidneys, and he was developing a bladder condition. It was attacking his teeth, his gums. They were beginning to see spots on his bones. The snowball was tumbling down the mountain [and] it was really getting to him. But he still was doing all he could."[1] That included his reappearance as Lennie Briscoe on *Trial by Jury*, the newest addition to the *Law & Order* franchise.

With shooting to commence in late September, *Trial by Jury* executive producer Walon Green was concerned about the unusually low profile Jerry had kept all summer: "No one had seen him. I ended up talking to a teamster [on the *Law & Order* crew] who had played a round of golf with him, who said, 'He's all excited about coming to work.'"[2] And the first day, there he was, gaunt and raspy-voiced, but eager to trade one-liners with his new partner, Kirk Acevedo, who played DA Investigator Hector Salazar. "He probably had a little cold and that was it," thought Acevedo. "Every day he was on time, worked, cracked jokes, knew his lines. He was a pro."[3] If he was feeling poorly, he never conveyed it. When he and Elaine celebrated their twenty-fifth wedding anniversary on October 7, he seemed tired but fine to their guests. Nevertheless, at the end of each workday, he would arrive home more exhausted than before, heading straight to bed until dinnertime. Frequently, while conversing at the table, Elaine had to ask him to clear his throat so she could understand what he was saying. The condition was getting so bad that he told Tony he was planning to get an evaluation by a voice specialist — that is, until his doctors uncovered the source of the problem: a tumor growing on his vocal cords. He was losing his voice, the tool of his trade.

A few days before Halloween, Chris received a call from his father. "How'd you like to play golf with me?" asked Jerry. "I'd love that," responded Chris eagerly. Though not a par golfer, he had always wanted to do the links with Jerry. Halloween morning, they golfed together for the first time. "It was an Indian summer day," Chris remembers,

> just a gorgeous, warm fall day. The golf course was more or less deserted and … he was showing me how to do things.… I made a couple of really good shots and when I made this one really good shot, he put on one of his funny voices and said, "Dat's my sonny boy!" But there were a couple times when I could see him getting tired. We were thinking of maybe playing eighteen holes, and we played about twelve. Then he

said, "I think I need to stop. I'm tired." I said, "Okay." That day was extra-special. But I knew that something must be up. It was like, "My God, he's invited me to the golf course. He's never done that before."[4]

On November 4, Jerry flew to Pittsburgh with Elaine. That evening at the annual gala for cancer research sponsored by the University of Pittsburgh Cancer Institute, he sang "Try to Remember" and won the audience's praise.[5] Somehow, to Elaine's amazement, he found the stamina—and the voice—to do justice to the song that had become his theme. But the next day, during takeoff on their return fight to New York, the price he paid was evident from the discomfort on his face, and she wondered how much more he could take.

No longer able to produce the distinctive timbre of Lumière, Jerry canceled his recording session for the Disney video game *Kingdom Hearts 2*. On the set of *Trial by Jury*, his voice was progressively more high-pitched and raspy, making it hard for him to deliver lines in the terse nasal Gothamese that was Briscoe's trademark. "When it got very hard for him, he still wouldn't stop," said Walon Green. "He would not be written out of scenes. A couple of times I thought, 'Well, I'll lighten his load a little bit and take away a scene,' and he'd call and be upset and want to know why I'd taken him out. He'd want the scene back. He was like the Energizer Bunny. He wanted to keep going."[6] That also became clear to Jon Olexy during an afternoon he spent with his cousin at the Lone Star Boat Club shortly before Thanksgiving.

"A boat club?" thought Olexy. Jerry had no yacht, nor was he into fishing or water sports. On the phone, Jerry explained that it was his gym and gave him directions as peculiar as the name itself that included a set of stairs leading nowhere: "Jonny, . . . once you're inside, don't go up the stairs. They don't go anywhere except into a wall. Just follow the small hallway to the left and press 4 in the tiny elevator." Olexy found the location but, once inside, automatically took the stairs and ran right into the wall. Then he remembered the elevator and took it to the fourth floor. There, a club employee led him to a large locker room where a half dozen cigar-chomping men in towels and briefs were playing in what appeared to be a high-stakes poker game. Jerry introduced him to them, finished his hand, and then gave him a tour of the facilities, which included a special room where they hit golf balls twenty yards into a mat, and a billiards room where Jerry showed him a series of trick shots made famous by Willie Mosconi. "After [that]," Olexy recalls, we swam in the pool and showered. It was there I really became aware of Jerry's failing body and how the cancer and chemotherapy were having a devastating effect—he had no hair, eyebrows were gone, muscle tone depleted. Looking in the mirror, he pretended to comb what little hair remained. "Looks like it's growing back," he said, always the optimist.... I offered—feebly—that shaved heads were the latest style. That night, we walked with our wives to nearby Ben Benson's, and Jerry looked like a million dollars—toupee, eyebrows, and makeup. He was ready for the public. And the patrons were calling to him from the bar the minute we entered. "We love you, Jerry.... Don't leave L&O.... You're the best." And he waved and joked with them. To one customer, he teased: "Look at the size of your prime rib...even Fred Flintstone couldn't eat one that big!" And then he ordered one just as big and could only eat a bite or two, while he kept us laughing with a slow-building joke about the Animal Super Bowl. No one would have detected anything wrong. And four weeks later he was gone.[7]

As filming began for the second episode of *Trial by Jury*, his voice gave out completely. "I can't hear him," confided the sound technician to Walon Green. With Jerry no longer able to project and his voice virtually reduced to a whisper, Green revamped the scene. He directed Jerry to pace nervously outside the courtroom doors, awaiting the verdict of the trial. With court still in session, it was only natural that Briscoe and his colleagues would communicate in whispers—and the actors did exactly that. When news of the judge's decision reached them, Briscoe showed his approval with an understated victory salute. For Jerry, the scene was a personal victory aided by a cast, crew, and staff determined to show him their loyalty and love. The scene would be his last, the finale of his career, played with his customary skill and proficiency. When it aired as part of the show's two-night premiere on March 4, 2005, it showed Lennie Briscoe in top form, seeking justice as effectively as ever. In living rooms across the nation, no one ever guessed that Jerry had no voice. But, just days after shooting the scene, he fell and had to face the fact that he was too ill to carry on. Just before Thanksgiving, his *Trial by Jury* colleagues threw him a farewell party. Brief as his time had been with them, the impression he had made was deep, and whether he realized it or not, as he took leave of them, he was also taking leave of his career. He had been an actor for fifty-two years.

Under these circumstances, a low-key Thanksgiving celebration seemed best. Elaine booked a reservation at Da Tommaso for four — Jerry, Emily, herself, and one of her friends. But come Thanksgiving Day, Jerry had no appetite and was too weak to walk to the restaurant, only steps away. He asked Elaine to take their guests to dinner while he rested. With the arrival of December, he began to hemorrhage and was immediately taken to Sloan-Kettering. The next day, his manager, Robert Malcolm, released a statement announcing that he had prostate cancer. Malcolm also told the *Daily News*, "We expect he'll be fine. He's been playing golf, shooting his episodes and doing real well." Dick Wolf covered for Jerry, too: "We hope he will make a full and swift recovery, and while he is receiving treatment, we will work around his schedule." In the hospital, Jerry refused to admit defeat. "I have to stay here and get this under control," he explained to Emily, Tony, Chris, and Elaine. "I'm going home. I'm going to go home." For the first two weeks of his hospitalization, that seemed possible as he joked with the nursing staff and traveled back and forth from his room to an adjoining sitting room where he chatted with visitors. "We had a two-room suite," Elaine explained, "and he walked around all hooked up. He'd have his coffee and sit in the window to get his tan. But little by little, he wasn't going into the other room; he was staying in bed as it got worse and worse."[8] Just before Christmas, Elaine asked one of the physicians she especially trusted if Jerry would be coming home. When she learned the answer, she steeled herself for what was ahead, taking up round-the-clock residence in the adjoining room as visits from family and friends increased.

On Christmas Eve, Jerry asked Chris to find a special gift he wanted to give to Elaine, and Chris found the very thing. Christmas morning, Jerry gave a small box to Elaine. "Don't be mad," he whispered to her, recalling their promise never to give gifts. Elaine opened it and found an angel pin, like the one she had given him ten years before. The next day, after farewells to family and friends, Jerry entered a coma induced by doctors to free him from pain. Three days later, on Tuesday, December 28, 2004, at six-thirty in the evening, Jerry succumbed to a ten-year battle with prostate cancer at age sixty-nine. Throughout life, he had enjoyed perfect vision — nearsighted in one eye and farsighted in the other. Consequently, he never had to wear glasses or contacts. That good fortune was not something he took for granted. Remembering Leo's struggle with glaucoma, he wanted to help people in danger of losing their vision. Hence, at his death, he donated his eyes to Manhattan's Eye Bank for Sight Restoration and gave the gift of sight to two anonymous recipients.

The evening following his death, Broadway paid homage to one of its greatest song-and-dance men by dimming its lights in his memory for one minute at curtain time. Friday morning, December 31, at eleven-thirty, as Jerry's body lay in a plain wooden coffin wreathed with white carnations in Riverside Memorial Chapel, his life was celebrated in a way he would have approved—with memories, meditation, music and a multitude of friends. Recalling their onstage alliance in *Chicago*, thirty years before, Chita Rivera said, "This huge silhouette would appear in a fedora, smoking a cigar. There was our anchor. There was our rock in a pinstriped suit."[9] Reflecting on his work and friendship with Jerry, first, as director of *6 Rms Riv Vu* and later as executive producer of *Law & Order*, Ed Sherin called him "my best friend" and echoed the sentiments of many in the assembly when he added, "I imagine there are a lot of people here who would say the same."[10] And Sam Waterston spoke of how in the weeks before his death Jerry continued to focus on enjoying the essentials of life—the companionship of family and friends, the view from his window at the hospital. "He chose a certain life, lived it as himself—and it worked out," he reflected, fighting to maintain his composure before an assembly of three hundred mourners, including Jerry's colleagues from the Friars Club, in which he had served as an honorary officer. A guided meditation led by Elaine's friend and interfaith minister Elizabeth Hepburn was beautifully complemented by a performance of John Denver's "Perhaps Love" on acoustic guitar. After the service concluded, with guitar renditions of "Lullaby of Broadway" and "Try to Remember," family and friends quietly filed out of the chapel and onto the corner of West Seventy-Sixth Street and Amsterdam Avenue—Danny Aiello, Brian Dennehy, Olympia Dukakis, Chris Noth, Tony Roberts, Benjamin Bratt, Michael Imperiolli, and Malachy McCourt among them. Per Jerry's instructions to Elaine, the executrix of his estate, his remains were cremated and later laid to rest in the only remaining active cemetery in Manhattan—the Mausoleum of Trinity Church Cemetery at the Church of the Intercession between Broadway and Riverside Drive on the Upper West Side. At his death, he left behind an estate valued at $10 million.

Honors and testimonials poured forth. In February 2005, Jerry was posthumously awarded a Screen Actor's Guild Award for Outstanding Performance by a Male Actor in a Drama Series. After his final *Trial by Jury* appearances aired March 3 and 4, his departure from the series was quietly acknowledged in a scene during the fifth episode in which members of the District Attorney's office returned from a memorial service for Briscoe reflecting on how he had looked tired but not gravely ill in his final days. At the fade-out of the final scene, the words "For Jerry" appeared in honor of his memory. On March 24, over one thousand people from the entertainment industry gathered at the Richard Rodgers Theatre on Forty-Sixth Street to pay Jerry final homage at a memorial emceed by Sam Waterston.[11] There, in the very theatre where Jerry and Elaine first met when performing in *Chicago*, Mayor Michael Bloomberg spoke of the "indelible character" Jerry created in Lennie Briscoe "with enough one-liners to fill a Centre Street holding cell," and praised the actor, who "symbolized New York," for the way "he used that position to help make the city an even better place to live and work." Ed Sherin and Professor Richard Brown shared highlights of their work and friendship with Jerry. Broadway's Karen Ziemba, recalling Jerry's congenial mentorship early in her career, sang "They Were You" from *The Fantasticks*. Angela Lansbury recalled how she and Jerry "shared some of the great golden years of Broadway … when the musical theatre reigned." Dick Wolf, praising Jerry's "unimpeachable" theatrical, film, and television legacy, noted that, "his real legacy is being the ultimate gentleman in the true sense of being a gentle man." Jane Alexander read eloquently from the poems he had written daily to Elaine, and Elaine warmly recollected the life she and Jerry had shared. But it was Sam Waterston who captured the essence of Jerry's life most memorably, stating, "Jerry knew how to do this: how to live simply in the midst of success and fame and how to never lose the habit of getting all the juice out of the orange. With Zorba the Greek, who used his last strength to haul himself to the window for one more look at the blue sky, the blinding light, and the Mediterranean Sea, Jerry was interested in everything life had to offer to the end. He didn't quit the show before it was over. He really showed us how it's done, and we can take from his example."[12]

Two years later, on June 21, 2007, one of two theatres in the Snapple Theatre Center, at Fiftieth and Broadway, was named the Jerry Orbach Theatre, where currently the revival of *The Fantasticks* plays. Yet, beyond the theatre marquees and street signs that bear his name, there is that personal legacy from Jerry that only his sons can express. "Before he would become known as the quintessential, wizened New Yorker," says Tony, "Jerry was the son of Emily Olexy and Leo Orbach: a product of the Bronx, but also of coal-mining towns and the Midwest. Before he was Chuck Baxter, Billy Flynn, and Lennie Briscoe, Jerry was Marta Curro's husband, and Chris and Tony's father, and they had a long, interesting run together at 232 West Twenty-Second Street. He was also grandpa to Sarah Kate and Peter. Though he made everything he did look easy—and savored the praise, success and fame—Jerry was at base a super hard-working professional who strove to be a good family man."[13]

Chris reflects,

> Dad *had* to shine—he had no choice. But walking around town with him, he was cool with everything and everyone. He got more of a kick out of being recognized by a guy loading beer into a supermarket than any paparazzo. I'll remember him as a charmingly confusing treasure of paradoxes: beatnik and baritone, pool shark and puppeteer, serious and silly, self-doubting and self-confident, Midwesterner and city boy, down-to-earth and brilliant. He equally loved Danny Kaye and Marlon Brando, dug Bob Dylan and Charles Aznavour, Kander and Ebb and Ray Charles, Lerner and Loewe and Roger Miller. He was a star, and a father—at times, a distant dream of a father. He gave his gifts to the world for as long as he could, and the world is better for them. But it's hard not to feel selfish.... I wish he hadn't worked as hard near the end. I wish he'd taken better care of himself. I wish he were still here.[14]

As for the rest of us, there is a treasury of works Jerry left behind, always as close as the remote beside our chair. The cast albums of *The Fantasticks*, *Carnival*, *Promises, Promises*, *Chicago*, and *42nd Street* preserve his splendid baritone, helping us to try to remember, or imagine, the glory of the American musical at the peak of its golden age. On DVD, Gus Levi and Jack Rosenthal continue to electrify us as much as Jake Houseman and Lumière touch and delight. Daily, on cable channel reruns of *Law & Order*, Det. Lennie Briscoe, Jerry's classic portrait of the world-weary New Yorker, lives on. In these ways, his talent, humanity, and affection for the city and its people remain immortal. "There's a feeling that I am a typical New Yorker" he once said, "and everyone else seems to agree."[15] In the years since his death, that reality has not changed a bit—and, because of the goodwill he radiated to the city and the world beyond, it never will.

EPILOGUE:
IT'S NICE TO REMEMBER

WITH THE ASSISTANCE OF FRIENDS AND FANS, ELAINE steadfastly waged a six-month campaign that finally achieved its goal on September 17, 2007. That afternoon, at the southwest corner of Fifty-Third and Eighth, at the site of the high rise where they had lived for nearly twenty-five years, the New York City Department of Transportation staged a dedication to unveil the street sign bearing Jerry's name. By 2:30 P.M., nearly seventy well wishers had gathered for the impromptu but heartfelt ceremony, among them Broadway's Len Cariou, *Law & Order: SVU*'s Christopher Meloni, *Homicide*'s Richard Belzer, and comedian Robert Klein, who remarked, "Jerry was a poker-playing, cigarette-smoking New York actor."[1] He was that and more. "New York is a city of heroes, some real and some fictional; Jerry Orbach represented both. [He was] a remarkable and unforgettable character, both on and off the screen,"[2] so read the Petition to Community Board 4 signed by scores of New Yorkers in support of the street naming. Then, as onlookers applauded, Elaine commenced the reveal, pulling a rope attached to a sleeve covering the sign. Moments later, the corner of West Fifty-Third and Eighth—where a new Fifty-Third Street condo called "Lumière" rose only feet away—was officially named in Jerry's honor.

Emily did not attend the ceremony; at age ninety-six it was unwise to risk exposure to the afternoon heat. But weeks later, sitting by the window of an uptown bus that stopped for a light at Fifty-Third and Eighth, she spotted the green sign with white lettering designating "Jerry Orbach Way." It was a bittersweet tribute, but one befitting her son, the risk-taker from the Bronx, who rose to become a distinguished actor, consummate New Yorker, and esteemed prince of the city.

NOTES

PROLOGUE

1. Harney 1997, 13.

CHAPTER 1

1. Orbach, Emily Olexy, interview with author, June 8, 2009.
2. Lewis 1975, B25.
3. Orbach, Emily Olexy, interview with Chris Orbach, March 21, 2005.
4. Orbach, Emily Olexy, interview with Chris Orbach, March 21, 2005.
5. Tallmer 1968, 33.
6. Lynch 2000.
7. Buckley 2003, 2–3.
8. Tallmer 1968, 33.
9. Lynch 2000.
10. Zailian, 1978.
11. Shouler 1994, 62.
12. Ibid.
13. Schwartz 1981, 29, and Harney 1997, 13.
14. "County Actor" 1989 and Emory 1975, B25.
15. Lynch 2000.
16. Buckley 2003, 2–3, and Schwartz 1981, 29.
17. Orbach, Jerry, interview with Rick McKay, August 8, 2002.
18. "County Actor" 1989 and Buckley 2003, 2.
19. Orbach, Jerry, interview with Rick McKay, August 8, 2002.
20. Schwartz 1981, 29
21. Orbach, Jerry, interview with Rick McKay, August 8, 2002.
22. "Jerry Orbach: The Singing Detective" 2000.
23. Dennis.
24. Lewis 1975, B25.
25. Provenzano 1988, 5.
26. http://MaeWest.blogspot.com
27. Orbach, Jerry, interview with Rick McKay, August 8, 2002.
28. Gould 1969, 79.
29. "Jerry Orbach: The Singing Detective" 2000.

CHAPTER 2

1. Orbach, Jerry, interview with Rick McKay, August 8, 2002.

2. Provenzano 1988, 5.

3. "Jerry Orbach: The Singing Detective" 2000.

4. Ibid.

5. Harney 1997, 16.

6. Farber and Viagas 1991, 140.

7. Burden 1980, 42.

8. Schwartz 1981, 29

9. Tallmer 1968, 33.

10. Orbach, Jerry, interview with Rick McKay, August 8, 2002.

11. "Jerry Orbach: The Singing Detective" 2000.

12. Blinn 1969, 45.

13. Gould 1969, 77.

14. Tallmer 1968, 33.

15. Lewis 1975, B25.

16. "Jerry Orbach: The Singing Detective" 2000.

17. Harney 1997, 16, and Buchalter 2002, 12.

18. Tallmer 1968, 48.

19. Schmidt, Harvey, interview with author, September 16, 2010.

20. Farber and Viagas 1991, 116.

21. Jones, Tom, interview with author, September 16, 2010.

22. Orbach, Jerry, in *Try to Remember: The Fantasticks*, 2003.

23. "Jerry Orbach: The Singing Detective" 2000.

24. Farber and Viagas 1991, 135.

25. Schmidt, Harvey, interview with author, September 16, 2010.

26. Farber and Viagas 1991, 139–140.

27. Ibid., 141.

28. Ibid., 144.

29. Ibid., 144–145.

30. Baram 2005, 3.

31. Tallmer 1968, 48, and Orbach, Jerry, in *Try to Remember: The Fantasticks*, 2003.

32. Kerr 1960.

33. Orbach, Emily Olexy, interview with author, June 8, 2009.

34. Rudolph 1999, 36.

35. Fields 1968 and Herridge 1961.

36. Orbach, Jerry, interview with author, June 11, 1992.

CHAPTER 3

1. Orbach, Jerry, interview with author, June 11, 1992.

2. Gilvey 2004, 100.

3. For more on Gower Champion, see the author's *Before the Parade Passes By: Gower Champion and the Glorious American Musical* (New York: St. Martin's Press, 2004).

4. Orbach, Jerry, interview with author, June 11, 1992.

5. Ibid.

6. Ibid.

7. "A History of the Musical" 1990.

8. Orbach, Emily Olexy, interview with author, June 8, 2009.

9. "Jerry Orbach: The Singing Detective" 2000.

10. Horwitz 1993, 42.

11. Buckley 2003, 2

12. Orbach, Jerry, interview with Rick McKay, August 8, 2002.

13. Olexy, Jon, correspondence to author, February 14, 2010.

14. Orbach, Jerry, interview with author, June 11, 1992.

15. Wahls 1972, 60.

16. "Jerry Orbach: The Singing Detective" 2000.

17. Orbach, Jerry, interview with Rick McKay, August 8, 2002.

18. Ibid.

19. Ibid.

20. Morehouse.

21. Dennis.

22. Okon 1969, 7.

23. Originally Jerry was to have played Arnstein to Anne Bancroft's Fanny Brice in *Funny Girl*, until producer David Merrick sold his rights to Ray Stark. Mrs. Stark, Fanny Brice's daughter, wanted Sidney Chaplin, who in her estimation was more mature.

24. Okon 1969, 7.

25. Gould 1969, 84–86.

26. Buckley 2003, 3.

27. Ibid.

28. Dennis 1966.

29. Buckley 2003, 3.

30. "Annie Get Your Gun" 1966.

31. Dennis 1966.

32. McGovern and Winer 1993, 154–155.

33. Orbach, Jerry, interview with Rick McKay, August 8, 2002.

34. Buckley 2003, 4.

35. Ibid.

36. Ibid.

CHAPTER 4

1. "Such Talk" 1967.

2. Barthel 1968, D1.

3. "A Hang-up Named Scuba" 1967, 122.

4. Ibid.

5. Barthel 1968, D5.

6. "Bruce Jay Friedman Interviewed by Derek Alger" 2004.

7. "Such Talk" 1967.

8. Gould 1969, 84.

9. Rodin, Rita Bird.

10. "Such Talk" 1967.

11. Ibid.

12. Gould 1969, 77.

13. Zadan 1969, 16.

14. Mordden 2001, 246.

15. Ibid.

16. Simon 1996, 297.

17. Buckley 2003, 4

18. Norton.

19. Orbach, Tony, interview with author, June 18, 2009.

20. McGovern and Winer 1993, 46.

21. Gould 1969, 84.

22. Ibid.

23. Barnes 1968.

24. Simon 1996, 298.

25. Orbach, Jerry, interview with Rick McKay, August 8, 2002.

26. "Asides and Ad-Libs" 1969.

27. Gould 1969, 74, 77.

28. Orbach, Jerry, interview with Rick McKay, August 8, 2002.

29. Zadan 1969, 16.

30. Gould 1969, 79.

31. Shouler 1994, 64.

32. Gould 1969, 77.

33. Blinn 1969, 45.

34. Gould 1969, 77.

35. Graham 1969.

36. Okon 1969, 6–7.

CHAPTER 5

1. Previous to *She Loves Me*, Laszlo's work was filmed twice, first in 1940 as *The Shop Around the Corner* with James Stewart and Margaret Sullivan, then later in 1949 as the musical *In the Good Old Summertime* with Judy Garland and Van Johnson, and in 1998 it received yet another treatment as *You've Got Mail* with Tom Hanks and Meg Ryan.

2. Provenzano 1988, 5.

3. Lewis 1975, B25.

4. Provenzano 1988, 5.

5. Zailian 1978. Although released in 1972, *A Fan's Notes* was actually filmed before the release of *The Gang That Couldn't Shoot Straight* in 1971.

6. Zailian 1978, and Provenzano 1988, 5.

7. Wilson 1972, 1G.

8. Folsom 2008, 8.

9. Goddard 1974, 18.

10. Folsom 2008, 8.

11. Meskil 1976, 63.

12. Goddard 1974, 47.

13. "Our Friend Joey Gallo" 1972.

14. Aronson 1974, 163.

15. Diapoulos and Linakis 1977, 108.

16. Goddard 1974, 383–387.

17. Ibid., 385.

18. Diapoulos and Linakis 1977, 108.

19. Aronson 1974, 163.

20. Diapoulos and Linakis 1977, 108.

21. Aronson 1974, 43.

22. Diapoulos and Linakis 1977, 108.

23. Goddard 1974, 388.

24. Ibid.

25. Curtis 1972, 87.

26. Goddard 1974, 388.

27. Ibid., 389.

28. "Our Friend Joey Gallo" 1972.

29. Curtis 1972, 87.

30. Steinberg 2007, 165–167.

31. Curtis 1972, 86.

32. Ibid.

33. Orbach, Tony, interview with author, June 18, 2009.

34. Orbach, Chris, interview with author, September 7, 2009.

35. Ibid.

36. Ibid.

37. Curtis 1972, 87.

38. Ibid.

39. Sheahan 1972, 1, 6.

40. Diopolous and Linakis 1977, 110.

41. Orbach, Emily Olexy, interview with author, May 12, 2010.

42. Curtis 1972, 86.

43. "Our Friend Joey Gallo" 1972.

44. Ibid.

45. Curtis 1972, 86.

46. Folsom 2008, 198.

47. Sheahan 1972, 6.

48. Friedman interview with Alger 2004.

49. "Our Friend Joey Gallo" 1972.

50. Sheahan 1972, 1.

51. Goddard 1974, 431–432.

52. Diapoulos and Linakis 1977, 111. As author Steven Linakis notes in *The Sixth Family*, "ubatz" (pronounced ooh-batz) is Mafia argot for *upazzo*, maning "crazy" or "the crazy one" (Diapoulos and Linakis, 1977, xiii).

53. Ibid.

54. "Our Friend Joey Gallo" 1972.

55. Sheahan 1972, 6.

56. Christeson 2007, 4.

57. "Our Friend Joey Gallo" 1972.

58. Goddard 1974, 435.

59. "Our Friend Joey Gallo" 1972.

60. Diapoulos and Linakis 1977, 141.

61. "Joe Gallo Rubbed Out" 8, 67.

62. Goddard 1974, 10.

63. Hamill 2005.

64. Baram 2005, 3.

65. "Our Friend Joey Gallo" 1972.

66. Sheahan 1972, 6.

67. "Jerry Orbach: The Singing Detective" 2000.

68. Pelleck 1972, 1, 3.

CHAPTER 6

1. Zailian, 1978.

2. Taylor 1972.

3. Buckley 2003, 6.

4. Sherin, Edwin, interview with author, November 19, 2010.

5. Ibid.

6. Buckley, 2003, 6.

7. Wahls 1972, 60.

8. Gottfried 1972, and Watts 1972.

9. Barnes 1972.

10. Kerr 1972, D3.

11. Alexander, Jane, interview, November 23, 2010.

12. Taylor 1972.

13. Orbach, Jerry, interview with Rick McKay, August 8, 2002.

14. Taylor 1972.

15. Wilson 1972, 1G.

16. Ibid.

17. Buckley 2003, 6.

18. Orbach, Jerry, interview with author, June 11, 1992.

19. Orbach, Chris, interview with author, September 7, 2009.

20. Raidy 1975.

21. Lewis 1975, B18.

22. Kander, John, interview with author, September 11, 2010.

23. Buckley 2003, 5.

24. Ibid.

25. Ibid., 2.

26. Raidy 1975.

27. Rivera, Chita, October 10, 2010.

28. Ibid.

29. Buckley 2004, 5.

30. Wilson 1977, 34.

31. Orbach, Jerry, interview with Rick McKay, August 8, 2002.

32. Ibid.

33. "One Man's Chicago" 1975, 1.

34. "Chicago' Lawyer Is Alive ..." 1976, 13.

35. Ibid.

36. Ibid.

37. Ibid.

38. Ibid.

39. Ibid.

40. Ibid.

41. Ibid.

42. Ibid.

43. Wilson 1977, 34. Marta moved in shortly after former tenant Mako, star of *Pacific Overtures*, moved out following the show's closing in June 1976. Like Jerry, Mako was a Tony nominee that year for Best Actor in a Musical. "I thought Jerry would win," he later recalled. "I didn't care for myself. If I got it, I'd have to get up and give a speech. George Rose and Ian Richardson were also nominated for *My Fair Lady*, but that was a revival, so I didn't think they stood a chance. But Rose won [for what was essentially a 'featured' role]. Anyway, I got home late, about 2:30 in the morning. At about 4:30, I heard Jerry Orbach shouting from the floor below, "Hey, Mako! What the f—happened? I can't believe it; we lost to a f——revival!" (Wong, Wayman, "Actors Remember Pacific Overtures," *The Sondheim Review*, Vol. 4, No. 4, Spring 1998).

44. "Jerry Orbach: The Singing Detective" 2000.

45. Wahls 1972, 60.

46. Orbach, Chris, interview with author, September 7, 2009.

47. Orbach, Tony, interview with author, June 18, 2009.

48. Ibid.

49. Wilson, 1975, 36.

50. "Rex Reed Rap of Jerry Orbach …" 1978, 455. Subsequently, the feud escalated after Jerry's appearance in *Mr. Words*, a gala performance with Kitty Carlisle Hart and Chita Rivera at Lincoln Center's Avery Fisher Hall on November 11, 1975, that honored lyricist Ira Gershwin and benefited the American Musical and Dramatic Academy. In his review of the event in the *Sunday News* of November 23, 1975, Reed, known for his acerbic style, referred to Jerry as "a tone-deaf mediocrity," adding that "poor ossified Orbach proved what league he belongs in by turning out to be the night's only non-professional embarrassment" by making two of Gershwin's greatest works, 'How Long Has This Been Going On' and ''S Wonderful,' into "dirges, his voice wandering unsteadily through several keys beyond his range and ability."

In December, the performer countered with a $6 million lawsuit against New York News, Inc. in which he claimed that Reed's remarks were "intended to expose him to public scandal, shame, degradation, contempt, scorn, ridicule, disgrace and infamy, and cause it to be believed he is a non-professional." The plaintiff further complained that the review exposed him to "ridicule and slander" by describing him "viciously and maliciously" in a "false and defamatory" manner and was made "carelessly and recklessly with actual malice for the purpose of injuring" his "well-being and professional reputation." (See "Jerry Orbach Sues Critic," *New York Post*, December 23, 1975, 16.)

Two and a half years later, the actor's libel suit was dismissed without trial by New York Supreme Court Judge Israel Rubin, because "no matter how severe, hostile, rough, caustic, bitter, sarcastic or satirical," a critic's assessment is protected from the sting of libel laws. "No doubt the writer's review was exaggerated," the judge observed. "However, the law of libel is not concerned with questions of exaggeration, taste or propriety in the use of language." (See "Court Decisions," *New York Law Journal*, May 4, 1978, 10.)

As attorney-journalist Robert L. Spellman explains in "The Critic's Delight: Constitutional Protection for Criticism" (*The Journal of Popular Culture*, Vol. 21, Issue 3 [Winter 1987], 47), "Reed benefited from a constitutional umbrella which has been placed over fine and popular arts critics during the past two decades. Two doctrinal pillars support the umbrella. One is total protection for opinion. The other is denial of recovery for false and defamatory statements of fact unless the critic either knew what he wrote was false or he entertained serious doubts as to its truth or falsity." In essence the lawsuit was pointless.

51. Orbach, Chris, interview with author, September 7, 2009.

52. "Jerry Orbach: The Singing Detective" 2000.

53. Ibid.

54. Orbach, Tony, interview with author, June 18, 2009.

55. "Jerry Orbach: The Singing Detective" 2000.

56. Orbach, Tony, interview with author, June 18, 2009.

57. Orbach, Chris, interview with author, September 7, 2009.

58. Ibid.

CHAPTER 7

1. Orbach, Elaine Cancilla, interview with author, October 13, 2008.

2. Orbach and Orbach with Bloom 2009, 16–17.

3. Lynch 2000.

4. "Jerry Orbach: The Singing Detective" 2000.

5. Orbach, Tony, interview with author, June 18, 2009.

6. Orbach, Chris, interview with author, September 7, 2009.

7. Orbach, Emily Olexy, interview with author, June 29, 2009.

8. "Jerry Orbach: The Singing Detective" 2000.

9. Ibid.

10. Baram 2005, 3.

11. McGovern and Winer 1993, xii.

12. Orbach, Chris, interview with author, September 7, 2009.

13. Ibid.

14. Orbach Cancilla, Elaine, interview with author, October 13, 2008.

15. "Sidney Lumet."

16. Klemesrud 1981.

17. Curry 1981, 5.

18. Curry 1981, 5, and Klemesrud 1981, C6.

19. Klemesrud 1981, C6.

20. "Jerry Orbach in '42nd Street'" 1984, C2.

21. Baram 2005, 3.

22. Ibid.

23. Orbach, Jerry, interview with author, June 11, 1992.

24. Ibid.

25. Orbach, Jerry, interview with Rick McKay, August 8, 2002.

26. Ibid.

27. Tallmer 1980, 29.

28. Kroll 1980, 85.

29. Shewey, Don 1986, also www.donshewey.com/theater_articles/jerry_orbach.html.

30. Orbach, Emily Olexy, interview with author, June 29, 2009.

31. Klemesrud 1981, C6.

32. "Jerry Orbach in '42nd Street'" 1984, C2.

33. La Ferla 1982, 6

34. Klemesrud 1981, C6.

CHAPTER 8

1. Shewey, 1986.

2. Ibid.

3. Orbach and Orbach with Bloom 2009, 26.

4. Barron, 2005, B3.

5. Rudolph, 2009, 42.

6. Barron 2005, B3.

7. Orbach and Orbach with Bloom 2009, 28.

8. Shewey 1986.

9. Ibid.

10. Provenzano 1988, 5.

11. Ibid.

12. Fretts 1992.

13. Greppi 1992, 61.

14. "Famous Movie Locations: Kellerman's Resort from 'Dirty Dancing,' and 'Dirty Dancing.'"

15. Lynch, 2000.

16. Orbach and Orbach with Bloom 2009, 35.

17. "Patrick Swayze Talks About …" 2009.

18. Ibid.

19. "Memorial for Jerry Orbach" 2005.

20. Orbach and Orbach with Bloom 2009, 38.

21. Provenzano 1988, 5.

22. Ibid.

23. Ibid.

24. Hiltbrand 2003, C4, and Buckley 2004, 5.

25. Orbach, Elaine Cancilla, interview with author, October 13, 2008.

26. Orbach, Tony, interview with author, June 18, 2009.

27. Orbach, Chris, interview with author, September 7, 2009.

28. Baxter 1998, 169.

29. Ibid., 370.

30. Buckley 2003.

31. Fallon, 1993, 4.

32. Hiltbrand 2003, C4.

33. Buckley 2003.

34. "Memorial for Jerry Orbach" 2005.

35. "The Making of 'Beauty and the Beast'" 1991.

36. Fretts 1992.

37. Ibid.

38. Fallon 1993, 4.

39. Roush 2009, 2.

40. Wolf, Dick, interview with author, November 9, 2010.

41. Orbach and Orbach with Bloom 2009, 40.

42. Flaherty 2009, 15.

43. Wolf, Dick, interview with author, November 9, 2010.

44. Baram 2005, 3.

45. Fretts 1992.

46. Greppi 1992, 61.

47. Horwitz 1993, 7.

48. Hochman 2009, 11.

49. Rudolph 2009, 2–3.

50. Roush 1992, 3D.

51. Ibid.

52. Fretts 1992.

53. Rosenthal, Herma M., 2009, 12.

54. Rudolph 2009, 42.

55. Orbach, Emily Olexy, interview with author, June 29, 2009.

56. "Memorial for Jerry Orbach" 2005.

CHAPTER 9

1. Orbach, Elaine Cancilla, interview with author, October 13, 2008.

2. Orbach, Tony, interview with author, June 18, 2009.

3. Orbach, Emily Olexy, interview with author, June 29, 2009.

4. Orbach, Chris, interview with author, September 7, 2009.

5. Gould, Lewis, interview with author, December 18, 2009.

6. "Special Tribute to Jerry Orbach" 2005.

7. Horowitz 1993, 7.

8. "Jerry Orbach Profile" 2005.

9. Orbach and Orbach with Bloom 2009, 89.

10. "Jerry Orbach Profile" 2005.

11. Hiltbrand, David 2004, C4.

12. Merkerson, S. Epatha, interview with author, October 29, 2010.

13. Rudolph 2009, 42.

14. Ibid.

15. "Jerry Orbach Profile" 2005.

16. Ibid.

17. Gould, Lewis, personal interview with author, December 18, 2009.

18. Ibid.

19. Wolf Dick, interview, November 9, 2010.

20. Deggans 2005.

21. Rudolph 1999, 36.

22. Lynch 2000.

23. Green 2003, B19.

24. Orbach and Orbach with Bloom 2009, 105.

25. Orbach, Elaine Cancilla, interview with author, October 13, 2008.

26. Orbach Ibid.

27. Ibid.

28. Ibid.

29. "Ebay Gets the Dirt on TV Cop" 2000.

30. Orbach, Elaine Cancilla, interview with author, October 13, 2008.

31. Lynch 2000.

32. Green 2003, B19.

33. Logan 2009, 29.

34. Rudolph 2009, 16.

35. Ibid., 40–41.

36. Ibid, 40.

37. Fallon 1993, 4.

38. Sod, Ted, correspondence to author, October 8, 2010

39. Robin 2004, A3.

40. Wilson 2004, B3.

41. Ibid., B3.

42. Brantley and Severo 2004.

43. "Biography for Jerry Orbach."

44. "Statement by Office of Emergency Management …" 2004.

45. Olexy, Jon, correspondence to author, February 14, 2010.

46. "Friends, Co-stars Remember Jerry Orbach" 2005.

47. Harney 1997, 13.

48. "Chinese Coffee: A Conversation with Al Pacino and Jerry Orbach …" 2007.

49. Orbach 2003, C4.

50. Wolf 2000.

51. Buckley 2003, 6. According to Wikipedia, the phrase "jump the shark" is an idiomatic expression describing "the moment of downturn for a previously successful enterprise [that was] originally used to denote the point in a television program's history where the plot spins off into absurd storylines or unlikely characterizations … [as a] result of efforts to revive interest in a show whose audience [has] begun to decline …." Specifically, it "refers to the climatic scene in 'Hollywood,' the third part of a three-part episode opening the fifth season of the American TV series *Happy Days* in September 1977 … [in which] Fonzie (Henry Winkler), wearing swimming trunks and his leather jacket, jumps over a confined shark on water skis, answering a challenge to demonstrate his bravery." (See http://en.wikipedia.org/wiki/Jumping_the_shark).

52. Hiltbrand 2003, C4.

53. Orbach, Elaine Cancilla, interview with author, October 13, 2008.

54. Used with permission of Rita Cancilla Hubbard.

55. Cancilla-Orbach interview.

56. Merkerson, S. Epatha, interview with author, October 29, 2010.

57. Orbach and Orbach with Bloom 2009, 163.

CHAPTER 10

1. Orbach, Elaine Cancilla, interview with author, October 13, 2008.

2. "Jerry Orbach's Last Days" 2005, 11.

3. Ibid.

4. Orbach, Emily Olexy, interview with Chris Orbach, March 21, 2005.

5. "Philanthropy Soars at Annual Cancer Gala," 2005, 10.

6. "Jerry Orbach's Last Days" 2005, 10.

7. Olexy, Jon, correspondence to author, February 14, 2010.

8. Orbach, Elaine Cancilla, interview with author, October 13, 2008.

9. "Friends, Co-stars Mourn Jerry Orbach" 2004.

10. "Friends, Co-stars Mourn Jerry Orbach" 2004.

11. That same day, the rehearsal studio adjacent to the theatre was named the Elaine Cancilla-Orbach Rehearsal Studio in Elaine's honor.

12. "Memorial for Jerry Orbach" 2005.

13. Orbach, Tony, correspondence to author, October 8, 2010.

14. Orbach, Chris, correspondence to author, October 8, 2010.

15. Robin 2004, A3.

EPILOGUE

1. McGeehan 2007.

2. "Petition: To the Members of New York City Community Board 4" 2007.

BIBLIOGRAPHY

BOOKS

Aronson, Harvey. 1974. *The Killing of Joey Gallo.* New York: Signet Classics.

Baxter, John. 1998. *Woody Allen: A Biography.* New York: Carroll & Graf Publishers.

Diapoulos, Peter, and Steven Linakis. 1977. *The Sixth Family.* New York: Bantam Books.

Farber, Donald C., and Robert Viagas, 1991. *The Amazing Story of "The Fantasticks."* New York: Citadel Press.

Folsom, Tom. 2008. *The Mad Ones: Joey Gallo and the Revolution at the Edge of the Underworld.* New York: Weinstein Books.

Gilvey, John Anthony. 2004. *Before the Parade Passes By: Gower Champion and the Glorious American Musical.* New York: St. Martin's Press.

Goddard, Donald. 1974. *Joey.* New York: Dell Publishing.

McGovern, Dennis, and Deborah Winer. 1993. *Sing Out, Louise! 150 Stars of the Musical Theatre Remember 50 Years on Broadway.* New York: Schirmer Books.

Meskil, Paul S. 1976. *The Luparelli Tapes: The True Story of the Mafia Hitman Who Contracted to Kill Both Joey Gallo and His Own Wife.* Chicago: Playboy Press.

Mordden, Ethan. 2001. *Open a New Window: The Broadway Musical in the 1960s.* New York: Palgrave.

Orbach, Jerry and Elaine, with Ken Bloom. 2009. *Remember How I Love You.* New York: Touchstone Press.

Shewey, Don. 1986. *Caught in the Act: New York Actors Face to Face.* New York: NAL Books.

Simon, Neil. 1996. *Rewrites: A Memoir.* New York: Simon & Schuster.

Steinberg, David. 2007. *The Book of David.* New York: Simon & Schuster.

ARTICLES

"A Hang-up Named Scuba." 1967. *Life Magazine* (November 17): 122.

"Annie Get Your Gun." 1966. *Playbill* (September 21).

"Asides and Ad-Libs." 1969. *Variety* (March 19).

Baram, Marcus. 2005. "The Transom: Remembering Jerry." *New York Observer* (January 10): 3–4.

Barron, James. 2005. "Jerry Orbach Still Belongs, and the Pinochle Goes On." *New York Times* (February 7): B3.

Barnes, Clive. 1968. "Promises, Promises." *New York Times* (December 2).

———. 1978. "'6 Rms Riv Vu,' a Diverting Place to Visit." *New York Times* (October 18.)

Barthel, Joan. 1968. "'Scuba Duba' Makes Him Manic." *New York Times* (June 2): D1.

Blinn, Johna. 1969. "At Home with Marta and Jerry Orbach." *New York Post* (June 7): 45.

Brantley, Ben, and Richard Severo. 2004. "Jerry Orbach, Star of 'Law & Order,' Dies at 69." *New York Times* (December 29).

Buchalter, Gail. 2002. "Now, I Do Whatever I Want." *Parade Magazine* (January 13): 12. Buckley, Michael. 2003. "Stage to Screens: A Chat with Theatre Veteran Jerry Orbach." *Playbill* (February): www.playbill.com.

Burden, Martin. 1980. "Last Night: In the Cards." *New York Post* (June 19): 42.

"'Chicago' Lawyer Is Alive and Living in New York." 1976. *Our Town* (September 17): 13.

"County Actor." 1989. *Waukegan News Sun* (July 28).

"Court Decisions." 1978. *New York Law Journal* (May 4): 10.

Christeson, Wayne. 2007. "Married to the Mob." *Nashville Scene* (May 3): 4 http://m.nashvillescene.com/gyrobase/married-to-the-mob/Content?oid=1194618.

Curry, Jack. 1981. "The Shady Side of Jerry Orbach." *New York Daily News* (August 14): 5.

Curtis, Charlotte. 1972. "The Last Delicious Days of Joey Gallo or Mafia Chic." *Harper's Baazar* (May 1972): 87.

Deggans, Eric. 2005. "Jerry Orbach: The Ultimate New Yorker." *St. Petersburg Times* (January 2).

Dennis, Charles. "Actor, Pool Player, Sharp Dresser." *New York Telegraph.*

"Ebay Gets the Dirt on TV Cop." 2000. *New York Observer* (April 3): 30.

Fallon, Lyn B. 1993. "Jerry Orbach: The Quintessential New York Actor." *The Hollywood Informant,* no. 2: 4.

Fields, Sidney. 1968. "Only Human: Actor with Promise." *New York Daily News* (November 27).

Flaherty, Mike. 2009. "'Law & Order': An Appreciation," *TV Guide: Special Collector's Issue — Law & Order: 20 Years of Arresting Drama* (Winter): 15.

Fretts, Bruce. 1992. "The Sum of All His Parts." *Entertainment Weekly* (November 27).

"Friends, Co-stars Mourn Jerry Orbach." 2004. *USA Today* (December 31).

"Friends, Co-stars Remember Jerry Orbach." 2005. *MSNBC* (January 1) http://www.msnbc.msn.com/id/6775797/.

Gottfried, Martin. 1972. "6 Rms Riv Vu." *Women's Wear Daily* (October 18).

Gould, Gordon. 1969. "…Jerry Orbach. That's O-R-B-A-C-H. You Know, the Famous Broadway Star." *Chicago Tribune Magazine* (April 20): 79, 84.

Graham, Sheilah. 1969. "Orbach Repeats." *Newark Evening News* (January 20).

Green, Blake. 2003. "Law & Order, Song & Dance." *Newsday* (February 17): B19.

Greppi, Michele, 1992. "New Yorker Orbach in Sole Drama Made Here." *New York Post* (November 24): 61.

Hamill, Pete. 2005. "Bright Lives, Big City." *New York Times* (January 2).

Harney, John. 1997. "Jerry Orbach, True Prince of the City." *New York Daily News* (April 12): 13.

Herridge, Frances. 1961. "Across the Footlights: 'Carnival' Lead Came Up Easy Way." *New York Post* (April 24).

Hiltbrand, David. 2003. "Jerry Orbach: Living Landmark." *Philadelphia Inquirer.* (December 10): C4.

Hochman, David. 2009. "'Law & Order': An Appreciation." *TV Guide: Special Collector's Issue-Law & Order: 20 Years of Arresting Drama* (Winter): 11.

Horwitz, Simi. 1993. "Jerry Orbach: His 'Law & Order' Role Fits Him Like a Glove." *Washington Post TV Week* (February 28–March 6): 42.

"Joe Gallo Rubbed Out." *New York Post*: 8, 67.

"Jerry Orbach in '42nd Street.' 1984. *New York Times* (August 31): C2.

"Jerry Orbach Sues Critic." 1975. *New York Post* (December 23): 16.

"Jerry Orbach's Last Days." 2005. *TV Guide* (February 27): 11.

Kerr, Walter. 1960. "'The Fantasticks' Offered at Sullivan St. Playhouse." *New York Times* (May 4).

———. 1972. "Orbach Makes It Fun." *New York Times* (October 29): D3.

Klemesrud, Judy. 1981. "At the Movies: From Song and Dance to Tough Cop." *New York Times* (August 28): C6.

Kroll, Jack. 1980. "Lullaby of Broadway." *Newsweek* (September 8): 85.

La Ferla, Ruth. 1982. "Jerry Orbach: A Closet Full of Characters." *Daily News-Record* (May 21): 6.

Lewis, Emory. 1975. "Jerry Orbach Just Won't Fit Into Any Mold." *Bergen Sunday Record* (June 29): B25.

Logan, Michael. 2009. "'Law & Order': An Appreciation." *TV Guide: Special Collector's Issue–Law & Order: 20 Years of Arresting Drama* (Winter): 29.

Lynch, Jason. 2000. "Made to Order." *People Magazine* (August 7).

McGeehan, Patrick. 2007. "In This Corner, Finally, It's Jerry Orbach Way." *New York Times* (September 17).

Morehouse, Ward. "Jerry Orbach Made It Without Trying." *Sunday Star-Ledger.*

Norton, Elliot. "New 'Promises' Musical Show Too Long Now, But Promising." *Boston Globe.*

Okon, May. 1969. "Wow! By Gosh, You're a Star!" *New York Sunday News* (March 2): 6. "One Man's Chicago." 1975. *Cue* (June 2): 1.

"Our Friend Joey Gallo." 1972. *Time* (April 17).

Pelleck, Carl J. 1972. "Police Guard Actor & Wife in the Gallo Slaying." *New York Post* (April 12): 1, 3.

"Philanthropy Soars at Annual Cancer Gala." 2005. *Cancer Discovery and Care* (Winter): 10.

Provenzano, Tom. 1988. "Always the Consummate Professional: 'The Law' of Jerry Orbach." *Hollywood Drama-Logue* (March 17–23): 5.

Raidy, William A. 1975. "Jerry Orbach, B'way's Mr. Chicago." *Chicago Daily News* (August 23).

"Rex Reed Rap of Jerry Orbach Not Libel, Even If Exaggerated." 1978. *Variety* (May 17): 455.

Robin, Joshua. 2004. "Actor Who Personified New York." *Newsday* (December 30): A3.

Rodin, Rita Bird. "Life on 22nd St. Has Its Zany Moments for Scuba Duba Star." *Chelsea Clinton News.*

Rosenthal, Herma M. 2009. "'Law & Order': An Appreciation." *TV Guide: Special Collector's Issue — Law & Order: 20 Years of Arresting Drama* (Winter): 12.

Roush, Matt. 2009. "Law & Order: An Appreciation." *TV Guide: Special Collector's Issue — Law & Order: 20 Years of Arresting Drama* (Winter): 2–3.

———. "A Richer 'Law and Order.'" *USA Today* (November 25): 3D.

Rudolph, Ileane, 2009. "Remembering Jerry Orbach: 1935–2004." *TV Guide: Special Collector's Issue — Law & Order: 20 Years of Arresting Drama* (Winter): 40–43.

———. 1999. "The Singing Detective." *TV Guide* (August 14): 36.

Schwartz, Richard. 1981. "Westsider Jerry Orbach: Star of 'Prince of the City.' *West Side TV Shopper* (September 19–25): 29.

Sheahan, Denis. 1972. "The Gang Shot Straight to Get Gallo." *Women's Wear Daily* (April 10): 1, 6.

Shouler, Kenneth. 1994. "Jerry Orbach: Spinning Tales and Cue Balls." *Billiards Digest* (June): 62.

Spellman, Robert L. 1987. "The Critic's Delight: Constitutional Protection for Criticism." *The Journal of Popular Culture* 21, no. 3 (Winter 1987): 47.

"Statement by Office of Emergency Management Commissioner Joseph F. Bruno on the Passing of Jerry Orbach." 2004. *OEM Press Release* 04-019 (December 29).

"Such Talk." 1967. *New York Times* (November 12).

Tallmer, Jerry. 1968. "Jerry Orbach: Poker, Poll & Promises," *New York Post* (December 14) 33.

———. 1980. "The Glorious Gulch They Call Broadway." *New York Post* (August 30): 29.

———. 2000. "A Fantasticks Journey" *Playbill* no. 5 (May 2000): 48.

Taylor, Nora E. 1972. "'6 Rms Riv Vu' star tks abt thr." *Christian Science Monitor* (September 29).

Wahls, Robert. 1972. "Footlights: In-Between Generation." *Sunday News* (November 19): 60.

Watts, Richard. 1972. "6 Rms Riv Vu," *New York Post* (October 29).

Wilson, Barbara L. 1972. "Comedy in Tryout: Orbach Furnishes '6 Rms Riv Vu.'" *Philadelphia Inquirer* (September 24): 1G.

Wilson, Earl. 1977. "Jerry's Broadway's Iron Man." *New York Post* (July 16): 34.

———. 1975. "Star-Spangled Feuds." *New York Post* (November 17): 36.

Wilson, Michael. 2004. "For Police, It's As If They'd Lost One of Their Own." *New York Times* (December 31): B3.

Wolf, William. 2000. "Special Reports: Weill Celebration." (February 11): http://www.wolfentertainmentguide.com/pub/specialdisplay.asp?record=650.

Wong, Wayman. 1998. "Actors Remember Pacific Overtures." *The Sondheim Review* 4, no. 4, (Spring).

Zadan, Craig. 1969. "Jerry Orbach's 'Promising' Broadway Career." *Hofstra Chronicle* (March 27): 16.

Zailian, Marian. 1978. "Jerry Orbach: 'I Was Too Lazy to Work, Too Scared to Steal.'" *San Francisco Examiner and Chronicle Datebook* (July 16).

INTERVIEWS

Alexander, Jane. Interview with author. November 23, 2010.

Gould, Lewis. Interview with author. December 18, 2009.

Jones, Tom. Interview with author. September 16, 2010.

Kander, John. Interview with author. September 11, 2010.

Merkerson, S. Epatha. Interview with author. October 29, 2010.

Orbach, Chris. Interview with author. September 7, 2009.

Orbach, Elaine Cancilla. Interview with author. October 13, 2008.

Orbach, Emily Olexy. Interview with author. June 8, 2009.

———. Interview with author. June 29, 2009.

———. Interview with author. May 12, 2010.

———. Interview with Chris Orbach. March 21, 2005.

Orbach, Jerry. Interview with Rick McKay. August 8, 2002

Orbach, Jerry. Interview with author. June 11, 1992 and February 4, 1994.

Orbach, Tony. Interview with author. June 18, 2009.

Rivera, Chita. Interview with author. October 22, 2010.

Schmidt, Harvey. Interview with author. September 16, 2010.

Sherin, Edwin. Interview with author. November 19, 2010.

Waterston, Sam. Interview with author. October 20, 2010.

Wolf, Dick. Interview with author. November 9, 2010.

CORRESPONDENCE

Olexy, Jon. Correspondence to author. February 14, 2010.

Orbach, Chris. Correspondence to author. October 8, 2010.

Orbach, Tony. Correspondence to author. October 8, 2010.

Sod, Ted. Correspondence to author. October 8, 2010.

WEBSITES, DOCUMENTARIES, AND TELEVISION PROGRAMS

"Biography for Jerry Orbach," IMDb-Internet Movie Database.
http://www.imdb.com/name/nm0001583/bio.

"Bruce Jay Friedman Interviewed by Derek Alger." 2004. *Pif Magazine* (October 8):
http://www.pifmagazine.com/2004/10/bruce-jay-friedman/.

"Chinese Coffee: A Conversation with Al Pacino and Jerry Orbach with Professor Richard Brown." 2007. *Pacino: An Actor's Vision.* 20th Century Fox. DVD Box Set.

"Dirty Dancing." Wikipedia.com. http://en.wikipedia.org/wiki/Dirty_Dancing#cite_note-asheville-8.

"Famous Movie Locations: Kellerman's Resort from 'Dirty Dancing.'" Moviefone. http://blog.moviefone.com/2010/04/09/kellermans-resort-from-dirty-dancing/.

A History of the Musical. 1990. Ron Husmann and Chesney Communications. Documentary. Ron Hussman, nar. DVD.

"Jerry Orbach Profile." 2005. *Law & Order: The Third Year — 1992–1993.* Universal. DVD. Disc 3, Side 2.

Jerry Orbach: The Singing Detective. 2000. A&E Biography. Documentary. VHS. "Mae West." http://MaeWest.blogspot.com.

"The Making of 'Beauty and the Beast.'" 1991. Walt Disney Productions. Disney Channel Documentary. DVD.

Memorial for Jerry Orbach. 2005. Gift of Elaine Cancilla Orbach to author. Richard Rodgers Theatre. DVD.

"Patrick Swayze Talks About Working with Jerry Orbach on 'Dirty Dancing.'" 2009. American Film Institute. http://www.youtube.com/watch?v=xPQlzKrqe6g&feature=fvw.

"Petition: To the Member of New York City Community Board 4." 2007. GoPetition: Fight to Have the Late Jerry Orbach's Name Adorn NYC Street Sign. Gillian, pub. (March 15). http://www.gopetition.us/petitions/jerry-orbach-name-for-nyc-street-sign.html.

"Sidney Lumet." Wikipedia.com. http://en.wikipedia.org/wiki/Sidney_Lumet.

"Special Tribute to Jerry Orbach." *Law & Order: The Third Year — 1992–1993.* Dick Wolf, prod. Universal. Disc 3, Side 2.

Try to Remember: "The Fantasticks." 2003. Zeitgeist Films. Eli Kabillio, dir. Documentary. DVD.

Wolf, William, "Special Reports: Weill Celebration," February 10, 2000, http://www.wolfentertainmentguide.com/pub/specialdisplayasp?record=650

INDEX